The
SETCHKO
HOLOCAUST
COLLECTION

Tormented Warrior

By the same author

Biographies:

CLAUSEWITZ
MOORE OF CORUNNA
ZAPATA
THE HUSSAR GENERAL – THE LIFE OF BLUCHER
THE FOX OF THE NORTH – THE LIFE OF KUTUZOV
THE AUK – AUCHINLECK, VICTOR AT ALAMEIN

Histories:

PEACE FOR OUR TIME
BLOOD, TOIL, TEARS AND SWEAT
A DAY'S MARCH NEARER HOME
THE PENINSULAR WAR
THE WAR IN THE DESERT
DAWN ON OUR DARKNESS
ENCYCLOPEDIA OF MODERN WAR

TORMENTED WARRIOR

LUDENDORFF
and the
SUPREME COMMAND

Roger Parkinson

STEIN AND DAY/*Publishers*/New York

First published in the United States of America in 1979
Copyright © 1978 by Roger Parkinson

Printed in the United States of America
Stein and Day/*Publishers*/Scarborough House
Briarcliff Manor, N.Y. 10510

Library of Congress Cataloging in Publication Data

Parkinson, Roger.
    Tormented warrior.
    Ludendorff and the Supreme Command

    Bibliography
    Includes index.
    1. Ludendorff, Erich, 1865-1937.   2.   Generals
—Germany—Biography.   I.   Title.
DD231.L8P37   1979   355.3′31′0924 [B]   78-24691
ISBN 0-8128-2597-7

Contents

Illustrations
& Maps

ACKNOWLEDGMENTS

1 Verlag Dr Hans Epstein, Leipzig and Vienna
2 Radio Times Hulton Picture Library
3 The Imperial War Museum
4 Verlag für Kulturpolitik, Berlin
5 Paul Popper Ltd

Introduction

FEW MILITARY COMMANDERS IN HISTORY HAVE WIELDED GREATER POWER than did General Erich Friedrich Wilhelm Ludendorff towards the end of the First World War. He directed armies totalling five million men. In addition, for over a year, he was virtually dictator of Germany, controlling the day-to-day policies of the state in the manner of Bismarck and eclipsing the Kaiser himself. Yet neither his military nor his political authority was officially conferred, and within weeks of the Armistice in November 1918 he was an exile, fleeing for his life from those who had previously looked to him for salvation.

From that moment Ludendorff has been largely ignored or reviled. Certainly he has suffered severe neglect from British writers. His reputation has been tarnished by wartime propaganda and by the fact that he gave the prestige of his name to the post-war Nazi movement.

It is easy to condemn Ludendorff. Even his appearance can be used against him: he seemed the archetypal Prussian officer, resembling the cartoons of the 'Hun' drawn to entertain his British, American, Russian and French opponents. Close-cropped hair undulated on the rolls of fat at the nape of his neck beneath his *Pickelhaube* helmet; his jowls hung slack beside his grim, thin-lipped mouth; his eyes were harsh, arrogant, staring; the belt of his tunic failed to restrain his paunch; his rages flushed his face first to crimson and then to purple.

He has therefore been represented as a dangerous buffoon, or as the evil influence behind Hindenburg, his nominal superior, or as a maniac whose sanity snapped in the final period of the war.

The time is long overdue for a more realistic appraisal, and it is this that my biography attempts. It is not put forward as a definitive study. I am conscious that there is much more to be said about each important aspect of Ludendorff's incredible career – his relationship with Hindenburg; his period as Chief of Staff on the Eastern Front, especially after the Battle of Tannenberg; his transfer to the Western Front for the final phase of the war; the economic programme he devised during his dictatorship; and, finally, his post-war relationship with Hitler. Nor is it easy to penetrate behind the outward façade of Ludendorff's character to reach the man beneath, since he made every effort to hide his private personality: in this respect he was no Wellington, still less a Blücher.

Nevertheless this book covers all the above subjects, albeit in limited form. I believe that what is said sufficiently justifies my conclusion that Ludendorff has been vastly misunderstood and underrated. There is so much to fascinate both the specialist and the non-specialist in his life: his extremes of elation and depression, his mania for work, his strategic and tactical concepts, above all the theories which would later be developed as *Blitzkrieg*. Though the object of Hitler's hero-worship, he was neither criminal nor mad. (As I emphasise in its place, his 'war aims' and Hitler's were completely different concepts.) But certainly his near breakdown in 1918, and the manner of his cure while Germany crumbled about him, make one of the strangest stories of any war. And through his 'stab-in-the-back' theory, which put the blame for Germany's defeat on the politicians, his influence was to live on.

Part of his importance lies in the fact that, upon him were thrown unprecedented burdens concerned with the conduct of modern total war, and the manner in which he attempted to solve those problems – which he was the first to face alone – established him as one of the most brilliant soldiers in history. In some respects he was a genius. He pointed the way to come. And behind the hitherto accepted image of the obstinate, obsessive, rude and ruthless general, lies a different man whom only now can we come to regard with some sympathy, as we partially uncover the tragic elements of his twisted career.

I take this opportunity to express my gratitude, once again, to Dr Fritz Bechtle, for his generosity and for his unfailing help in finding German-language material; I thank also Norman Stone, for his incisive comments on the earlier manuscript; Mrs Christa Carne, for her translation work; John Castle, for his cross-examination of my opinions, often to my disadvantage but always beneficial; Rivers Scott for his understanding, patience and helpful remarks; and to Betty, for keeping me going.

Tormented Warrior

CHAPTER ONE

Planning for War

LUDENDORFF'S LIFE BEGAN IN ONE ERA – BISMARCK'S – AND ENDED IN another – that of Hitler and the Third Reich. He was a child of the first and in many ways the unwilling father of the second. His origins were relatively humble, in contrast to those of the aristocratic Prussians who made up the bulk of the military caste: his mother's family, the von Tempelhoffs, occupied a higher position in the social scale than that of his father, but lacked money. Not that his father was rich. Descended from a family of Pomeranian merchants, he was a small landowner who owned meagre acres of pasture and woodland and an unpretentious white-washed farmhouse. There, at Kruschevnia in Posen, on 9 April 1865, Erich Friedrich Wilhelm Ludendorff was born.

This future military dictator of Germany was the third of six children, all of whom throve in the quiet Posen countryside. But despite the peace of the fields, the temper of the country was warlike. Friedrich III and his wife Victoria, formerly Princess Royal of England, ruled in Berlin; and six years before Erich Ludendorff was born the Empress had given birth to the son, Friedrich Wilhelm, who was to be Kaiser Wilhelm II, one of Ludendorff's most damaging critics. The old Prussian Field-Marshal, 'Papa' Wrangel, rushed to inform the crowd of the royal birth: too impatient to fumble with the catch, he smashed the Palace window with his fist and bawled: 'Children – it's a braw recruit!'[1]

During these years Otto von Bismarck finally achieved his aim of welding Prussia and her neighbours into a Germanic nation by 'blood and iron'. The Austro-Prussian War broke out in June 1866, the year after Ludendorff's birth. The Austrians were shattered at Sadowa on 3 July, thanks to plans conceived by Helmuth von Moltke, and the war ended after barely six weeks – thereby enhancing the reputation of Moltke and the Prussian military machine as a whole.

Prussia's next leap forward came in Ludendorff's fifth year, with the Franco-Prussian War. Moltke repeated his spectacular perform-

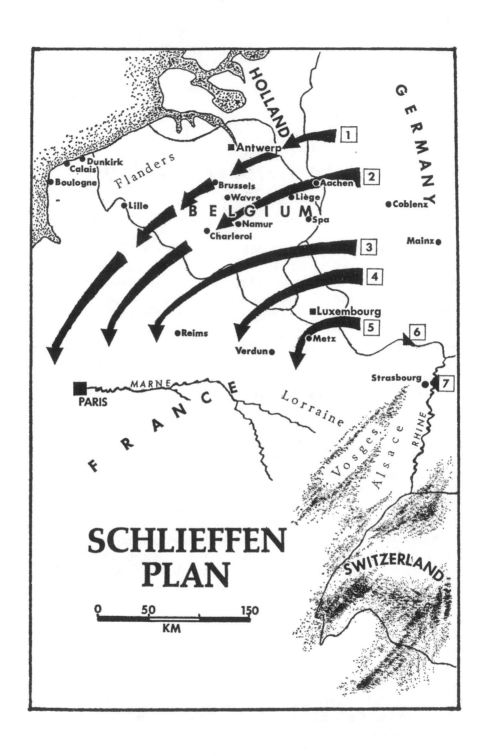

SCHLIEFFEN PLAN

ance, and redoubled German prestige. But the victory also brought an unquenchable desire for revenge on the part of France. The years of peace, which saw the final establishment of the German state with Prussia at its centre, did nothing to dispel the military atmosphere: Germany began to prepare for the next war, this time likely to be against two enemies, France and Russia. This two-front problem would become Ludendorff's greatest concern, and his final failure to master it would send Bismarck's proud Germany crashing to defeat.

Meanwhile Ludendorff began his education at the local school. He seemed a lonely boy and he later admitted how difficult he had always found it to make friends; he suffered almost an obsession about cleanliness which prevented him from joining in the rough-and-tumble with other children, and he preferred instead to study mathematics with a self-discipline which would always remain with him. He soon decided on a soldiering career – a choice which was welcome at home since the farm could not support the entire family. In 1877, in his twelfth year, Erich therefore entered the Cadet School at Plön after passing through the entrance examination with distinction, mainly due to his brilliant marks in mathematics. He kept himself apart from the other cadets and showed a minimum of aptitude or inclination for sports and gymnastics, but his schoolroom performance remained outstanding – even though he had to hold his own in a class two years above his normal age group.[2]

After only three years, in 1880, Ludendorff left Plön to enter the senior Military Academy at Lichterfelde on the outskirts of Berlin. His isolation continued. He declined to join in the usual teenage pranks, and preferred studying to gambling, drinking and duelling.

Ludendorff's mind always seemed unable to accept compromise. He clamped himself to convictions and pursued them with an awesome doggedness. Later this trait would take fanatical form in his hatred of Jews and of the German politicians whom he claimed stabbed Germany in the back by their acceptance of Allied terms in 1918–19. Now, as a teenager, he thought of nothing but work. Nothing must be wasted; no time must be lost, whether in the cold lecture halls, in his bare and inhospitable room, or on the parade ground and riding area. His every activity was directed towards being a soldier, able to fulfil the oath he had sworn on his sword-knot to serve the Kaiser and the Fatherland.

The first true Kaiser of modern Germany began his rule in 1888. Wilhelm II already displayed a complete contrast in character to the young soldier Ludendorff. As a child he had been restless and excitable, revealing a nervous irritability: perhaps his behaviour was linked with physical defects suffered at birth, when his left arm had been pulled from its socket, leaving this limb slightly deformed and sometimes painful. Beyond this, his manner could be theatrical, as though he were seeking an escape from his everyday routine.

Within two years conflict arose between the dour, seventy-four-year-old 'Iron Chancellor' and the twenty-nine-year-old Kaiser, as the latter determined to exercise his own rule. Bismarck resigned in 1890, and under the inconsistent and often irresponsible Wilhelm and his advisers Germany became increasingly isolated from all other European nations except Austria. At the same time, the Kaiser's attempt to pursue a policy of *Weltpolitik* – world politics – brought dangers of fresh friction.

After nearly five years at the Military Academy Ludendorff gained his commission as a second-lieutenant and travelled to Wesel to join his first regiment, the 57th Infantry. During the next eight years he served his soldiering apprenticeship, moving to the 2nd Marine Battalion at Kiel and then to the 8th Grenadier Guards at Frankfurt on the Oder. His determination and single-mindedness continued as strong as ever; no enduring friendships were made; his service reports proved consistently excellent, with commendations for his diligence. He carried no vivid memories of these years into later life, and he only seemed conscious of working steadily towards some unspecified role.

Ludendorff's application made him obvious material for further education, and in 1893 he attended the *Kriegsakademie* in Berlin. This establishment, successor to the institution founded by the great Prussian reformer Gerhard von Scharnhorst in 1810, had been developed by Moltke as a breeding ground for General Staff officers; the commandant, General Meckel, took note of Ludendorff's potential and recommended him to the General Staff. Promoted to captain in 1895, Ludendorff first commanded an infantry company at Gorn, then moved on to staff appointments with the 9th Division at Glogau and the 5th Corps at Posen.

He responded well to the change in duties, and later described this period as 'a time I shall never forget'.[3] Promotion to major came in 1900. He remained in his native province of Posen, to which he would return in far less happy circumstances a few years later. He gained experience in administration and served as a senior staff officer of the HQ staff of the 5th Corps from 1902 to 1904.

In March 1904 he received an appointment which marked him as a soldier with a highly promising career ahead of him: he was ordered to move to Berlin, where he would join the Great General Staff under Moltke's successor, Alfred von Schlieffen. The following year Ludendorff began detailed work in the *Aufmarschabteilung* (Concentration) Department, thereby becoming closely associated with the famous plans for war which bore Schlieffen's name.

Schlieffen, Chief of the General Staff since 1891 and described by Ludendorff as 'one of the greatest soldiers who ever lived', had been working on his scheme for a decade. Behind the so-called Schlieffen Plan lay the attempt to solve Germany's basic strategic problem: how to handle war both with Russia in the East and France in the West. Germany's increasing isolation had aggravated this concern: in June 1890 Wilhelm had declined to renew the German-Russian Reinsurance Treaty, and three years later the Franco-Russian Alliance was signed. Moltke's recommended answer had been for Germany to conduct a defensive war in the West and an offensive campaign in the East. Schlieffen reversed this plan. A stalemate against France in the West, combined with a protracted war in the East where the vast plains allowed evasive Russian strategy, would enable Britain to intervene. Schlieffen therefore urged a campaign which would overrun France in minimum time whilst a Russian invasion was blocked in the East.

In 1905, less than twelve months after Ludendorff joined the Great General Staff, Schlieffen embodied his ideas into a memorandum. This amounted to a compilation of schemes drawn up by him since 1897, and it stated that Germany would only deploy one-ninth of her forces against Russia, her overwhelming might being thrown against France. The Russians would clearly attempt to make use of German preoccupation with the West: in answer, the outnumbered German forces on this front would attempt a limited offensive when the enemy separated to filter through the Masurian Lakes area, and would then fall back behind fortresses on the Vistula. Meanwhile, all would depend on a speedy victory over the French, and to obtain this Schlieffen was prepared to take maximum risks. Rather than attempt to push through the more difficult terrain to the south, the German armies would thrust against France from the north – even though this would violate Belgian neutrality and hence precipitate British intervention.

Ludendorff himself had no scruples over a German invasion of Belgium. He wrote that the Schlieffen Plan was 'based on the assumption that France would not respect Belgian neutrality or that Belgium would join France. On this assumption the advance of the German main forces through Belgium followed as a matter of course. Any other plan of campaign would have been crippled.'[4]

Schlieffen's 1905 memorandum therefore advocated that the ratio of strength between the German right (north) and left (south) wings against France should be about seven to one. This would leave southern Alsace virtually unprotected, as a consequence of mustering all available strength further along the front. The offensive would aim at sweeping forward from a line running Verdun–Dunkirk, then swinging round Paris to throw the French against their own fortresses and the Swiss frontier.

'We were all convinced of the soundness of this plan,' wrote Ludendorff. 'In our unfavourable military-political position in the centre of Europe, surrounded by enemies, we had to reckon with foes greatly superior in numbers and prepare ourselves accordingly, if we did not wish to allow ourselves to be crushed.'[5]

Count Schlieffen retired soon after presenting his memorandum.

The Kaiser insisted his place should be taken by Colonel-General Helmuth von Moltke, known as 'Moltke the Younger' and nephew of the hero of the Franco-Prussian War. The newcomer accepted the appointment with considerable reluctance; he confided to the Chancellor, Prince Bernhard von Bülow: 'Everything in me dislikes the thought of the appointment. I do not lack personal courage but I lack the power of rapid decision. I am too reflective, too scrupulous, or, if you like, too conscientious for such a post. I lack the capacity for risking all on a single throw.'[6]

Moltke's words proved perceptive. Lacking confidence in himself, the new Chief of the General Staff relied heavily upon his subordinates. Among his assistants, Ludendorff soon rose to a prominence beyond that of his rank. In 1907 he stepped up to lieutenant-colonel; the following year he became Head of the *Aufmarschabteilung*, overcoming strong opposition from his nearest rival, Wilhelm Groener, and with this appointment he became even more closely involved in the final adaptations of the Schlieffen memorandum prior to war. Moltke rightly considered that the changing international situation necessitated alterations, indeed even in retirement Schlieffen himself continued to work on his ideas. Russia gained additional strength; this, combined with the development of railways in the East, meant that the threat on this front might be more powerful than Schlieffen had originally calculated. Accordingly Moltke increased the size of German forces deployed against this enemy.

More important, Moltke altered Schlieffen's conception of the wheeling right wing against France, reducing the north-south ratio from seven to one to three to one. He feared a determined French offensive in Alsace-Lorraine; on the other hand he believed that such an attack could work to Germany's advantage – a decisive battle might be possible with the French driven against the Vosges and the Rhine.[7] Ludendorff agreed with this alteration, with the important proviso that extra strength for the southern German wing should be acquired from new divisions, rather than by depleting the northern wing.[8]

Manpower therefore assumed ever-increasing importance, and the demand for a larger German army would very soon precipitate conflict between Ludendorff and his political superiors, which without the advent of war would have shattered his career. But before this clash, Ludendorff emerged briefly from his preoccupation with plans and war games and railway networks. In August 1909 this sober, grim-faced officer married the beautiful and vivacious Margarethe Pernet.

The meeting was romantic. Ludendorff preferred to walk rather than drive home from the General Staff HQ on the Königsplatz since the exercise was beneficial. One rainy evening he noticed a woman sheltering in a doorway; he marched across and offered to share his umbrella. Walking together beneath this protection, the couple found themselves attracted to each other; the forty-four-year-old lieutenant-colonel pushed friendship into courtship in his usual brusque, efficient fashion, and declared his love. Margarethe was already married, to a businessman whom she had met soon after leaving school. A divorce was arranged, and the marriage to Ludendorff followed soon after.

Margarethe proved popular amongst Ludendorff's fellow-officers, with her dark curling hair and finely-drawn features. Before, she seems to have been lonely: her mother was dead and soon afterwards she lost her father; her only near relation, a sister, lived some way from Berlin and visits were infrequent. Now her life was changed.

Ludendorff had another side to his strict, military character. He enjoyed family life. His own relations welcomed Margarethe, and their reaction reveals the hidden Ludendorff through his background. He introduced his wife to his three married sisters and to his mother. 'They gave me such a warm welcome that I was able to face the future with less misgivings,' wrote Margarethe. 'And then that first time when we stayed with his dear mother ... How groundless had been my fears! I found a lady of such charm and distinction that she took my heart by storm. I was devoted to her.'

Margarethe had also to face Ludendorff's seven elderly aunts, which she did with strong apprehension – again soon dispelled. 'They would have taken me to their arms if I had been the biggest monster in the world, because my husband was their obvious favourite – the idol at whom they gazed with fanatical adoration. Such simple kindly old ladies I had never met before.'[9]

So began a marriage which would survive the strain of war, but which would be destroyed by the subsequent peace. Ludendorff displayed deep affection to his wife: his letters were warm and tender, with frequent reference to 'my dearest' and expressions of loneliness at being parted from her. Margarethe and Ludendorff had no children, but instead Margarethe brought three sons and a daughter from her first marriage – Franz, Heinz, Erich and Margot. Margarethe constantly expressed her delight at the way Ludendorff felt for them as if they were his own, and she wrote: 'From the beginning my children had a warm liking for their new father, and this in the course of the war deepened into love and admiration.'

But marriage failed to alter Ludendorff's approach to work. 'My husband's position involved a formidable mass of work,' Margarethe recalled. His day in the Königsplatz office began early, and although he returned home during the mid-afternoon, his activity continued. 'Every afternoon at five o'clock an orderly appeared with a bulging despatch case, which Ludendorff awaited with impatience; frequently he stayed in his study deep into the night.'[10]

War seemed to be drawing closer. In 1905 Kaiser Wilhelm had travelled to Tangier to challenge French influence in Morocco; Russia and Britain backed France. At the same time the Anglo-German naval

B

race was accelerating, and an Anglo-French Convention of 1904 was followed by the Anglo-Russian Entente, August 1907: this Triple Entente now balanced the Triple Alliance signed between Austria, Germany and Italy in 1882. In October 1908 Austria annexed Bosnia and Herzegovina; Russia, weakened by her conflict with Japan and her 1905 Revolution, was in no state for war, and Austria was allowed to undertake her annexation without hindrance. But Russia immediately increased her arms programmes ready for the next crisis.

Belligerent declarations became common. The *German Military Review* stated in July 1909: 'If we do not decide for war, that war in which we shall have to engage at the latest in two or three years will be begun in far less propitious circumstances. At this moment the initiative rests with us: Russia is not ready, moral factors and right are on our side, as well as might ...'[11] Also in 1909 the Austrian *Danzers Armee-Zeitung* declared: 'Never was a war more just. And never yet was our confidence in a victorious issue more firmly grounded. We are being driven into war ...'

Another Moroccan crisis erupted in 1911, and although Germany edged away from full confrontation this supposed humiliation aggravated the militants in the country. Tension rose in the Balkans. The German politician Ernst von Heydebrand stormed in the Reichstag on 9 November: 'When the hour of decision comes we are prepared for sacrifices, both of blood and treasure.'

But Ludendorff became dissatisfied with Germany's preparations. The army had been increased in size, yet he believed manpower still to be critically short. Although Prussia had been a pioneer of universal military service, politicians had allowed the practice to lapse whilst paying homage to the principle. The Reichstag specified the number of recruits which the army authorities could take each year, and the main political parties were hostile to the services, which they regarded as the domain of the aristocracy. Liability to service ended at the age of 45, compared with 48 in France; in Germany less than 50 per cent of liable young men were conscripted and trained, in France 85 per cent.[12]

Ludendorff was convinced that additional troops were essential, especially if the strengthening of the south wing in France was not to be at the expense of the north; moreover, Russia's latest increases in military strength necessitated stronger German forces on the Eastern Front. Schlieffen had urged the Reichstag to allow substantial extra manpower drafts, without significant success; Moltke resumed pressure, managing to obtain some additional allocations, yet Karl von Einem, War Minister, informed the Chief of General Staff in 1909: 'An increase in the peacetime effective strength of 6,500–7,000 men, spread over the five years from 1 April 1911, is the absolute maximum which, under present conditions, can be demanded and which it is at all possible to achieve.'[13]

Also in 1909 Moltke further committed Germany to a two-front war. In January he received a communication from the Austrian Chief of General Staff, Field-Marshal Baron Conrad von Hötzendorf, claiming that his Austrian armies might be obliged to occupy Serbia: he assumed that if Russia intervened, Germany would fulfil her 1879 treaty obligation and would lend support. Moltke agreed on 21 January, adding that agreement presumably existed between France and Russia in the event of a Russo-German war: France would therefore take similar mobilisation measures.[14] This in fact meant that if Germany helped Austria, she would be involved not only against Russia but France – and, under the war plans, France would be attacked first.

Ludendorff's work-load became greater and more urgent. By now his wife had come to appreciate his rigid self-discipline. 'He was a man of iron principles. Whether his work kept him up late at night or we had been at a ball or a party, it made no difference: next morning, winter or summer, he was in the saddle by seven o'clock. He always rode the same way along a track in the Tiergarten or the Grünwald.' After this exercise Ludendorff walked to the office, arriving at exactly the same moment each day; he ruled himself and those around him with machine-like efficiency. 'He was punctual to the minute,' commented Margarethe. 'Time was not reckoned in our house by hours, but by minutes. He would say, for instance, "Today I shall be back at four o'clock for some food." He would come back on the stroke of four, change his clothes and walk straight into the dining-room. If the soup was not on the table already he would say teasingly, "Well, that's a nice thing, there's nothing to eat in your well-managed home today." '[15]

Von Einem was succeeded by General von Heeringen, but the new War Minister proved just as obstructive. In early 1911 Moltke sought an increase of 300,000 men, claiming such a figure was a 'precondition for survival'; in reply the Reichstag met in February to approve an increase of 10,000.[16]

Ludendorff decided that the normal channels of communication for seeking extra strength had failed. Other means must be found. At the same time the international situation deteriorated still further with the Moroccan crisis of 1911, with Germany pressing for compensation for French gains in this territory. Negotiations lagged and in July Germany despatched the cruiser *Panther* to Agadir. War seemed imminent: Ludendorff requested three more army corps to be authorised immediately, plus another three in 1913 or 1914. The Agadir crisis passed slowly without Ludendorff's proposals meeting success. He then took the controversial step of involving himself in political intrigue, completely contrary to normal military traditions.

First, Ludendorff approached General Keim, a retired officer. Keim supported the president of the nationalist Pan-German League, Heinrich Class, who immediately took up Ludendorff's proposal for more troops. The War Ministry reacted violently. Both Heeringen and

General Wandel, Director of the General War Department, knew that Ludendorff had implicated himself and the errant staff officer received a stiff reprimand from Wandel.

The uneasy situation continued. Then, in summer 1912, tension increased in the Balkans. In October the combined forces of Montenegro, Bulgaria, Serbia and Greece attacked Turkey. The conflict, which would end with a Turkish defeat the following May, immediately caused repercussions elsewhere: troops in Russia and Austria were alerted, and the Austrian Chief of General Staff again reverted to his scheme for a Serbian invasion.

With Moltke's approval Ludendorff drafted a plan for an increase in the army budget, which included a renewed request for three more army corps. Ludendorff then prodded his superior into action. 'I was able to induce General von Moltke to approach the Imperial Chancellor with the plan.' Once again the War Ministry was therefore being by-passed.[17] The Chancellor, Bethmann Hollweg, gave his reluctant approval; the Kaiser hesitated. Indeed, from a political point of view such caution was understandable with regard to the possible effects of Germany's warlike preparations on foreign governments. The tense international situation dictated a careful balance between belligerent acts and the means whereby such acts could be successfully accomplished. The Kaiser, for all his arrogance – which played such an important part in provoking war in 1914 – was fully aware that Germany must not be forced to move too soon; Bethmann Hollweg was even more hesitant, fearing that the increases in army strength being urged by the General Staff would be an unnecessary provocation of other European powers at that time.

For its part the General Staff, represented in this instance by Ludendorff, considered that the very tension in the international situation necessitated all possible increases in German military strength: Germany must stand ready to fight; the army must be given the power to undertake those tasks which might soon be demanded of it. To Ludendorff – and to Moltke – the issue was simple: sufficient forces must be available to carry out the Schlieffen Plan, upon which depended Germany's survival. Yet other complications existed, even beyond this straight military-political argument: some army officers, with whom the Kaiser had considerable sympathy, opposed a massive expansion in the army since they believed this would destroy the old élite force. Exclusiveness would be removed.

Ludendorff's attitude towards this whole important question provided a key to his beliefs. He held that if the army was assigned certain missions by the politicians – in this case the defence of the Fatherland through the Schlieffen Plan – then the politicians in turn should provide the army with all possible backing, and he was to maintain this conviction in even stronger form during the war. Moreover, for all his respect for old army traditions, his fight for large manpower increases revealed that he considered other factors to be more important than the maintenance of an *ancien régime* based on class. He always recognised the impact of modern technology: the age of mass armies with modern weapons had outdated small, élite forces. To Ludendorff, it was more critical to preserve the Fatherland than to preserve the old army. Once again, his intense patriotism – eventually to lead him to fanatical heights – was his prime motivating principle.

Now, in the actutely uneasy situation existing in winter 1912, the demand for army increases caused further bitter debates. Eventually the latest plan for a boost in the army budget was handed to the War Ministry, and a prolonged discussion began in the Reichstag. The result was a decision in April 1913 for approval for the budget increase and for an additional 4,000 officers, 14,850 NCOs and 117,000 troops. But this number was far fewer than Ludendorff had sought, and from this point of view the result was a compromise which satisfied no one, least of all Ludendorff himself.

By now Ludendorff had left the Great General Staff. His career seemed shattered. He departed from Berlin in virtual disgrace, criticised for his attitudes and for his political manoeuvring by the War Ministry and by the Kaiser himself. Only a few months before, his future had seemed dazzling: promoted full colonel in 1911 he had in fact been acting in a capacity above this rank. Moltke's reliance upon him, combined with his intimate knowledge of war plans and his undoubted competence as a senior staff officer, had seemed to indicate that he would be selected Chief of Operations if war broke out – Moltke's chief assistant. Events might have been far different if this partnership had come about. Likewise the situation in 1914 could have been radically altered if the politicians and the War Ministry had shared Ludendorff's belief in the need for more troops. As it was, Germany would march to the two-front war vastly outnumbered in both East and West. French, Belgian and British troops on the one front totalled more than the entire German strength on both; France's army in 1914 represented a tenth of her population, the German forces one-twentieth.[18]

On a personal level, Ludendorff's failure to obtain more troops encouraged in him the belief that the military would always be in danger of receiving inadequate backing from the politicians. Ludendorff's suspicions of politicians and of others with vested interests steadily grew from this moment onwards, and these uneasy emotions would play an increasingly important part in his subsequent actions.

Ludendorff received his orders to quit the General Staff in January 1913. The new posting would be to Düsseldorf as commanding officer of a line regiment; he confided to his wife that he hoped to be given an élite Brandenburger Regiment, but even this was denied. Instead he was posted to the Lower Rhenish Fusilier Regiment No. 39. Nor

was the garrison at Düsseldorf even at full strength, having been reduced by the previous War Minister, von Einem.[19]

For the last thirteen years Ludendorff had been away from regimental duties. During this period his work had concentrated on strategic
troop deployment at the highest level. Now, in Ludendorff's words,
'my chief work was the inspection of recruits'. As an additional insult,
many officers and politicians who had opposed his insistence on army
increases emerged with promotion and honours after the Reichstag
debate: several, including Wandel, were ennobled.[20] Ludendorff
merely grunted to Margarethe: 'The soldier has no personal ends to
pursue. He goes where he's sent. That's enough about it.'

Just before Ludendorff left Berlin he heard that the great Schlieffen
had died. The eighty-year-old Field-Marshal worked on his plans to
the end. Scribbling a note on 28 December which stressed the importance of taking the Belgian fortified towns, especially Liège, as
early as possible. A few moments before he died on 4 January his eyes
flickered open and he reportedly whispered: 'It must come to a fight.
Only make the right wing strong.'

CHAPTER TWO

Slide to Conflict

UNKNOWN TO LUDENDORFF A BRIEF NOTE OVERTOOK HIM ON HIS JOUR-
ney to Düsseldorf. It was addressed to his divisional commander from
the Military Cabinet in Berlin, and it declared: 'This Colonel should be
taught some discipline.'[1] Ironically, Ludendorff arrived at his new
posting with the conviction that only through strict supervision and
control could his regiment be prepared for inevitable war.

'My aim was to turn highly-disciplined troops into responsible men
possessed of initiative,' wrote Ludendorff in his memoirs. 'Discipline
is not intended to kill character, but to develop it ... Discipline, to
which officer and private alike were subjected, was, in my opinion,
the only basis on which an army could be effectively trained for war.'
Above all, Ludendorff was possessed with a sense of urgency. 'I realised all the more the great responsibility which rested on me as Commanding Officer of the regiment, as I saw the coming war rapidly
approaching.'[2] 'He worked at the minutest detail,' commented Wilhelm
Breucker, a battalion adjutant, 'with the same accuracy with which
up to now he had worked out the exact deployment plans for the whole
army.'

Ludendorff's painstaking method was revealed in his attitude to
garrison regulations; he criticised these for being outdated and revised
page after page. 'Regulations which aren't amended weekly are no
longer alive,' he declared.[3] Breucker considered that Ludendorff appeared to be a 'narrow-minded bureaucrat' to some senior officers at
the garrison, with these gentlemen smirking at the newcomer's enthusiasm and joking about him behind his back. By contrast junior
officers responded to the attention which Ludendorff gave them.

After only a few weeks Ludendorff felt reasonably satisfied with
progress so far. 'First of all I had to use a firm hand,' he told General
von Stein, Quartermaster-General. 'Very much has to be made up for.
I've started immediately.' He added: 'I've been educated in a hard
and simple manner. I also appreciate moderate pleasures, but beyond

that I cannot go. Here we advance along the road which we presume to be correct. Perhaps others might follow.'⁴

Nor, despite outward appearances, was the Colonel the complete autocrat. According to Breucker, now beginning many months of service with Ludendorff: 'He would listen to any argument if it was put to him backed by reason: he never changed in that respect, and even found pleasure in doing so . . . He preferred upright to servile people.'⁵

Ludendorff enjoyed the social aspects of being a regimental commander: his pleasures may have been moderate, but were nonetheless appreciated. Slowly he came to feel at home, helped by Margarethe. Soon after their arrival they found a suitable house close to the Royal Park and the Rhine. The house had a large garden, 'which particularly pleased us', remembered Margarethe. 'In front of the dining-room was a cosy veranda with a terrace from which broad steps led down.' She also wrote: 'We had certainly nothing to grumble about in Düsseldorf. From the very beginning we were delighted with the lovely city on the Rhine.' She excelled at being the Colonel's wife and manoeuvred her way through social difficulties – including the attentions of the previous commander's widow, who proffered imperious advice. 'I was ordered to report to her and received the usual lesson in deportment. I was instructed how to conduct myself . . . I was not, however, much edified by this lecture, because I imagined that I had already mastered the rules of good manners. I had not come from a small garrison but from Berlin.'⁶

Entertainment at the Ludendorff house remained simple yet effective. The Colonel unbent slightly. 'His family happiness was conveyed to all the guests,' commented Breucker. He added:

> If the number of guests was small enough, Ludendorff retired after the meal to his study, and if his young lieutenants followed him he occasionally gave them glimpses of the work of the General Staff, and he told them of his difficult fights for the war readiness of Germany as well as about his worries for the safety of the Fatherland. In such hours the lieutenants grew to know quite a different character than the severe and rather restrained regimental character.⁷

Fighting in the Balkans subsided in April 1913 with the Turkish defeat at Scutari, only to flare again the following month in even more dangerous proportions. The victorious participants squabbled over spoils, with Serbia joining Greece and Rumania against her former ally Bulgaria and emerging triumphant in July. Success encouraged Serbian-Slav extremists in their policy of 'liberating' the Austrian territories of Bosnia and Herzegovina, despite the massive conflict which would almost certainly result. Already, in May, Kaiser Wilhelm wrote in a despatch: 'The fight between Slavs and Germans is no longer avoidable. It is bound to come. When? We shall soon see.' Field-Marshal Sir John French, British Chief of the Imperial General

Staff who had been invited to watch German summer manoeuvres, was informed by the Kaiser: 'You have seen how long my sword is – you may find it is just as sharp.'[8]

Also during the summer Ludendorff took part in local exercises with his regiment. Too often, these manoeuvres merely amounted to an excuse for officers to ride from one Rhine village to another sampling the wine. Not so under Ludendorff. His regiment formed part of the 'Blue' forces engaged against the 'Red' enemy, and Breucker recollected that Ludendorff 'who, in peace, lived as if war had already begun', expected conditions to be as realistic as possible. One morning the commander of a hussar patrol brought him an exact sketch of the enemy situation. Ludendorff asked the cavalryman how he had managed to obtain such details.

'Yesterday evening,' replied the young officer, 'I dined with my cousin Fürstenberg of the 4th Cuirassiers at Löffelmann. He commands a Red cavalry patrol. We exchanged our sketches over a good bottle of wine.'

Ludendorff, according to Breucker, was made 'sad rather than angry' by the disclosure. But he also took strong exception to the behaviour of some senior officers. One morning the corps commander, General von Einem, had invited a large group of Westphalian aristocracy to watch an attack against Red position on a nearby hill. Einem had carefully arranged the performance so that the assault would be made frontally in full view of the distinguished spectators.

This audience arrived early in the morning. The hours passed, one after another, with the aristocrats becoming increasingly wet and miserable. Finally, news arrived that the assault had been launched by Ludendorff much earlier, against a distant flank rather than the front. Von Einem complained; Ludendorff merely answered: 'One glance at the map would have revealed that my decision was the only possible warlike answer.'[9]

Despite touches of self-righteousness, outward prickliness and sudden rages, Ludendorff was regarded by the ordinary soldiers with respect and even affection, and amongst the officers the younger element especially responded to his leadership. Breucker, who believed Ludendorff to be an 'unusually soft person' beneath his harsh exterior, wrote: 'Is it not wonderful for a regimental commander when his young lieutenants call him "Father"?'[10]

International affairs pressed forward again as 1914 opened. Serbian extremists had continued to agitate for occupation of Bosnia and Herzegovina, and far from attempting to restrain preventive Austrian action, the German Kaiser seemed to encourage such a drastic step. He told Conrad in October: 'I go with you. The other Powers are not ready and will not attempt any counter-action.' In February 1914 Wilhelm informed the Belgian King that war between Germany and France was near at hand.[11]

Ludendorff's next posting arrived in early spring. His latest orders resulted in promotion to brigade commander, yet the Military Cabinet in Berlin still apparently viewed him with disfavour: he asked for the Infantry Brigade at Frankfurt, available at that time and allowing him to be near his mother, but the request was refused. Instead Ludendorff travelled with his wife to Strasbourg, where he would command the 85th Infantry Brigade.[12]

Troops and young officers at Düsseldorf were sorry to see the Ludendorffs leave – 'nothing which happened later was able to wipe out the picture of their happy and harmonious family-life,' commented Breucker, soon to rejoin Ludendorff. Never again would he obtain the quiet contentment which he enjoyed at Düsseldorf: within a few months colossal responsibilities would be heaped upon him, and would remain to torment him for the rest of his career. Margarethe wrote: 'In Düsseldorf, free from all worry, I passed the happiest days of my life. I shall never, I fear, look on the like again ... The officers for the most part were killed.' Ludendorff also expressed his regret at departure in his own, brusque fashion: 'I missed the direct intercourse with the troops.' At Strasbourg he would chiefly be occupied with organisational affairs.[13]

The weather during these fateful months of 1914 remained hot and calm. In May Ludendorff left Margarethe to take part in a staff ride from Freiburg-im-Breisgau to Cologne; once again the question of his possible reappointment to the General Staff had arisen, perhaps even as Quartermaster-General, but no news reached him during this staff excursion.

In June Ludendorff spent some time with his stepsons Franz and Erich, at home on leave from their military school at Lichterfelde. As always, he enjoyed their company. Franz, the eldest of the four children, had joined the military cadets when aged only ten, at his own request. Now his education was almost finished, and his progress had been extremely satisfactory. In some ways he resembled his stepfather, with a passion for tidiness, and he had recently been awarded the Kaiser's prize for diligence and smartness. In other respects his character contained facets which Ludendorff sadly lacked: his adoring mother believed the keynote to his personality to be 'his sunny cheerfulness. There was something triumphant about it which won him all hearts, and from his childhood onwards he possessed this touch of radiance.' Erich, tall and slender, was the most handsome of the three boys, extremely serious and with a strong sense of duty; Heinz, absent from this summer holiday, was an ensign in the 31st Infantry Regiment stationed at Altona.[14]

'It was one of my favourite dreams,' wrote Margarethe, 'to see Ludendorff and my three boys sitting round our table as officers. How differently everything turned out.'

The holiday passed without hint of tragedy. Excursions were made into the Vosges mountains – to Molsheim, Schirmeck, Schlettsstadt, and higher into the peaks of Donon and Hohkönigsburg. The family climbed together 'in really incredible heat'. They visited Zabern, peacefully embedded in the hills, surrounded by woods and pastures which were hazy in the sunshine.

On 28 June the portly Archduke Franz Ferdinand, Heir Apparent to the Austrian throne, was visiting Sarajevo, capital of Bosnia, where he wished to inspect his Austro-Hungarian troops. One personal reason for his presence stemmed from his desire to ride beside his wife in an open car on an official occasion, with the crowds waving and cheering. Franz Ferdinand had married beneath him: his wife, Countess Sophie Chotek, was barred by rules of social etiquette from sitting beside him on public occasions, unless he happened to be acting in a military capacity. Now, at 11 o'clock this Sunday morning an Austrian schoolboy named Gavrilo Princip fired two shots into the car, killing both occupants, and setting in motion the chain of events which started the final slide to the First World War.

Princip and his young associates had been trained and armed in Serbia by the Slav extremist group known as the Black Hand secret society, but it appeared that as yet no evidence existed of complicity by the Serbian Government itself.

At Kiel, Kaiser Wilhelm was attending Regatta Week on board his yacht *Meteor*. Present at the festivities was a British naval squadron, paying the first courtesy visit to a German port for many years. British and German sailors had been drinking together in the local beergardens, and highly successful parties had been thrown in respective wardrooms.

Shortly after 2 pm this Sunday a fast motor launch pulled alongside *Meteor* and a telegram was handed to the Kaiser. He read that his friend the Archduke, whom he had visited at Konopischt only a few weeks previously, had been killed. Within hours the regatta had been cancelled at the Kaiser's command; coded Admiralty messages ordered the Royal Naval squadron to sail for home. Not only had the Kaiser lost a friend, but he considered the assassination to be a violation of the position of all monarchs. He disregarded the lack of evidence at that time of official Serbian involvement, and he believed that the Austrians had every right to inflict punishment. Conrad, the fiery Austrian Chief of Staff, agreed whole-heartedly and began to enlist support.

Publicly, the murders seemed not to have caused a serious crisis. Germans continued to enjoy the holiday weather, and no trace of war hysteria could be detected. Yet there seemed to be a subtle difference in the atmosphere. 'The light had grown more livid', commented Theodor Wolff, editor of the *Berliner Tageblatt*.[15]

Margarethe left with Franz and Erich for an additional holiday at Lucerne; Ludendorff, to his regret, was unable to accompany them since he had to conduct a 'supply ride' designed to examine the plans for maintenance of an army in the field. Afterwards came autumn manoeuvres; meanwhile Margarethe continued to enjoy her 'last weeks of untroubled happiness' at Lucerne. 'With open hearts and open eyes we gave ourselves up to enjoy the beauties of nature. My children were young and energetic, and every day they stirred me up to some excursion, by rail or boat or car or on foot . . .'[16]

The Kaiser had previously arranged a tour of Norwegian fiords in the royal yacht *Hohenzollern*. The cruise carried on as scheduled, but Wilhelm's manipulation of international affairs also continued. He believed Russia to be militarily and financially incapable of fighting to protect the Serbs against an Austrian attack – moreover, the Tsar was unlikely to offer help since Serbia 'has stained itself by an assassination'. On the other hand, time must not be wasted. According to Gottlieb von Jagow, German Foreign Secretary: 'In a few years, according to all competent authorities, Russia will be ready to strike. Then she will crush us with her numbers.' Moltke had journeyed to Karlsbad to take a cure for his diseased kidneys, yet for some time he had been saying that such an excellent opportunity for war was unlikely to be repeated.

At 6 pm, 23 July, Austria delivered an ultimatum to Serbia. The date and time were precisely chosen: at that moment the French President, Raymond Poincaré, and French Premier René Viviani were at sea returning from a state visit to Russia, and the actual delivery of the Note was delayed to allow them to be away from efficient communications facilities. The ultimatum had only a forty-eight-hour time limit, preventing adequate liaison between the Serbs and their Russian allies. Austria demanded that Serbia should formally condemn and cease all Pan-Serb propaganda, expel from office anyone implicated in such activity, instigate legal action against certain officials whom the Austrians would name, and allow Austrian investigation of the Sarajevo assassination. Serbia sent an apparently conciliatory answer just before the time limit expired on 25 July, prompting Wilhelm to declare four days later: 'A great moral victory for Vienna but it removes any reason for war.'

Yet the brakes had been loosened. Austria rejected the Serbian reply; tension began to soar in European capitals. News of the serious diplomatic situation reached Ludendorff, who immediately telephoned Margarethe, still in Lucerne. Over the crackling, long-distance line he told her to return immediately to Germany with the children: war was likely at any moment. Margarethe had been ignorant of the international crisis since her landlady had kept the news secret, not wishing to spoil the holiday season; now Margarethe reacted with 'horror and alarm . . . For a time I was unable to collect my thoughts.' The family packed as quickly as they could and left Lucerne on the next train. 'Quite indescribable confusion reigned. The Germans were streaming in feverish haste to the frontier of their land.'

Ludendorff met his wife and stepsons at Strasbourg station, his manoeuvres prematurely ended and troops recalled to garrisons. Franz and Erich pestered him with questions, and Margarethe felt renewed horror when her sons shouted in excitement: 'Hurrah – war! We shall soon get to the Front!'[17]

Serbia had already mobilised, anticipating the Austrian rejection of her reply; Austria reacted by ordering her own counter-mobilisation, and on 28 July she declared war. Frail hopes remained of peace between the great powers, but these rapidly diminished; on 29 July Austrian gunboats bombarded Belgrade and on the same day Russia ordered general mobilisation, altered to partial measures against Austria alone after urgent telephone calls between Tsar Nicholas II and Kaiser Wilhelm, then reverting to full mobilisation on 31 July following pressure on the Tsar from his military chiefs. The effects of the elaborate system of alliances and mobilisation schemes now began to be seen: Russia bound to Serbia and hence hostile to Austria; Germany bound to Austria and hence hostile to Russia; France bound to Russia. As Ludendorff knew better than most, the intricate German plans specified an assault against France in order to protect herself in a two-front war, with the Schlieffen scheme making it virtually impossible to mobilise German forces against Russia alone. An offensive against France meant invasion of Belgium, almost certain to bring British participation.

At 1 pm, 31 July, the German General Staff issued orders for the preliminary step to complete mobilisation, known as the state of *drohende Kriegsgefahr*, DK – 'threatening danger of war'. The news reached Ludendorff as he ate his midday meal with Margarethe. They sat alone at the table: shortly before, they had stood on Strasbourg station saying goodbye to Franz and Erich, whom Ludendorff had sent back to their cadet corps. Margarethe wrote: 'Silent and without a tear, I stared at the train which bore them away.' Yet as the midday meal began it seemed for a moment that some hope remained: Ludendorff believed negotiations could still avert conflict. 'It looks as though the black storm-clouds are passing away.'

Then an orderly brought in a flimsy piece of paper. Printed on the sheet were just two letters – DK. 'It was no longer possible to avert the evil thing,' wrote Margarethe, 'and I felt myself go white to the lips.' Ludendorff insisted that she leave for Berlin immediately, since Strasbourg lay too near the frontier.

Before leaving, Margarethe joined her husband in pushing all the furniture and belongings into one room, so allowing the flat to be used as a hospital if necessary. She departed for Berlin on the 6 pm train, journeying in a packed carriage through this hot July night with fellow-travellers collapsing from the stuffiness.[18] Also during the night of 31 July, Germany delivered an ultimatum to Russia demanding a suspension of all war measures; the Russians failed to reply. At about 4.45 pm next day, 1 August, France ordered her own general mobilisation. Germany followed suit about 15 minutes later. War was declared on Russia during the evening.

Ludendorff found time to write a note to Margarethe, dated 31 July.

My own wife. You've just gone, and it gives me a feeling of emptiness which never leaves me. Let me tell you once again that I love you more than anything in the world. How heavy those last hours were! Our life lies behind us, though we parted with the heartening consciousness of our mutual affection. But it is hard, hard for the husband and far harder for the wife, who stays at home and knows that husband and children are facing the foe. Do not, however, allow yourself to give way ... Yes, my own wife, the task laid on you is terribly difficult, and in my thoughts I shall always be near you, hold you and support you. I am waiting eagerly for your letters ...

I wonder what your journey was like, and what sort of rooms you have found in Berlin. I wonder if you have seen the boys. I should think it would be unlikely ... I am thirsting for a man's work to do, and it will be given me in full measure. Pray for me beloved, that my efforts may be crowned with success. I send you many warm kisses. In deep affection, Your Own Husband.[19]

Two nights before, Margarethe records, she had lain wide awake next to her sleeping husband. 'I stared with open eyes into the darkness and my heart was heavy with grim forebodings ... I knew only too well the meaning of war on two fronts.' She whispered into the darkness: 'God in heaven stand by me in my need.'[20]

CHAPTER THREE

Invasion

BELLS BOOMED IN BERLIN ON SATURDAY, 1 AUGUST 1914. THE PREVIOUS evening Kaiser Wilhelm had appeared on the balcony of his Royal Palace and shouted to the massive crowd: 'The sword is being pressed into our hands! Now I commend you to God!'

Ludendorff had played a major part in the detailed planning for the outbreak of war; mobilisation now proceeded according to exact schemes drawn up so meticulously by him and his colleagues the previous year. And, after his isolation, the time had come for Ludendorff's talents to be put to better use again: his own mobilisation orders declared that he should assume the post of Deputy Chief of Staff to the 2nd Army, based on Aachen and commanded by General Karl von Bülow. Ludendorff had been closely involved with the preparation of tasks for the 2nd Army, which formed one of the five German armies in the right wing – this, under the Schlieffen Plan, must undertake the gigantic wheeling movement in the north through Belgium.

Ludendorff also knew that the 2nd Army, and the 1st Army forming the end of the whole German line, would have to carry out a more difficult and crucial offensive than the other three in the German right wing. Amongst Moltke's changes to the Schlieffen Plan had been the decision not to violate Dutch as well as Belgian neutrality. Space would therefore be more restricted than Schlieffen had envisaged: the 1st and 2nd German armies would be obliged to fight a way through the narrow and strongly-defended fortress area of Liège in Belgium – hence the statement made in Schlieffen's last notes that Liège must be taken in minimum time. Failure would mean the vital right wing being disastrously delayed and the whole wheeling movement endangered.

But for the moment Ludendorff could journey in an almost leisurely manner to his posting: war against France had still to be declared. He left Strasbourg in the early morning of Sunday, 2 August, travelling with his horses via Cologne. There he watched the crammed troop

trains clattering through the station regularly each ten minutes, all
rushing north for the invasion of Belgium.

Ludendorff reached Aachen during the evening. Immediately, he
received fresh orders: he was to be temporarily seconded to General
von Emmich, commander of the six mixed infantry brigades allocated
for the initial surprise attack on Liège. This force would have the responsibility of clearing a way for the main armies.[1] Ludendorff found
a room in the Hotel Union in Aachen and waited for von Emmich,
who arrived next morning, 3 August; the two men had never met before, but from the first they established an excellent relationship.
'From that time onwards,' wrote Ludendorff, 'I cherished a feeling of
deep esteem for him which lasted until the day of his death.'

Also on this Monday, the Prussian Cabinet met in Berlin. The decision had to be taken whether war should be declared on France,
and no more time could be spared since hostilities would begin at any
moment on the Eastern Front. Bethmann Hollweg reported the latest
situation, his face strained. Instructions had been sent to the German
Ambassador in Belgium, Claus von Below-Saleske, to present an ultimatum demanding passage of German troops through the country:
Belgium was asked to view this invasion, undertaken through the
'dictates of self-preservation', with 'benevolent neutrality'. The curt
Belgian rejection had been received at 7 o'clock that morning. The
Chancellor continued by declaring that British participation in the
war now seemed certain. Admiral von Tirpitz, head of the German
Navy, reportedly shocked those present by exclaiming: 'All is lost
then!'

A few hours later Germany declared war on France. During the
afternoon the British Foreign Secretary, Sir Edward Grey, informed
the House of Commons of the imminent threat to Belgian neutrality
and of Britain's 'obligations of honour'. Enthusiastic applause greeted
his words.

In the early hours of Tuesday, 4 August, the first German cavalry
patrols trotted over the Belgian frontier. Close behind moved the remainder of the brigades under Emmich, advancing towards the massive fortress of Liège and thereby opening the first hostile acts in the
First World War. With these advance troops rode Ludendorff.

Ludendorff had recently celebrated his forty-ninth birthday. He enjoyed perfect physical fitness, despite the thickening round his waist.
He had been expecting war for months and even years, and had
readied himself accordingly: his life so far had been spent preparing
for this moment; he apparently felt neither elation nor fear, simply a
sense of the inevitable. He never expressed in public his opinions as
to the justification of the war, contrary to the volumes of statements
he would make regarding the eventual peace. Such opinions, at this
moment, would have seemed to him entirely unsoldierly.

In many respects Ludendorff's personal position was unique. Many still believed he should be employed as the Chief of Operations alongside Moltke, and that Moltke would benefit to a drastic degree from his presence. Instead, Ludendorff's career had been checked, but even this could be used to advantage. His more recent regimental and brigade experience enabled him to view the German plans from both strategic and tactical aspects; during the last twenty months he had gained greater knowledge of the problems amongst the line regiments – lack of training in some cases, shortages of officers, even lack of sufficient support artillery.

His present post highlighted the problematical nature of Ludendorff's employment. He lacked precise instructions except 'to co-ordinate General von Emmich's plans with General von Bülow's probable dispositions'.[2] Emmich had his own chief of staff, General von Lauenstein, in fact superior in rank to Ludendorff. Ludendorff himself had no official position, nor could he issue orders; his own superior, Bülow, remained many miles away at Hanover, his intention being to move his HQ forward when battle developed. Ludendorff therefore enjoyed a degree of independence, but he had to avoid the suspicion of being an interfering outsider.

Uhlans from General von der Marwitz's 2nd and 4th Cavalry Divisions probed down the narrow lanes beneath the poplars; the sun rose to glint on lances and square-topped helmets, and still no enemy fire had been received. Then, at the small cobbled hamlet of Battice, rifles cracked from the houses and perhaps four of the German cavalrymen slumped from their saddles: their companions charged and overran the hamlet. No uniformed enemy soldiers were found, and instead the defenders all seemed to be civilians. The discovery immediately stimulated anger amongst the invaders, who considered this practice of guerrilla warfare to be barbaric. They replied in kind, driving out the inhabitants of Battice and burning the houses – such civilian warfare prompted memories of 1870–71 when German troops suffered from the hated French patriots, the *franc-tireurs*.

Similar guerrilla actions were repeated elsewhere bringing ruthless German reaction including six hostages shot at the village of Warsage. Ludendorff joined in the condemnation of the use of civilians. 'Such action was not in keeping with the usages of war; our troops cannot be blamed if they took the sternest measures to suppress it.' Overlooking the flagrant violation of Belgian neutrality, he added: 'For my part, I had taken the field with chivalrous and humane conceptions of warfare. This *franc-tireur* warfare was bound to disgust any soldier. My soldierly spirit suffered bitter disillusion.'[3]

Ludendorff rode forward during the day to investigate progress. By now opposition had stiffened, and near the village of Visé, fifteen miles from Liège, Ludendorff came under fire from Belgians hidden in the hedgerows – his first active engagement, from which he escaped unscathed. Occupation of Visé was essential in order to secure the nearby Meuse crossing before the assault on Liège, but one barricade after another blocked the road to the village and the cavalry made slow progress. At Ludendorff's request a cyclist company was sent to reconnoitre: soon afterwards a message came back that the entire company had been slaughtered in the village.

Ludendorff displayed considerable courage, moving forward himself with only two men. They crept into the village, where they found the cyclists in fact still alive. The houses were taken one by one, and the Germans continued their advance, but only to discover that the Meuse bridge had been blown. Ludendorff returned to von Emmich's HQ and reported the cavalry positions; the German commander ordered the infantry forward and the marching battalions filtered down the lanes like columns of scurrying grey ants. Ludendorff slept that night at Hervé, about ten miles from Liège on the main Aachen road. This night of 4–5 August, Ludendorff's first on enemy soil, proved disturbed: civilians fired at the inn in which he slept, fetching him from his bed in the early hours.

Ahead lay the grim Liège fortress system. Tactical schemes for the assault had been drafted in 1911, with Ludendorff giving detailed advice to Moltke; now these plans must be put into effect, and Ludendorff, so closely concerned with the conception, would be even more involved with the execution.

The Liège defences presented a formidable obstacle. Designed by the brilliant military engineer H. A. Brialmont, the forts were constructed between 1888 and 1891, and were far in advance of any other fortified system at that time. Brialmont abandoned the traditional idea of encircling the city with a continuous curtain, and instead moved the forts outside to cover every approach and also to cover each other. The dozen forts were therefore situated about four miles from the city; artillery totalled 400 pieces, and the garrison numbered over 20,000 men. Each fort had an immense concrete shield, based on a triangular plan, with a surrounded ditch filled with barbed wire. Turreted guns – like those on a battleship – were positioned to supply maximum firepower, and beneath the forts lay a complex structure of tunnels, underground chambers and store rooms, all protected by thick concrete.

German plans envisaged making use of the undulating ground in the vicinity of the forts, which allowed some cover for infantry attacks. But the latter would not be directed at the forts themselves; instead the attempt would be made to infiltrate between them to reach the city beyond – the Belgians had neglected to deploy sufficient strength between the concrete bastions. Nevertheless, heavy German casualties were expected, since the attackers would still have to endure concentrated fire from the multitude of loopholes in the fortress walls, apart from the troops in the defensive lines between them. As for the forts, these would be left for the moment: later they would be dealt with by using a method so far kept tightly secret. Ludendorff was one of the few people who knew of an awesome weapon in Germany's arsenal.

After an early breakfast on 5 August Ludendorff rode from Hervé to visit forward units. 'The troops felt nervous,' he wrote. 'From conversations with the officers, I gathered that their faith in the success of this undertaking was only slight.'[4] First, the outnumbered Germans attempted to gain possession peacefully, but the Belgian commander, General Gérard Leman, quietly refused; he preferred to carry out his orders received from King Albert: 'I charge you to hold to the end ...'[5] One hour later, just before noon, the German guns began to thump and thunder from the woods east of Liège. High explosive shells burst among the forts and thick smoke swept over the city, and shrapnel blasted into the enemy infantry deployed between the main defensive works. The bombardment continued throughout the afternoon: from a distance it seemed the enemy walls must be shattered, yet each time the smoke drifted away the defences could be seen still intact.

Towards evening orders were given to the German infantry for the advance. The men stood to form line, humping on their equipment and even dragging their field kitchens with them. Ludendorff, still with Emmich's staff in the centre, watched the formations begin to move forward. Perhaps he spared a thought for his wife – this day was her birthday. Within seconds the Belgian *mitrailleuse* machine guns opened fire and were ripping into the German ranks, spewing 150 rounds per gun each 60 seconds; enemy riflemen began to fire steadily from the trenches and for the first time Ludendorff witnessed men dying *en masse* and heard the cacophony of screams, harsh rattling machine guns and the hollow crump of mortars.

The first assaults were driven back. Fresh lines were formed and ordered forward. The men displayed lack of training and experience – formations were ragged and unco-ordinated – yet their courage and determination impressed even their enemy.

> They made no attempt at deploying but came on [wrote one Belgian officer] until, as we shot them down, the fallen were heaped on top of each other in an awful barricade of dead and wounded that threatened to mask our guns and cause us trouble. So high did the barricade become that we did not know whether to fire through it or to go out and clear openings with our hands ... But would you believe it? This veritable wall of dead and dying enabled those wonderful Germans to creep closer.[6]

Darkness provided extra cover. The Germans gained ground, and just before midnight Ludendorff rode out from Hervé with Emmich and the rest of the staff. Wounded men, cars, and soldiers waiting to go into action crammed the highway. Ludendorff reached Micheroux, about two miles from the nearest Belgian positions at Fort Fléron, where von Wussow's 14th Infantry Brigade was trying to assemble for the advance. Ludendorff noted that the troops 'were collecting in a very unsoldierly manner on a road which could easily have been swept by the fortress guns'. Fortunately the latter failed to seize the opportunity, but rifle shots nevertheless flashed from houses south of the road; the 14th Infantry Brigade continued to struggle into line, stumbling in the dark, and at 1 o'clock the advance began. Emmich and Ludendorff rode with the marching troops.

Wussow's brigade formed part of a renewed attempt to break through the fortress circle east of Liège: the 14th Infantry Brigade would aim north of Fort Fléron striking via the hamlet of Rétinne, then, if the fort could be successfully skirted, the troops would push to the higher ground at La Chartreuse almost in the Liège suburbs. Almost immediately Ludendorff found himself thrown into the midst of battle. Emmich and his staff moved towards the rear of one of the brigade columns when the advance began, but soon afterwards the men halted, cramming together in the darkness and cursing as they tried to discover the reason for the delay. Ludendorff pushed his way to the front and discovered the halt followed a misunderstanding of orders; despite his own lack of authority to issue commands 'I put the column in motion again and remained at its head'. Meanwhile the brigade units further to the flank had continued their advance and Ludendorff's column lost contact. The troops suddenly came under concentrated fire. 'Men fell right and left. I shall never forget hearing the thud of bullets striking human bodies. We made some rushes at the invisible enemy, but the firing became more intense.'

Ludendorff ordered withdrawal out of range and the men crept and crawled back to Rétinne, eventually finding the correct road. But the situation seemed as confused as ever. Taking only a handful of men, Ludendorff probed forward. 'Suddenly there was firing ahead. Machine-gun bullets swept the road but did not harm us.' Only a few yards further Ludendorff blundered into a heap of dead and dying Germans, victims of machine-gun fire, and with the Brigade Commander Wussow among them.

Taking command himself, Ludendorff collected men around him and hurriedly organised an attack on the nearby machine guns: men filtered across the fields on either side of the road, closed in on the enemy, and the guns were silenced. Ludendorff ordered continued advance but almost immediately his troops came under fire again; and so the painful progress continued until the sky at last began to lighten, and the soldiers filed on towards the Meuse with the heights around La Chartreuse rising beyond. A way had been prised between the chain of forts.

We could see the works on the north side of Liège as we climbed out of the Meuse valley to the heights ... It was about two o'clock when the brigade arrived there. Guns were at once trained on the town, and a shot was fired now and again, partly as a signal to the other brigades, partly to intimidate the Governor of the fortress and the inhabitants. But I had to be exceedingly sparing of ammunition, for we were very short. The troops were exhausted and much weakened by the hard fighting; officers had lost their horses, and the field kitchens had been left behind ...

Suddenly white flags began to flutter from the city and for a while it seemed the battle was over. But by 7 o'clock it had become known that the flags were flown contrary to the command of the Belgian Governor, and resistance continued. Moreover, Ludendorff's improvised units were in an extremely precarious situation, lacking support.

'It became increasingly clear that the brigade was isolated within the circle of forts, cut off from the outer world. We had to reckon with hostile attacks.' The nerves of the troops began to suffer as night fell; Ludendorff wrote later:

I shall never forget the night of the 6th–7th August. It was cold and as I had left my kit behind, Major von Marcard gave me his cloak. I was very anxious and listened feverishly for the sound of fighting. I still hoped at least one brigade had broken through the girdle of forts. But all was quiet, though every half-hour or so a howitzer shell fell into the town. The suspense was unbearable.

At last day began to break. Ludendorff managed to find his way back to Emmich to discuss the situation: the General agreed that Ludendorff's units should continue to strike for the city regardless of lack of support. Soon after returning to his men a message reached Ludendorff from Emmich saying the attack must begin immediately: troops were ordered to their feet and they moved wearily into line.

The key point in Liège was the citadel. Ludendorff's plans envisaged this strongpoint being taken by his advance guard under Colonel von Oven, and this moved off; the remainder of the troops followed some way behind, winding down the slopes towards the city. Much to their relief they encountered only stray sniper bullets, and some Belgian troops even walked forward with hands raised in surrender. Ludendorff believed von Oven must have taken the citadel and he commandeered a Belgian car to drive there as quickly as possible, only taking with him the brigade adjutant. The car stopped outside the citadel doors, and the startled Ludendorff could see no signs of German troops – only Belgian. It was already too late for him to seek safety.

Instead Ludendorff stepped from the car, walked to the massive fortress gates and thudded on the wood for entrance. The doors swung open. Ludendorff strode through and stood alone amongst the several hundred Belgian soldiers sheltering inside. One by one they surrendered.[7]

Within hours, this act made Ludendorff a hero. Newspapers printed descriptions of his exploit and the story gained added colour – this unknown soldier had captured Liège single-handed, merely by pounding on the gates with the hilt of his sword. In reality Ludendorff's accomplishment was far less noteworthy. General Leman had already ordered the withdrawal of his mobile troops from the Liège city area, and late the previous day these valuable units had begun pulling out of line to join the rest of the Belgian Army on the Gette. Left at Liège were the garrisons manning the fortresses, together with a small number of troops in the city. Leman had moved his HQ from the rue Sainte-Foi to Fort Loncin on the far side of the city.

Oven, ordered to take the citadel, realised the situation when he entered Liège and had hurried his advance guard to the north-west exit, hoping to trap stragglers. Remaining Belgian troops, including those in the citadel, were in no fit state to continue the fight – hence Ludendorff's deliverance and his easy, single-handed conquest. The adventure therefore lacked the daring which it first seemed to have. But while not deserving the propaganda praise it received at the time in German newspapers, it did not by contrast merit the ungracious detraction levelled at it later. Since he had no means of knowing the real situation amidst the confusion, Ludendorff's act demanded a courage which, both now and in the assault on Liège as a whole, he displayed to the full. He showed himself to be a good tactical commander, clear-headed and decisive; he had conducted himself well in his first battle.

CHAPTER FOUR

To Prevent the Worst

Now Ludendorff had to leave Liege. The brigade was spreading out through the city and the citadel was secured; prisoners were being herded together. Ludendorff felt it necessary to report to his superior, General von Bülow – whom he had so far not met since the start of the campaign. 'I wanted to report what had happened to Army Headquarters, ascertain the whereabouts of the other brigades, and give directions for the bringing up of the artillery against the forts.'[1] The latter point was of vital importance and urgency. So far the huge fortress walls had survived German artillery bombardments; now was the moment for the secret weapon to be employed against them – a gun of unprecedented power.

For the past two decades the Krupp armaments works had been developing a succession of monster guns, each bigger than the last. After 1900 these artillery pieces were given code-names – Alpha, Beta, and, in about 1908, the Gamma, a version of which would now be used against the Liège forts. Soon these guns would become famous with the nickname Big Bertha, called after Frau Krupp. The latest form of Gamma had a 42-cm calibre and a range of 10,250 yards, over which it was deadly accurate; the weapon was so massive and heavy – over 42 tons – that it had to be transported in five loads towed by Daimler Benz tractors. Only one battery was so far developed, comprising two guns and manned by 200 gunners plus 80 drivers and mechanics. This unit, titled *Kurz Marin Kanone* Battery 3, awaited orders to move ponderously forward from Germany.[2] And now Ludendorff considered the early presence of the fearful KMK 3 to be essential.

He left at 7 pm, 7 August. His journey, for all its importance, proved chaotic and dangerous amidst the confusion of advancing troops and streams of prisoners and wounded. He was unable to find army transport or even a German driver, and was obliged to accept the services of a member of the Belgian civil guard. For a time all went well; they passed through Hervé, where Ludendorff noted that his former HQ and the station had been burnt down, and then they reached the German frontier. 'The driver stopped suddenly and told me he could not go any further.'

Ludendorff hitched lifts and finally managed to reach Aachen very late at night. His colleagues thought him dead. Then officers at the Hotel Union informed him that von Bülow and the 2nd Army HQ had still to arrive by train from Hanover and that they were expected next day. Ludendorff therefore snatched a meal and rushed out into the night to try to find brigade commanders – troops had to be hurried forward to Liège as soon as possible. In fact reinforcements were already moving towards the city: by nightfall elements of the 34th, 11th and 27th Brigades had joined von Emmich. Ludendorff returned to the hotel and to the ministrations of his batman Rudolph Peters, who had remained behind with the heavy baggage. Ludendorff stripped off his filthy uniform – 'I had not had my clothes off for nearly ninety hours' – and sank on to his bed for his first sleep in three nights. Outside, the reinforcements for von Emmich continued to tramp through the streets; further to the rear the bulk of Bülow's 2nd Army, deployed between Coblenz and the frontier, awaited news that the Liège gap had been cleared for the full-scale advance.

Von Bülow reached Aachen next morning, 8 August, and immediately agreed that the siege artillery must be brought up. So huge were these weapons that it would take four days for them to arrive and be positioned. Meanwhile Ludendorff remained at the 2nd Army HQ assisting with staff work. Fierce fighting continued around the Liège fortresses, with the Belgian commander and his remaining troops putting up desperate resistance. Time remained a vital factor if the sweeping German right wing was to gain momentum before French and British troops deployed in maximum strength.

And, during the night of the 9th, Fort Barchon at the north-east corner of the city finally fell to German infantry. Next night the emphasis switched to Fort d'Evegnée, immediately to the north of Rétinne hamlet: once again the attackers emerged victorious after fearful hand-to-hand fighting. Infantry assaults continued to swirl round surviving forts for the next forty-eight hours, then, during the 12th, the Krupp Big Bertha howitzers at last arrived.

Suitable sites were selected about 9,500 yards from the initial targets, Forts Pontisse and Embourg. The complicated procedure of unloading and erecting the gun sections was completed with maximum efficiency. Observers were posted as close as possible to the first target, Pontisse, with field telephone links back to the guns; command post personnel calculated bearing and range and the guns were orientated. Small cranes lifted the shells from their packing. By 6.30 pm all was ready.

Ludendorff had returned to Liège with von Bülow and his staff. Now he stood with these senior officers on a nearby vantage point:

Bülow gave the order to fire, and the staff officers lifted their field-glasses in anticipation. The breech block of the first gun slid back from the massive chamber; the first 1,800-lb shell swung into the breech; six men rammed the shell home. A soldier standing on the firing platform yanked the four-foot lanyard and at 6.40 pm the first shell screamed towards the Belgian target, arching three miles high and taking 60 seconds to arrive.[3]

Ludendorff and the other officers saw the eruption of earth and flame some way from the fort, and the roar swept back. Belgian defenders at Pontisse believed the explosion must have been caused by a German underground mine. Then the second shell landed, closer this time, and a third even nearer, and the Belgians realised they were about to be subjected to a more devastating artillery bombardment than any previously known. Four more shells landed, each creeping towards Pontisse.

The eighth landed on target, slicing through the massive concrete walls protecting the central keep and inflicting ghastly casualties. Then Big Bertha ceased to fire. The Belgians would have to wait in almost unbearable anticipation for another salvo.

Not until the following morning, 13 August, did firing recommence. Meanwhile the second howitzer had been supplied with data gained by the first, and both immediately found their target. One shell after another exploded in the fort, stripping away the concrete like a knife carving cheese and exposing the defenders to the blast. Carnage resulted amidst the deadly fumes and flying rubble. And, at 12.30, a white flag fluttered through the dust.

Firing immediately switched to Fort Embourg. This surrendered at 5.30 pm, allowing sufficient daylight for ranging rounds to be despatched at Forts Liers and Fléron. Destruction continued on the 14th, and on the 15th Forts Boncelles and Loncin were shattered. Loncin housed General Leman's HQ, and after 19 shells had landed the magazine had suffered a direct hit, making the whole structure seem like a volcano.

Ludendorff and von Emmich accompanied German troops clambering over the ruins of Loncin; the air hung heavy with fumes. 'A number of dazed and blackened Belgian soldiers crawled out of the ruins,' wrote Ludendorff. 'All bleeding, they came towards us with their hands up, stammering out *"Ne pas tuer, ne pas tuer!"* – Don't kill, don't kill!' He added: 'We were no Huns. Our men fetched water to refresh our enemies.'[4] Amidst the destruction lay the Belgian commander, Leman. He appeared dead, but medical orderlies crouched over the body and found him to be still breathing, although nearly suffocated from the fumes of the explosion. Ludendorff and Emmich stood by the stretcher while he came to life again: Emmich congratulated his opponent on the gallant Belgian resistance and insisted he kept his sword. Leman whispered: 'I ask you to bear witness that you found me unconscious.'

Still the Belgians refused to surrender and the bombardment continued. The next day, 16 August, Forts Flémalle and Hollogne were battered into submission, so ending all resistance. Already, on the 14th, von Bülow's 2nd Army had begun to sweep across the Belgian border joined by General von Kluck's 1st Army; together they pushed through the Liège corridor striking for Brussels; Ludendorff accompanied the HQ staff. Once through the Liège corridor the two armies spread wide across the Belgian countryside: hastily improvised defences were brushed aside north of Tirlemont on 18 and 19 August, and next day German troops entered the enemy capital. The Big Berthas were dragged forward, joined now by another new artillery piece, the more mobile Skoda 30-cm.

On 21 August Ludendorff witnessed the crossing of the Sambre west of Namur by the 2nd Guards Division, part of the 2nd Army. He believed everything to be going 'quite smoothly'. The German public as a whole celebrated the apparent successes, chief among which was the Liège victory. In Berlin, Margarethe waited anxious for news in her rooms at the Westens Hospice: General von Stein, the Quartermaster-General who also rented a flat in the building, had been the first to tell her the story. 'Your husband is the hero of Liège!' Margarethe exclaimed: 'My husband, my own husband the conqueror, the hero of Liège ... My head was in a whirl. I went to my room. I had to be alone.'[5]

All Germany seemed to be in a whirl over the situation in the West. In the East, everything depended on the blocking of Russia's expected advance into East Prussia with the enemy held as near to the border as possible. Responsible for this task was the German 8th Army under General Max von Prittwitz, spread south from the Baltic to Frankenau and based on Königsberg. Further south, the Austrians would push into Russian Poland from Galicia.

Russian forces for the invasion of East Prussia, the North-west Army Group, comprised the 1st Army under General Pavel Rennenkampf and the 2nd Army under General Alexander Samsonov. Overall commander was General Yakov Zhilinsky; on 12 August the Russian 1st Cavalry Division under General Basil Gourko began to move into East Prussia to open the campaign.

German plans entailed one Russian army being held by a weak screen while all available forces were thrown against the other. By 17 August it had become apparent to Prittwitz that the Russian 1st Army would arrive before the 2nd, and he elected to attack this force; he believed he had acquired a favourable position behind the river Rominte. Unfortunately General Hermann von François, commanding the 1st Corps in Prittwitz's army, objected to these dispositions: François was fanatical in his determination not to allow Russians to march on Prussian soil, and he insisted on remaining further forward: on 17 August his troops were deployed north and south of Stalluponen less than halfway between the border and the Rominte.

Elements in François's corps clashed with the advancing 1st Russian Army during the 17th; Prittwitz, taken by surprise by this independent action, feared the 1st Corps might become isolated; irate telegraph messages ordered François to break off immediately, and the corps commander eventually withdrew his forces during the evening, having inflicted about 3,000 casualties on the enemy.

Prittwitz issued orders during the evening of the 19th for a decisive battle. François was instructed to strike from the north against the Russian 3rd Corps, still disorganised after the engagements on the 17th, while von Below's 1st Reserve Corps and von Mackensen's 17th Corps were to attack frontally further south in the Gumbinnen region. Artillery in François's Corps opened fire at 3.30 am, 20 August, taking the Russians on this flank by surprise. The enemy began to retreat and although engagements further south were less successful it still seemed that victory could be gained the following day. Instead Prittwitz made the fateful decision which cost him his career and which threw Ludendorff into prominence.

During the previous night, 19 August, reports reached Prittwitz that the Russian 2nd Army had advanced westwards as far as Ostrokenka, thus bringing forward the moment when it could join with the 1st. And, during the 20th, the pilot of a German reconnaissance aircraft informed HQ that strong elements were moving north from Warsaw and that these would cross the frontier within 24 hours. Meanwhile the fighting against the Russian 1st Army on the 20th had failed to inflict decisive defeat, and with the Russian 2nd Army apparently approaching, Prittwitz believed acute danger existed of a gigantic enemy pincer movement.

Tension increased rapidly at the German 8th Army HQ, now at Nordenburg. During the evening of the 20th von Prittwitz called his senior officers into the Operations Room. 'Gentlemen,' he declared, 'I see you have also received the message and know that the Russian army from Warsaw will advance in our rear if we continue the battle, and cut us off from the Vistula. The army will, therefore, break off the fight and will retire behind the Vistula.'[6] Objections were immediately raised. Among those who protested was Lieutenant-Colonel Max Hoffmann, First General Staff Officer, who believed Gumbinnen could still result in a decisive victory. But Prittwitz's nerves were obviously unsteady; he refused to change his mind and left the room.

Back in his quarters, Prittwitz telephoned Supreme HQ at Coblenz informing Moltke of his decision: he said he must retreat as far as the Vistula, abandoning East Prussia completely, and even the Vistula might be difficult to hold since 'it can be waded across everywhere'.[7]

The 8th Army staff officers had continued to discuss the situation, ignorant of their commander's telephone call to Moltke, and they pressed their objections with renewed vehemence when Prittwitz returned. By now the commander had recovered some of his calm, and he eventually agreed to abandon his plans for withdrawal although he still refused to resume battle. Members of his staff immediately prepared orders for the fresh 8th Army deployment, but no message was sent to Coblenz concerning the latest change of plan.[8]

Moltke, himself harassed and ill, had reacted violently to Prittwitz's decision to retreat. The German Supreme Command already lacked confidence in the 8th Army leader, and Moltke had attempted to appoint another to his post even before war began, but had been overruled by the Kaiser. Now his views were seemingly reinforced by telephone conversations with 8th Army Corps commanders including François, and Moltke seized his opportunity to seek a replacement.

No less important than the post of 8th Army commander was that of Chief of Staff. Count von Waldersee, presently occupying this appointment, also had to go: Moltke knew someone who would be highly suitable for such employment, his colleague and principal assistant before the war. An officer carrying a letter from Moltke was despatched immediately, reaching Ludendorff at Bülow's HQ halfway between Wavre and Namur at 9 am, 22 August.

> You have before you a new and difficult task, perhaps even more difficult than that of storming Liège . . . I know no other man in whom I have such absolute trust. You may yet be able to save the situation in the east. You must not be angry with me for calling you away from a post in which you are, perhaps, on the threshold of a decisive action, which, please God, will be conclusive. This is yet another sacrifice you are called upon to make for the Fatherland. The Kaiser, too, has confidence in you. Of course, you will not be made responsible for what has happened already, but with your energy you can prevent the worst from happening. So answer this new call, which is the greatest compliment that can be paid any soldier. I know that you will not belie the trust reposed in you.

With this letter came a message from General von Stein, Quartermaster-General: 'You must go, therefore. The interests of the State make it imperative. Your task is a difficult one, but you are equal to it.'[9]

Ludendorff learnt that the new commander of the 8th Army would most likely be Infantry-General Paul von Hindenburg, whom he had never met and knew little about. The messenger from Moltke, Captain von Rochow, added that Hindenburg's whereabouts were unknown, and the retired General might not even accept the offer. Rochow also declared that Ludendorff's presence was required immediately at Supreme HQ.

'I was proud of my new task and of the trust placed in me,' wrote

Ludendorff in his memoirs. 'I was exalted at the thought of serving my Emperor, Army and Fatherland, in a position of great responsibility at a most critical point ... No soldier could have had a better chance given him. But I was deeply distressed that my appointment was the outcome of such a serious situation for my country.'

Within fifteen minutes Ludendorff had thrown a few belongings into a valise and scrambled into the waiting car. As the vehicle passed through Wavre, where houses still smouldered from damage inflicted by the German advance in the west, his thoughts were already ranging ahead to the distant Eastern Front.

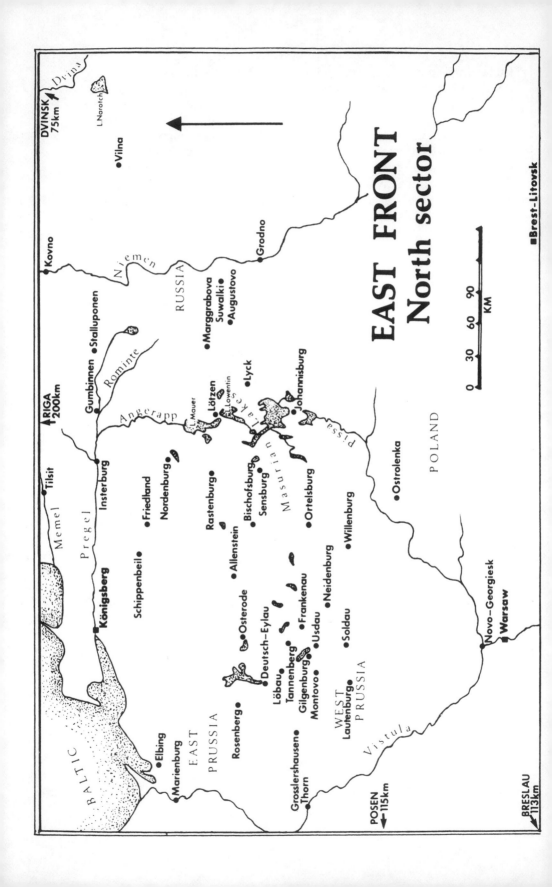

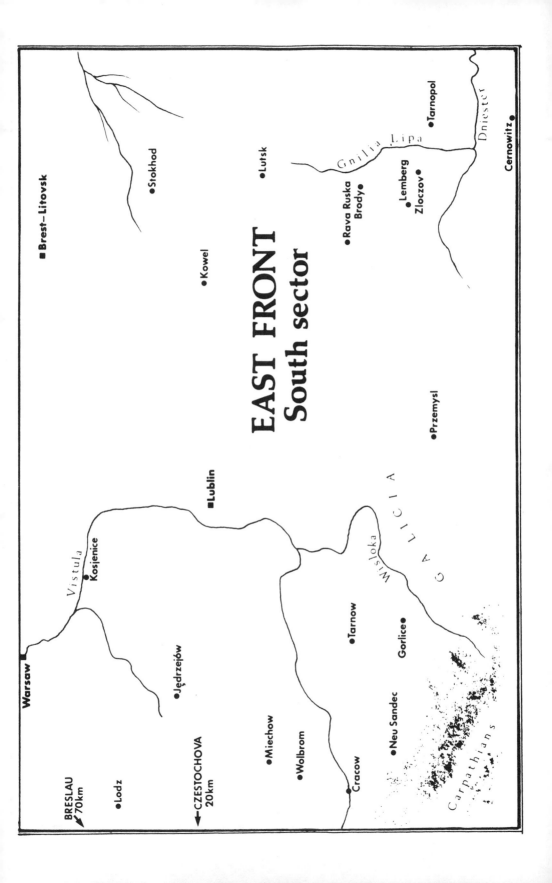

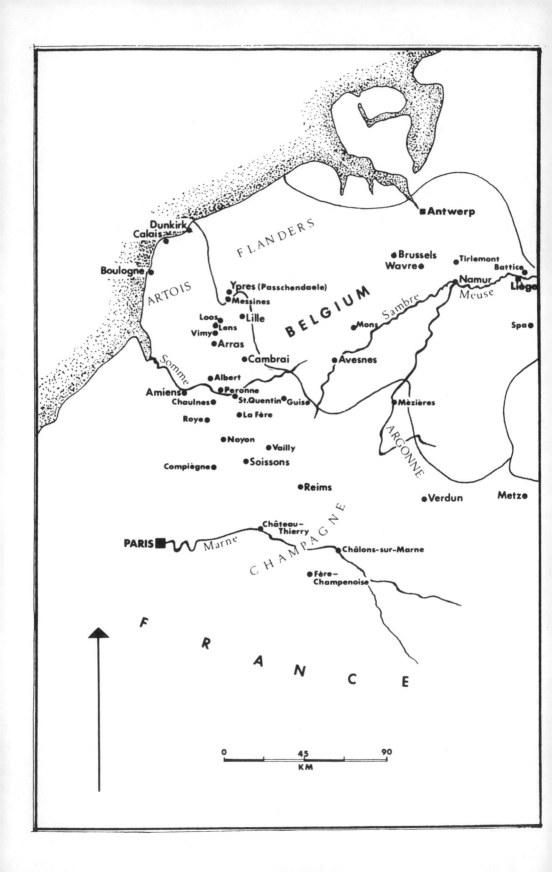

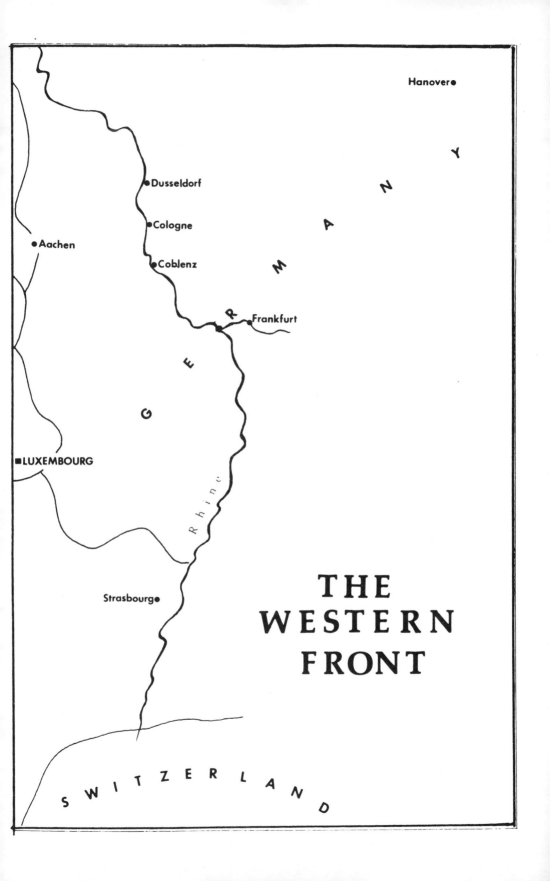

Hanover•

•Dusseldorf

•Cologne

•Aachen

•Coblenz

G E R M A N Y

•Frankfurt

G E R

■LUXEMBOURG

Rhine

Strasbourg•

THE
WESTERN
FRONT

S W I T Z E R L A N D

CHAPTER FIVE

Moves for Battle

FOR FOUR YEARS GENERAL PAUL VON HINDENBURG HAD LIVED IN PEACE-ful retirement in his Hanover flat. Life had seemed monotonous after an energetic career and his health showed signs of failing, but he enjoyed his favourite hobbies of shooting and collecting paintings of the Madonna and Child, and above all he found delight in watching the military progress of his son Oskar. The latter, an officer in the family regiment, had taken over from his sixty-seven-year-old father in con-tinuing the Hindenburg traditions. These stretched back to the thir-teenth century and to the Knights of the Teutonic Order, progressing through the years to Frederick the Great and the award of Prussian estates for services in the Silesian War. Hindenburg's childhood had been the epitome of the Prussian military caste system – his nurse, it was said, quelled infant protests by bawling: 'Silence in the ranks!' Hindenburg first saw service in the Seven Weeks' War against Austria, when Ludendorff was just one year old; four years later he won the coveted Iron Cross for bravery during the Franco-Prussian War.

Peace after 1871 brought a steady rise through the ranks, until Hindenburg reached his apparent summit in 1904 with command of the 4th Army Corps based at Magdeburg. According to rumours he fell out of favour with the Kaiser in 1908, when enthusiasm eclipsed discretion during Imperial manoeuvres and he allowed troops com-manded by the ruler to lose the mock battle. This was said to have prompted his retirement from the army three years later, but Hinden-burg denied the story. 'There was no prospect of a war,' he explained, adding that in consequence he believed it his duty to make way for younger men.

But the outbreak of war in 1914 made Hindenburg impatient to be employed again. 'I placed myself in the hands of fate and waited in longing expectations.'[1] Yet no summons came, and it seemed that his retirement was complete and that he was forgotten.

Then suddenly, during the late afternoon of 22 August, a knock sounded on his door. Hindenburg was handed a telegram from the

Kaiser himself, despatched from the Imperial HQ at Coblenz and asking if he was available for immediate service. The General sent two words in reply: 'Am ready'. He knew nothing of his appointment until further telegrams informed him of the 8th Army Command in East Prussia; Ludendorff, his Chief of Staff, would be travelling through Hanover during that night and contact between the two men could be made at the station. Hindenburg packed his bags and pulled out his old uniform, ruefully noticing that his tunic was now completely out of date.[2]

During the early hours of 23 August he slipped from his flat with his wife and took a taxi to Hanover station. There, while Frau von Hindenburg stood nervous and quiet, her husband paced up and down on the cold, dark platform, impatient to see the lights of Ludendorff's train and to begin his eastwards journey.

Meanwhile, during the previous afternoon, 22 August, Ludendorff's dark grey staff car had travelled at maximum speed along the crowded roads to Coblenz. The driver frequently sounded his horn to scatter troops out of the way: unit after unit was marching through Belgium, all forming part of the 1st and 2nd Army offensive against France. Suddenly Ludendorff noticed one particular regiment – the 31st Infantry – and with them his seventeen-year-old stepson Heinz, now an ensign. He ordered his driver to stop and they shook hands beside the road. As Margarethe commented later: 'What a strange meeting between father and son in the enemy's territory! One on his way to Russia, the other to France.'[3]

Margarethe herself was preparing to make a journey. The telephone had rung in her Westens Hospice rooms during the afternoon. 'It was urgent ... A general staff officer, whom I knew, gave me instructions on behalf of my husband to be at the Tiergarten station at eight o'clock next morning.'

Ludendorff's car reached Coblenz during the early evening of the 22nd. At 6 pm he entered Moltke's office, and immediately noted the haggard appearance of the Chief of General Staff. Moltke provided details of the eastern situation – the initial clashes with the Russian 1st Army, the battle at Gumbinnen, the approach of the 2nd Russian Army, and now von Prittwitz's decision to withdraw to the Vistula; Moltke was apparently still unaware that this decision had been changed and Prittwitz now intended merely to disengage from battle. Ludendorff had some sympathy with the policy of retirement, but realised that it neglected the psychological and political effects of retreat. Moreover, the situation differed from that envisaged in Schlieffen's war games, when such a withdrawal had been contemplated. Now, the 8th Army might not be allowed to spare itself for a subsequent counter-attack. 'As events were shaping, retreat behind the Vistula would have spelt ruin,' wrote Ludendorff in his memoirs.

'We should not have been able to hold the Vistula line against the numerically superior forces of the Russians, and it would certainly have been impossible for us to give direct help to the Austrians ...'⁴

Ludendorff therefore reached the same conclusions as those of Max Hoffmann and other members of Prittwitz's staff. Now he took it upon himself to despatch urgent orders without prior consultation with Hindenburg. In fact the commands were almost identical to those already issued by the 8th Army HQ to the corps commanders: battle would not be resumed at Gumbinnen, instead, the opportunity would be taken to make a fresh strike at the other Russian army. Thus Ludendorff envisaged a general movement south-east, to start next day 23 August. This would shift the 8th Army away from Rennenkampf's 1st Army and towards Samsonov's approaching 2nd Army – having blocked the one, forcing it temporarily on to the defensive, Ludendorff intended to move into a position offering an assault on the other. Hoffmann had also ordered a movement south-east, although to a deployment leaving the options open for attacks on either the Russian 1st or 2nd Army: according to Ludendorff's telegraphed instructions direct to the 8th Army corps commanders, the 1st Corps should reinforce 20th Corps further south, with this grouping in the Deutsch-Eylau area; Hoffmann ordered a similar reinforcement although slightly further west at Grosslershausen.

Similarities between the two sets of orders have been used as an example of the closely co-ordinated thinking generated by the Great General Staff system. Indeed, Ludendorff knew Hoffmann well, having lived in the same quarters when both were staff officers in Berlin. On the other hand, too much credit can be given to the Great General Staff aspect in accounting for the parallel lines of thought. Abandonment of the decision to withdraw left only two choices: either a renewed attack on the Russian 1st or a switch to be in a position to attack the 2nd. The former assault would be expected and therefore prolonged, allowing the threat from the south to grow. It seemed more logical to disengage from Rennenkampf and to prepare a strike against Samsonov's wing, without fear of a Russian attack from the rear. Plans for such an offensive had in fact been prepared prior to 1914. Now, in Ludendorff's words: 'No staff officer would miss such a chance of turning to good advantage the fact that their two armies were separated.'⁵

Ludendorff was anxious to leave Coblenz, but his impatience had to be contained: first the Kaiser requested his presence. Apparently the black shadow of disapproval, which had hung over Ludendorff since 1911, had blown away. Yet faint wisps of Imperial suspicion might still remain – hence Moltke's attempted reassurance in his letter when he stated categorically: 'The Kaiser, too, has confidence in you.' In fact Wilhelm was far from satisfied with the appointments of both Hindenburg and Ludendorff: these two had been forced upon him and were certainly not his own choice. He disliked Hindenburg's 'dry, solid simplicity' and he considered Ludendorff to be brusque, humourless and meddlesome.[6]

Outwardly all seemed well, for the moment. The Kaiser had already awarded Ludendorff the '*Pour le Mérite*', the first of the war, and now he insisted on summoning the new 8th Army Chief of Staff so that he could invest him in person.[7] Only as he prepared to leave did Ludendorff learn that Hindenburg had accepted the post of 8th Army commander, and that he would be boarding the train at Hanover. Moltke bade him farewell and turned back to his consideration of the Western Front, where all seemed to be going satisfactorily yet not sufficiently fast to ease nagging doubts. At 9 pm, just three hours after his arrival at Coblenz, Ludendorff boarded his special train and began his eastwards journey through the night.

The train contained three hastily prepared carriages: one served as sleeping and living room for Hindenburg, another as the same for Ludendorff, and the third acted as office and dining room. Ludendorff sat alone. The train rattled through stations and over points, with the latter always thrown to allow priority. At 4 o'clock in the morning, 23 August, the engine pulled into Hanover station.

Hindenburg waited beneath the harsh lights as Ludendorff stepped down on to the platform. The two men saluted, and then Hindenburg took the Chief of Staff's hand in both his own; Ludendorff stood aside respectfully as the General said his goodbyes to his wife, and they boarded the train. Ludendorff explained the situation in short, factual terms, and revealing the orders which he had already issued. Hindenburg's reaction was to prove typical. 'I can't think of anything better,' he declared. 'For heaven's sake, we'll do it.'[8] In his memoirs Ludendorff described this first meeting in one dismissive sentence: 'I explained the situation shortly and we then went to bed.'[9]

So began the famous partnership, made all the more interesting because of the contrast between the two men. Both had been born in Posen, but there the similarity ended. Hindenburg was the true Prussian aristocrat; Ludendorff the son of a small landowner. Those who met Hindenburg felt attracted to his kindliness and his childlike appeal; Ludendorff by comparison seemed stern and bull-like. But their personalities fitted them for their respective roles – one the beloved figurehead, the other an almost Machiavellian figure standing by his shoulder. Both were fully aware of the traditional parts played by Commander and Chief of Staff in the Prussian Army – the partnerships which had been forged in the Napoleonic past between Blücher and Scharnhorst and Gneisenau, Kleist and Grolman, Yorck and Rauch...

'For four years the Field-Marshal and I worked together like one man in the most perfect harmony,' wrote Ludendorff later. 'Our strategical and tactical views were in complete agreement, and harmonious

D

and confident co-operation was the natural result . . . He always agreed with my views and approved my draft orders.'[10] 'From now on we were to be united for years in common thought and action,' wrote Hindenburg. He characterised their relationship as being like a happy marriage and added: 'I realised that one of my principal tasks was, as far as possible, to give free scope to the intellectual powers, the almost superhuman capacity for work and untiring resolution of my Chief of Staff.'[11]

In Berlin, Margarethe found herself unable to control her impatience. She left her rooms in the early hours of the 23rd and hurried to the Tiergarten station; the minutes dragged by. 'I had come much too early, my anxiety having driven me out of the house. Finally, the train came in. A door was opened. I was pulled inside and away went the train towards the east.' Husband and wife remained alone for an hour. At 9 o'clock they walked to the office carriage where breakfast had been prepared, and where Margarethe met Hindenburg. He made an immediate and deep impression: his hulking, bear-like stature, deep chiselled face and kind, gentle eyes.

'After all these years,' remembered Margarethe, 'I realise all the loyalty and reliability, all the kindness and knowledge of human nature which was mirrored in his countenance. From the first moment I saw him my heart went out to him in confidence and admiration.'

They sat together at the meal table, and Hindenburg revealed how he had waited impatiently for employment in the war, adding that when the summons actually came it had still caught him unprepared. 'Look,' he confided, almost shamefaced, 'my uniform and boots are not according to the regulations.'[12]

The special train was steaming past ammunition trucks and transports, all heading east; carriages were decked with flowers, and from every window could be seen 'the fresh, smiling faces' of young soldiers. To Margarethe 'the whole thing seemed a dream'. She disembarked at Kustrin and waited for a train back to Berlin. 'Men, horses, cannons and war material of every kind – everything streamed by unceasingly to the Russian front.'[13]

Ludendorff and Hindenburg reached Marienburg at about 2 pm, with the Chief of Staff having already telegraphed that the 8th Army HQ should move to this town. Waiting at the station were Hoffmann and Grünert, 8th Army Quartermaster-General. Neither was particularly pleased by the change in command: Hoffmann continued to support Prittwitz once the withdrawal to the Vistula had been cancelled, and also disagreed with Ludendorff's action in issuing orders direct to corps commanders rather than through the army HQ.[14]

'Our reception in Marienburg was anything but cheerful,' commented Ludendorff. 'It seemed like entering another world to come into this depressing atmosphere after Liège and the rapid advance in the West.'[15]

Prittwitz and the former Chief of Staff, Waldersee, had already gone – having only learnt of their dismissal when the transport chief reported arrangements for their successors' special train. Ludendorff was introduced to the staff officers at the improvised HQ, then he dismissed them with the exception of Hoffmann. The latter supplied a full briefing. Later he wrote: 'I found him extremely surprised that all the instructions and orders necessary for the intended attack had already been given.' Hoffmann had still to overcome the suspicions of the newcomer, but soon this debonair, cynical, and highly intelligent officer would form an excellent assistant.

Within a few hours would emerge the results of long years of preparation both in Russia and Germany. In Russia, planning had been hampered by internal politics and wrangling, especially over whether the intricate fortress system should be maintained. This system, created in the late nineteenth century to offset the likelihood of speedier German mobilisation, had been the basis of Russian strategic thinking until critics maintained such defences had been rendered obsolete. In 1910 the War Minister V. A. Sukhomlinov and his chief assistant Danilov replaced the existing scheme with Plan 19: this proposed a Russian offensive in the first weeks of war to save France from isolation; an attack on East Prussia should be launched from south and east. At the same time Danilov realised that the East Prussian salient presented strong tactical difficulties – the broken countryside covered with lakes, forests and rivers, would oblige attacking forces to dissipate strength. Plan 19 therefore called for four armies being deployed, including 19 army corps: by comparison only 9 army corps would be allotted against the Austrians further south; fortresses should be disbanded since these would merely consume manpower.

Plan 19 met with fierce opposition, especially from those who believed that the fortresses should be kept. The scheme had to be amended, with serious results: under the revised Plan A, the emphasis was switched to a larger offensive against the Austrians, employing over 46 divisions compared with 30 against the Germans; the fortresses were retained, thus fostering a defensive mentality.[16]

Neither East Prussia nor Galicia was provided with sufficient strength; links between north and south were unsatisfactory. Moreover the Russian staff system compared unfavourably with the German, and the post of an independent Chief of the General Staff had only been created after the Russo-Japanese War. Personality clashes were intensified; senior officers represented different cliques in the faction-riddled Russian army: Zhilinsky, overall commander of the north front, was a keen supporter of Sukhomlinov's offensive ideas; Rennenkampf, 1st Army Commander, hated Sukhomlinov, while his Chief of Staff, Mileant, agreed with Zhilinsky – so much so that Rennenkampf would only communicate with him in writing. Samsonov, commanding the 2nd Army, was a Sukhomlinovite appointment, but his Chief of Staff, Postovski, was in the opposite camp.[17]

Co-operation was essential between the two Russian armies in the north if the plan for a pincer-movement could be accomplished, yet lack of adequate liaison existed from the beginning; moreover the Russians dissipated strength by detaching troops to guard against flank attacks and by failing to bring up reserves. On paper the Russian 2nd Army deployed 14.5 infantry divisions and four cavalry divisions, together with 1,160 guns, but by the time of Ludendorff's arrival this strength was 9.5 infantry divisions, 3 cavalry divisions and 738 guns. The German 8th Army contained 13 infantry divisions, 1 cavalry division and 774 guns.[18]

Even with improved odds Ludendorff could ill afford to fight without adequate concentration of his own corps: the complicated disentanglement from Rennenkampf's 1st Army front had to be achieved in minimum time. Troops were moved south throughout the night of 24 August and during the 25th, unit after unit filing to the railheads. Once at their destination these elements, comprising the 1st Reserve Corps and part of the 17th Army Corps, were positioned between Scholtz's 20th Corps already facing Samsonov's approach and the remainder of the 8th Army facing Rennenkampf.

Reports of these troop movements reached Rennenkampf – some German units were boarding their trains less than 25 miles from the front at Gumbinnen – but he believed these forces to be retreating. The Russian 1st Army remained immobile, since Rennenkampf preferred to rest his troops and reorganise supplies prior to a march on Königsberg: some of his staff officers even considered a Russian withdrawal to be necessary.[19] Samsonov displayed a direct contrast: he had pushed his 2nd Army troops too hard. His advance to the frontier had begun on 17 August, with the first units crossing on the 20th. Zhilinsky, his superior, sent a succession of messages ordering him to move faster, and on 19 August Samsonov snapped back: 'The Army is advancing according to the timetable in your orders, without halting, covering marches of more than 12 miles over the sand; therefore I cannot go more quickly.' Russian soldiers were exhausted even before they reached the frontier, toiling in the summer heat, yet Zhilinsky kept up his pressure. 'I demand immediate and resolute operations,' he telegraphed on 22 August. By nightfall on the 22nd leading units of the 2nd Army lay about 30 miles into East Prussia. But the Russian line stretched wide – 6th Corps at Ortelsburg, 13th Corps near Willenburg, 15th Corps at Neidenburg and 1st Corps at Soldau. A gap of over 40 miles had opened between Samsonov's two wings.[20]

Hoffmann and Ludendorff talked late into the night on the 23rd, the day of Ludendorff's arrival. Latest reports indicated activity in both the Russian 1st and 2nd Army sectors: in the north, Rennenkampf appeared to be moving at last; in the south, the first significant contact had been made with Samsonov's forward units. At 5 pm German troops in 20th Corps clashed with the enemy between Orlau and Frankenau; Russian troops from the 15th Corps were slaughtered as they tried to advance across potato fields against German machine guns.

Fresh news was handed to Ludendorff when he awoke soon after dawn, 24 August: Russian troops in the engagement between Orlau and Frankenau had launched repeated suicidal attacks in the half-light, and had succeeded in pushing back some German defences. Scholtz, 20th Corps commander, remained confident and believed his withdrawal would only be temporary.

Samsonov lost direct contact with the Germans and confusion increased; at the same time Zhilinsky pestered the 2nd Army commander with further orders. Optimistic reports from Rennenkampf indicated a full-scale German retreat in the north, and Zhilinsky therefore commanded Samsonov to hurry forward and trap the fleeing 8th Army. 'The enemy has apparently only left insignificant forces facing you. Leaving one corps at Soldau and securing the safety of your left flank by echeloning it back as necessary, you are to execute a most energetic offensive against Sensburg–Allenstein...The object of your manoeuvre is to attack and intercept the enemy retiring before General Rennenkampf and to cut off his retreat to the Vistula.'[21]

This message was transmitted over the Russian wireless early in the morning of the 24th. At that moment Ludendorff was driving south from Marienburg with Hindenburg to visit the 20th Corps. German signallers intercepted the Russian communication and handed the content to Ludendorff en route. He immediately realised the importance of the message, 'which gave a clear idea of our opponents' dispositions for the next few days. The Narev [2nd] Army was advancing, its left wing in echelon, its 6th Corps directed via Ortelsburg on Bischofsburg.'[22]

Hoffmann wrote later that the intercepted signal was not received until the following day, 25 August; Ludendorff stated in his memoirs that the event took place on the 24th. Whichever is correct, Ludendorff now issued orders to take advantage of such a Russian plan: he aimed to trap the Russian 2nd Army between German forces to the north, around Bischofsburg, and Scholtz's 20th Corps and other elements to the south. Scholtz assured him that the 20th Corps remained in good heart and proposed a limited withdrawal of his left flank. In effect this would either entice the Russians on, or would make them veer further north-west to avoid an engagement – and the more northerly direction would take the enemy into a region of small lakes and forests, beyond which lay Bischofsburg. The trap would be prepared.

Ludendorff proceeded to close this trap tight. During the evening of the 24th, instructions were sent from the 8th Army HQ, now at Rosenberg, to the 1st Reserve Corps and to part of 17th Corps for

deployment in the Bischofsburg area. Meanwhile the 1st Corps and
the 3rd Reserve Corps would reinforce the 20th Corps further south.

These orders took considerable courage. Only a thin screen remained in the north with units already on their way south: the latest
commands committed these units to battle deployment against the
2nd Army, making it virtually impossible for the movement to be
reversed back against the Russian 1st Army. Aggressive action by
Rennenkampf would have caught the Germans completely exposed.
'Few knew the anxiety with which I watched the Niemen [Russian 1st]
Army during those long days,' wrote Ludendorff.[23] Tension rose high
during the night of the 24th; Hoffmann commented: 'From the point
of view of the High Command, that evening was the most difficult of
the whole battle.' Nor could the Germans move into position as quickly
as Ludendorff hoped. 'All the troops were exceedingly exhausted,
and strength had been reduced by continual fighting. Many difficulties
were met with in the transmission of orders to the 1st RC and the
17th AC. Enemy cavalry patrols rendered that zone unsafe. It was
doubtful whether the enemy would give us time to carry out our plans.'

Ludendorff spent these nerve-racking hours drafting detailed plans
for battle, especially regarding deployment of forces in Scholtz's area.
Two options were open: either a full-scale strike into the Russian left
flank as the enemy moved north-west, or an even more ambitious
scheme to surround the enemy by thrusting southwards via Soldau.
'The defeat of the Narev Army, in conjunction with the advance of
the 17th AC and the 1st RC, could thus have been absolutely annihilating.' But Ludendorff added: 'The forces at my disposal were insufficient.' Germans in the southern sector would be outnumbered,
and the 20th Corps would be especially vulnerable if the enemy decided to engage rather than moving north-west. To guard against this,
and to undertake a more limited encirclement, Ludendorff ordered
François's 1st Corps to strike south-east via Usdau.[24]

This wise choice impressed Hoffmann, who described Ludendorff's
assessment as 'the most decisive point of the whole battle'. Moreover,
fears of a move by the Russians in the north were dispelled next morning: fresh reports revealed that Rennenkampf's advance was exceedingly slow; the gap between the two Russian armies remained wide.[25]

Soon after dawn on the 25th Ludendorff, Hindenburg and other
staff officers hurried from Army HQ to meet François, 1st Corps commander, at his battle headquarters near Montovo. A course of action
had to be agreed for the attack by this corps scheduled to take place
next morning. Ludendorff immediately encountered von François's
arrogance and obstinacy, which had already resulted in his independent action at the start of the campaign. Hindenburg told the corps
commander that he must launch a direct attack on the town of Usdau
at 5 am on the 26th, to cover an offensive by Scholtz towards Gilgenburg. François protested violently that the bulk of his artillery and

ammunition columns would still be absent. 'My corps will not be ready for action,' he declared; he later claimed that Ludendorff retorted: 'In that case you must attack with infantry alone.' A stiff discussion followed, which Ludendorff brought to a close by snapping: 'The corps must attack.' He then added, as if as an afterthought: 'The final decision, however, rests with the Commander-in-Chief.' Hindenburg apparently said nothing, and his silence was taken to mean agreement.[26]

The group left François at his hill-top battle HQ. Only a few miles down the road Hindenburg asked the cars to halt at Montovo station, from which the Army HQ could be telephoned for latest news. There seemed to be nothing of interest; the commander and his Chief of Staff climbed back into their vehicle, leaving Hoffmann to finish the telephone conversation. Moments later a signal was handed to Hoffmann who read the note, ran to his car and urged the driver to overtake the army commander. Hoffmann leant over the side to pass the signal: another Russian wireless communication had been intercepted.[27] The cars pulled on to the verge of the road and maps were spread across the bonnets.

Samsonov had ordered his centre to push in the direction of Osterode, north-west of the present position. Details were given of the movement of each enemy corps. Ludendorff therefore enjoyed exact knowledge of enemy intentions: Samsonov still believed the enemy to be retreating; fears for a premature attack by the Russians on the 20th Corps in the Gilgenburg area were removed, and instead Samsonov was marching to the north of Scholtz – almost directly into the net which Ludendorff was spreading.

Back at the HQ, Ludendorff sent copies of the Russian intercept by hand to François and Scholtz. He insisted that the attack by 1st Corps must still be launched early next morning as scheduled: although the threat to Scholtz had been removed by Samsonov's move north-west, the assault by François could now stand even better chances of a limited encirclement behind the enemy. Orders to this effect were despatched during the evening, signed by Hindenburg and received by François at 8.30 pm. 'Once more I voiced my objection,' he wrote, 'but once more was overruled.' His proposal for a wider flanking movement via Mlava was rejected since this might have meant loss of contact with Scholtz.

By nightfall on the 25th Ludendorff believed all possible steps had been taken for battle next day. Last-minute details had still to be settled, and in any case Ludendorff felt too tense for sleep. Hindenburg, on the other hand, stood from his chair and declared happily: 'Gentlemen, our preparations are so well in hand that we can sleep soundly tonight.' He walked in a leisurely way from the room.

Seventy-five miles away the Russian HQ displayed a complete contrast. Samsonov had begun to doubt the wisdom of the north-west march. Reports indicated enemy concentrations in the area just to the north of Gilgenburg and of large forces marching towards his exposed left wing in the Lautenburg region. Further north, cavalry patrols had sighted enemy movement through Rastenburg towards Bischofsburg. Such messages seemed to contradict the earlier belief that the Germans had embarked on full retreat. Nevertheless Samsonov allowed his north-westerly advance to continue, perhaps persuaded to do so by his staff, although he eased his fears slightly by ordering extra strength for his left wing.[28]

Samsonov's soldiers were exhausted, and supplies to them were deficient. A new logistical system had been introduced just before the war, more complicated than previous methods, and too few officers knew how this worked. Similar chaos surrounded Russian communications: telegrams to the army commander went first to the Warsaw post-office and then in bundles by car to Samsonov. In addition the 2nd Army front spread over 75 miles, with only minimal contact between the various sectors: only 25 field telephones were available plus a few Morse-coding machines and one Hughes patent apparatus, a primitive teleprinter discharging 1,200 words per hour which broke down at frequent intervals. And, at this moment, the 6th Corps on the right flank was unable to read messages from HQ since the communications staff did not possess the correct code.[29]

Ludendorff had been at the Eastern Front for just 48 hours. During this brief period troops had been extricated from one region to face another enemy army in a completely different direction; plans were laid for a carefully calculated trap, involving the movement of thousands of men and hundreds of guns. The whole focus of the army had been shifted, and the initiative grasped. Ludendorff owed much to Hoffmann, but his own achievement can only be considered brilliant, a superb example of decision-making and staff work.

Now, on the night of 25 August 1914, he was obliged to watch his plans being executed by others. German divisions continued to wheel and deploy in the darkness to the north, west and south-west of the approaching Russians.

CHAPTER SIX

The Trap Sprung

LUDENDORFF ESTABLISHED THE ARMY'S BATTLE HQ AT LÖBAU BEFORE
dawn, 26 August. The sun rose with the sky continuing clear and blue
as it had been for many days – the weather seemed perfect for a rapid,
devastating attack; Ludendorff waited impatiently for news from
François which would indicate that battle had begun. But the telephone remained silent.

> A general has much to bear and needs strong nerves [wrote Ludendorff].
> The civilian is too inclined to think that war is only like the working out
> of an arithmetical problem with given numbers. It is anything but that.
> On both sides it is a case of wrestling with powerful, unknown physical
> and psychological forces, a struggle which inferiority in numbers makes
> all the more difficult. It means working with men of varying force of
> character and with their own views ...[1]

Such an individual was General Hermann von François. During
the night the 1st Corps commander had telephoned the 20th Corps
HQ and asked Scholtz if any Russian threat to his position warranted
premature action by the 1st Corps. Scholtz, as always, expressed confidence: his men could look after themselves. François checked his
own situation. Ludendorff's plans stipulated an attack on the commanding Seeben heights at dawn prior to the assault on Usdau at
10 am. But the leading 1st Corps division had still to reach a position
confronting the enemy at Seeben; artillery remained lacking; troops
were exhausted. Moreover, François believed that the interception of
Samsonov's orders removed the urgency of his own assault.

Nevertheless, a message from the 1st Corps HQ to the Army HQ
at Löbau, timed 7.30 am, implied that the attack on Seeben was in
progress. Then communications fell silent. By 10.30 am Ludendorff
could contain his impatience no longer: he snatched up the telephone
and contacted François – and discovered that the 1st Corps had still
to launch its assault. For the first time the 8th Army staff officers witnessed one of Ludendorff's violent rages – the purple face, quivering

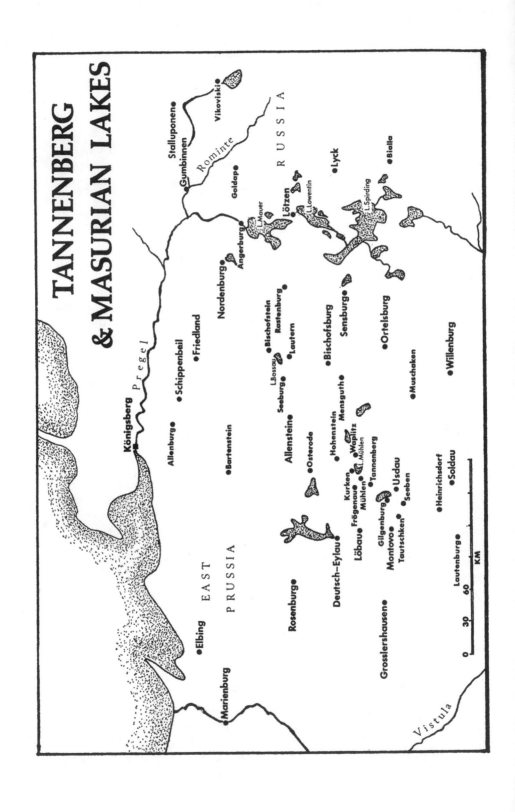

jowls, bullish bellows. François tried to explain his decision but found himself shouted down: Ludendorff demanded the attack to be launched no later than noon, less than ninety minutes away.

This time François obeyed. His units were still arriving as battle commenced, with men running from the railway depots and forming ranks as they did so. One regiment, the 3rd Grenadiers, off-loaded horses and baggages at Montovo, then the train steamed on to carry the men almost into battle; near Tautschken shells began to explode on either side of the track and earth splattered against the carriages. The driver continued as far as possible, then the men scrambled out, unslung their rifles, and advanced.[2]

Seeben fell within an hour. Ludendorff's orders were for François to move on immediately against Usdau, exposed by this initial success. General von Conta, commanding the 1st Corps leading division, informed François that the weariness of his troops, combined with absence of sufficient artillery ammunition, rendered an immediate operation out of the question; François agreed and declared that battle would be resumed the following morning. This time Ludendorff's anger and disappointment remained under control: other divisions were also unready for general battle, and later Ludendorff himself declared: 'General von François ... quite rightly insisted on concentrating the whole of his corps before attacking.'[3]

Hoffmann pointed out afterwards that François's decision was one of the greatest contributions to the outcome of the battle: had he attacked and failed, Samsonov might have appreciated German intentions and altered his plans accordingly. Instead the Russians continued to move north-west into broken country which restricted contact between local commanders. Extra time had already been allowed for the German left wing to come into position, nearly sixty miles to the north-east in the Bischofsburg region. These units, von Below's 1st Reserve Corps and von Mackensen's 17th Corps elements, had been marching continuously for the last three days in sweltering weather conditions; the vanguard only reached Seeburg and Bischofsburg during the previous evening, 25 August, and the men crumpled exhausted to the ground, snatching a few precious hours of rest before battle.

Mackensen's men marched forward soon after dawn on the 26th, hoping to find the Russian right flank; further to the west Below began a similar advance at 10 am, aiming to block the Russians from Allenstein. German columns stretched mile upon mile along the roads which wound between the heavy forests; the sun pierced through the trees, and dust from the soldiers' boots rose high in the air, turning grey uniforms to dirty white.

Opposite this advance lay the Russian 6th Corps, spread thinly south of Bischofsburg and comprising the 16th and 4th Divisions under General Blagoveshchensky. The 4th Division had moved northwards during the previous night, away from the 16th, having heard of German troops in the Lautern-Seeburg area: these units were believed to be retreating from Rennenkampf in the north and were thought to be an easy target.

Just before 11 am units from the Russian 4th Division clashed with Mackensen's advancing 17th Corps. Initial fighting took place near Lautern village, and at first it seemed the Russians would overwhelm the enemy column; then more German guns were dragged up and hastily unlimbered in the woods and fields, and the heavy barrage drove back the 4th Division troops down the road to Lake Bössau. Trapped against the shore of this lake, groups of Russians were overrun by the gathering momentum of the German advance – some soldiers drowned attempting to swim for safety. Fighting continued throughout the day. The Russian 16th Division had started to move towards Allenstein as planned when news of the 4th Division engagement reached Blagoveshchensky: first he ordered a turn-about, then split the 16th Division into two parts, neither of which reached Lake Bössau in time. By 6 pm 4th Division units were in full retreat, having lost 5,350 men, two batteries of artillery and numerous vehicles. So disorganised was the divisional command that its report of events could not be written until a week later; the remainder of the Russian corps retreated south.[4]

News of this success did not reach Ludendorff until nightfall. Meanwhile other reports caused him disquiet. Progress seemed indecisive in the centre, where the Russian 13th Corps under Klyuev was allowed to continue its north-westerly advance from Kurken, and by nightfall had reached the vicinity of Kellaren. To Klyuev's left the Russian 15th Corps under General Martos had run into greater opposition and suffered high casualties attempting to pass through German 20th Corps positions, but by nightfall these units under Martos had reached the vicinity of Mühlen.

Ludendorff's communications system, although more efficient than Samsonov's, was nevertheless inadequate, and frail contact broke down under the multiple pressures of battle. Throughout the day German signallers had intercepted requests from Samsonov to Rennenkampf seeking assistance. The German 8th Army no longer enjoyed the advantage of surprise, and a rapid decision had not been reached. Rennenkampf might turn from the north; the 8th Army might itself be trapped.

Dinner in the mess at Löbau that evening, 26 August, proved extremely depressing. The spectre of defeat seemed to be haunting Ludendorff; he sat silent at the table; his fingers tugged and twisted pieces of bread which he rolled between both hands – a habit which his staff soon came to recognise as a sign of acute nerves. Then he pushed aside his food barely touched, and waited impatiently for Hindenburg to finish. As soon as he could he rose abruptly from the table and asked to see Hindenburg privately, and the two men left the room together.[5]

Hoffmann believed that Ludendorff had 'lost his nerve a little'. If so, then Hindenburg restored the Chief of Staff's confidence and in doing so rendered Germany great service. Ludendorff emerged from the General's room and prepared orders for the following day: battle would be continued. At the same time fresh reports provided a much clearer picture of the day's events – and these were far more satisfactory than had first been thought: in the north the Russian 6th Corps was in full retreat, and the consequent German advance by Mackensen's 17th Corps, combined with Below's 1st Reserve Corps movements, promised to stab deep into the Russian front.

Ludendorff's temporary disillusionment on the night of the 26th clearly formed the basis of inferences in Hindenburg's memoirs after the war that the Chief of Staff favoured withdrawal. Only the two men knew the words spoken between them in private after dinner: perhaps Hindenburg did indeed save the battle by insisting on continued attacks. If this is true, then Hindenburg's stolid, concrete calm showed the value of his side of the partnership. If Hindenburg gave the order for a resumption of the battle next day, then Ludendorff most certainly agreed with this decision: he showed no signs of hesitation. Credit for the battle probably belongs to both men: neither could have brought success without the other.

One further incident took place in the 8th Army HQ on the night of 26 August. The telephone rang whilst Ludendorff and Hoffmann continued to draft the orders for the following morning: Colonel Gerhard Tappen, Chief of Operations at Moltke's Supreme HQ, wished to speak to Ludendorff. The latter asked Hoffmann to pick up the second receiver so that he could hear the conversation. Then the astonished Ludendorff heard that Moltke had decided to reinforce the 8th Army with three whole corps plus a cavalry division, all from the Western Front. The announcement caused Ludendorff immediate anxiety: however much he might welcome these reinforcements, they would surely be needed to an even greater degree in the West. He expressed gratitude but added that these units would not arrive in time for battle, and he would willingly forgo the extra strength if needs were greater in the West. Tappen assured him that the corps could be spared.[6]

German corps prepared for the next day's battle along the whole Russian front. To the south, on the far German right, lay General von Mühlmann's troops; next stood François's 1st Corps, and during the night François issued orders for his guns to open fire on Usdau at 4 am with the infantry to attack an hour later. Scholtz's 20th Corps was positioned in the German centre, reinforced by recent arrivals and ready to thrust in the Frankenau region. Further along the line the 3rd Reserve Division had the task of sweeping west via Riechenau.

Skirmishing continued throughout the hot, sultry night as individual regiments moved into forward positions. Ludendorff stayed awake: as always, he found it impossible to be calm and controlled on the eve of battle, and he paced nervously backwards and forwards, grasping each report as it arrived. As usual, Hindenburg slept; Hoffmann dozed.

Guns began to fire before dawn, 27 August, steady barrages which split the greying sky and echoed through the forests and over the swampy, lake-strewn terrain. Early in the morning Ludendorff called for his car: the attack on Usdau was planned to begin at 4 am and he wanted to be present. Almost immediately, excellent news reached the convoy of staff vehicles: Usdau had fallen. 'I considered the battle won,' remembered Ludendorff. Disappointment followed: the report was premature.[7]

Shells from the 1st Corps guns were bursting in Usdau when the cars arrived from the 8th Army HQ. Hindenburg and Ludendorff climbed on to an observation platform in a fir tree, situated on a small hill halfway between Gilgenburg and Usdau itself. Bombardment continued for almost five hours; German infantry advanced across the fields in long lines shortly before 10 am to find the enemy trenches abandoned except for the heaps of dead and wounded. By 11 am the town had been completely cleared; François halted his weary troops east of Usdau during the afternoon. The road to Neidenburg lay open, enabling a sweeping movement behind the Russian centre, but the 1st Corps lacked sufficient strength to continue.

Ludendorff returned to Löbau, 'not altogether satisfied' with reports of the battle. He entered the HQ building – where he received shattering information. 'News came through that the 1st Army Corps had been routed and that the relics of this corps were arriving in Montovo. Such news was difficult to believe.' An urgent telephone call by Hoffmann to the railway commandant at Montovo failed to bring complete reassurance: apparently only one regiment had retreated to the town, but no news was available of the remainder of François's corps.

Hoffmann immediately ordered the regimental commander at Montovo to turn and march back to the enemy; at the same time an aide was despatched in a car with instructions to drive until he came across troops – either Russian or German – and then to report back, if he could. This crude method of discovering essential information proved successful: after sixty tense minutes the aide returned. All was apparently well with the 1st Corps; the isolated regiment had been mauled by a Russian counter-attack at Heinrichsdorf, but the remainder of François's units stood intact.[8]

Other news was less satisfactory. An attack had been launched by 20th Corps, aiming south of Lake Mühlen against the Russian centre, but confusion had developed when Scholtz diverted his forces to deal with a supposed enemy breakthrough, which turned out to be false.

In the north, the 17th and 1st Reserve Corps had continued their pursuit of the Russian right wing; by nightfall the 17th Corps troops had taken Mensguth, while Below's 1st Reserve had shifted direction towards the Russian centre.

Decisive victory was still being denied. The battle had become a steady grind: men rising to attack and falling under machine-gun fire and massive artillery barrages. Ludendorff had no real idea about detailed progress, merely obtaining fragmentary and often conflicting scraps of information. But from the confusion emerged one or two salient features which hinted at ultimate victory: both Russian wings had been badly damaged, and the southern flank had been prised from the centre by the German 1st Corps advance. The Russian centre stood reasonably firm, yet this could still be destroyed by a determined 20th Corps assault and by the 1st Corps moving behind to slice enemy communications upon which modern armies so much depended.

Ludendorff issued orders for 28 August: 20th Corps would make a vigorous thrust into the Russian centre, with the 41st Division leading, while the 1st Corps would resume the advance on Neidenburg. The 20th Corps attack would be strengthened by General von der Goltz's *Landwehr* Division launching an offensive against Hohenstein, and the 1st Reserve Corps and 17th Corps would push in from the north-west.

After another tense, restless night Ludendorff left Army HQ in the early morning, 28 August. This time he established a field command post near the 20th Corps HQ at Frögenau. As always, he wanted to be as near as possible to the fighting, but communications were still deficient. 'A very ineffective field-telephone connected us with the 1st Army Corps, but no communication at all was possible with the other forces.' He sat on a camp stool or walked a few yards this way and that waiting for news; thick clammy mist muffled the sound of the guns.

> Our first impressions were by no means favourable [wrote Ludendorff]. Neidenburg had certainly been taken, but the 41st Infantry Division had attacked Waplitz in a fog and been driven back ... I sent an officer there by car to give me a report on the condition of the division, and his account was not encouraging. The *Landwehr* near Mühlen were not making progress. If the enemy attacked the right wing of the 20th AC in great force, a grave crisis might result. At the best, the battle would be prolonged.

Ludendorff repeated his recurring fear: 'Finally, Rennenkampf might march ...'[9]

Trouble arose again with François, now at Soldau. At 8.30 am the 1st Corps commander received urgent orders to despatch help to the 20th Corps, and especially to the 41st Division. François therefore sent his 2nd Division, and at the same time he continued his attempt to cut off the enemy centre by directing his 1st Division towards Neidenburg. Then another order arrived. François must change the direction of the 1st Division to a line further north. He immediately objected, saying this route would take him into difficult country and would allow the enemy to escape; he refused to alter his original plans. François later paid himself great credit. 'In consequence of these measures my troops captured 60,000 unwounded prisoners and 231 guns.' In fact he merely acted in the light of local tactical information denied to Ludendorff – and the latter altered his opinion when the 41st Division managed to recover.[10]

By then the atmosphere had undergone radical change. Realisation at last reached Ludendorff and the HQ staff that the Russians were crumbling. Increasing numbers of prisoners were reported; indeed, in the confused situation the sight of these captives caused panic amongst Germans, who believed the enemy had broken through. Roads everywhere were blocked by overturned vehicles and abandoned carts, yet from the chaos shone the increasing light of victory.

Even greater confusion existed amongst the enemy, and with it the stench of defeat. Samsonov had remained optimistic, and this proved fatal. His right wing, 6th Corps, had been shattered and thrown eastwards; his left wing, 1st Corps, had been split from the centre by François's seizure of Usdau and Soldau; his centre forces were either being decimated or surrounded: the 13th Corps under Klyuev was trapped near Hohenstein, unable to give support to the 15th Corps under Martos, now being slaughtered by the German centre north of Mühlen; further south the Russian 23rd Corps under Kondratovich was being encircled by François. The latter pushed steadily towards Willenburg, and if this town could be reached contact would be possible with the German right wing, Mackensen's 17th Corps. The Russians would then be encircled.

During the late afternoon Samsonov's HQ was positioned at Neidenburg; the thunder of François's guns crashed closer. Samsonov ordered his HQ to disperse, and he himself drove towards the front until the roads became impassable for his car, then he mounted a horse to continue his tragic journey. He spoke briefly to the British Military Attaché, General Knox: 'The enemy has luck one day. We will have luck another.'[11] Samsonov rode on, heading for 15th Corps in the centre, and everywhere were signs of the disintegration of his army: groups of men stumbling to the rear, unarmed, seeking only safety – and ignorant of the German troops creeping across their line of retreat; weeping soldiers, slumped in the ditches with their heads on their hands, covered with the filth of battle; shell-shocked soldiers, their eyes staring, inane grins on their faces. Shells constantly screeched overhead as the Germans probed and prodded the body of the dying Russian army.

Ludendorff, now at Osterode, allowed himself some satisfaction.

'We were not at all clear as to how things stood with the individual units; but there was no doubt that the battle was won.'[12]

August 29 was the day of victory. Russian units threw themselves backwards and forwards seeking escape through the German mesh; full retreat started during the early hours. Forces from the 13th Corps managed to reach a defile near Morken which seemed to be deserted, and the troops began to pass cautiously through. Machine guns suddenly began to clatter from all sides and scores of Russians fell; others tried to turn back, only to be pressed forward again by those advancing in a close-packed column. Survivors from the ambush tried to find another escape route; other remnants managed to reach Kurken. Meanwhile the 15th and 23rd Corps also succeeded in pulling back from the front, then they found further retreat impossible across the Neidenburg–Willenburg road: François had positioned a thin but deadly screen of guns and machine guns with the fire positions covering every exit from the forest. Repeated Russian attempts to cross were met by vicious bursts of fire; troops milled in confusion on the narrow forest paths, which were increasingly heaped with bodies, broken waggons and dead horses.[13]

In the midst of this Russian disaster news emerged to cause Ludendorff fresh anxiety. Early on the 29th a reconnaissance aircraft droned low over the HQ at Osterode and dropped a message: the pilot had seen a large body of Russian soldiers marching on Neidenburg from the south. Such an advance posed an acute threat to the German 1st Corps whose front faced north, blocking the main Russian retreat.[14]

These approaching Russians comprised the 1st Corps, severed from Samsonov's left wing by François's advance on Usdau and Soldau on the 27th and 28th. Recapture of Neidenburg might prise open an escape route; Ludendorff immediately issued orders for three divisions from the 20th Corps to rush to this sector. François had already received the same message from the reconnaissance aircraft and remained determined to cling to the Neidenburg–Willenburg road: the Russians took Neidenburg during the early afternoon, but were obliged to withdraw next day with the battle drawing to its agonising finish.

Samsonov's end came during the night of the 29th, in a pitiful fashion later revealed by General Postovski, his Chief of Staff. The Army commander tried to find escape by making for Willenburg with just seven officers, one NCO, no maps and only one compass. They rode as far as they could then trudged on foot through the forests. Samsonov, a sick man even before the invasion of East Prussia, staggered with exhaustion. Once or twice he whispered: 'The Tsar trusted me. How can I face him?' The small party blundered on in the darkness, the compass now useless since they no longer possessed matches to see the face, and often they linked hands to keep together. At 1 am the group halted for a short rest. Samsonov slipped away and a moment later the noise of a pistol shot reverberated from the trees. A German patrol later found the General's body, with a bullet-hole in the head.[15]

Other senior Russian officers were captured one by one. General Martos, the gallant 15th Corps commander, witnessed the gradual whittling down of the small group trying to escape with him, and he finally fell into German hands near Muschaken. He had a brief interview with François on 30 August before being driven to the 8th Army HQ at Osterode. There, in the 'dirty little inn', the Russian General was subjected to a stiff interrogation conducted by Ludendorff before being rescued by Hindenburg. The latter noticed the weariness and misery in the old man's face and walked quickly across the room to grasp the prisoner's hands in both his own.[16]

Minor clashes continued on the last day of August. The Germans seemed to be too exhausted to feel elation, and around them spread the worst miseries of war. 'I set out for Hohenstein,' wrote Ludendorff, 'and on the way went over the battlefield, which made a deep impression on me.' Wounded men lay everywhere, Russians and Germans so close together that no distinction existed between them. Estimates of casualty totals vary considerably. Some German authorities claimed nearly 130,000 prisoners taken, plus 500 guns; figures put forward by the Russians are in the region of 60,000 prisoners and up to 190 guns and at least 70,000 men killed or wounded. German losses were between 10,000 and 15,000 men. Ludendorff hesitated to state a figure; at the time Hoffmann estimated captured enemy troops at around 40,000.

Whatever the true totals, the Russian 2nd Army had ceased to exist. On 31 August Hindenburg sent the official despatch to the Kaiser: 'I have the honour to report to Your Majesty that a ring was yesterday closed around the greater part of the Russian Army. The 13th, 15th and 17th Corps have been annihilated . . .'[17]

Yet Ludendorff remained depressed. 'I could not rejoice wholeheartedly at our mighty victory, for the strain imposed on my nerves by the uncertainty about Rennenkampf's army had been too great.' He expressed his gratitude in typical fashion, providing an interesting insight into his priorities. 'I thought of General Count von Schlieffen and thanked him for his teaching. In the Protestant Church at Allenstein General von Hindenburg and I rendered thanks to Almighty God.'[18]

Already, on 28 August, Ludendorff's restless, unquiet mind had begun to flicker towards the next step. At 5.30 pm on this day he had dictated a preliminary order for the regrouping of the 8th Army: now Rennenkampf must be faced. In the course of this dictation a name was found for the present battle: Ludendorff first addressed the order from their present location, Frögenau, but Hoffmann interrupted suggesting the name of a nearby hamlet. There, in 1410, the old Teutonic Knights had been defeated by the barbaric Poles and Lithuanians: using the name now would wipe out the dishonour of that distant defeat inflicted on the ancestors of the Prussian military caste. Ludendorff agreed, and later claimed the name as his own idea – Tannenberg.

CHAPTER SEVEN

The Masurian Lakes

FIRST REPORTS OF THE TANNENBERG VICTORY WERE SCARCELY BELIEVED at home. Attention remained fixed on the Western Front: all still seemed to be going well, with the British and French pushed back from the Mons area at the end of August by Kluck's 1st Army. But beneath the surface lay ominous signs of difficulties soon to come. Ludendorff's previous commander Bülow had encountered stiff resistance at Guise, 29 August, against the French 5th Army; Kluck, partly to help Bülow and partly because he believed the French 5th now constituted the enemy's flank force, shifted direction more to the south on 31 August. This would lead him in front of Paris rather than behind it, according to both the original Schlieffen Plan and to Moltke's variations. Moltke sent his approval two days later. By this manoeuvre the scything right wing of the German advance would lose its sharpness; the French were by no means beaten; German troops were suffering from exhaustion, and the momentum of the forward movement might soon slacken. The promise by Tappen on 26 August that three army corps would be sent to the East had already been reduced to two corps and a cavalry division.

News of Tannenberg reached the Western Front on the first day of September. One officer, Hans Frentz, described the reaction. 'During the late evening I read the following to the Sergeant sharing quarters with me and who lies like a corpse on his mattress through exhaustion: "Under General Hindenburg in the East at Tannenberg, the Narev Army has been completely annihilated and survivors have been taken prisoner – 100,000 men. It is the greatest victory in recorded time. This news is to be reported to the troops immediately." ' Frentz's account continued: 'One knew that things were going badly in the East ... The news of such a victory just could not be right ... Hindenburg? The name was unknown to me. The Sergeant said: "How childish to tell battle-weary troops such jokes." He lifted himself wearily. "100,000 men, hmm, that just isn't possible." He slumped back to sleep again muttering: "It's just blue smoke." '[1]

Reaction would soon turn from numbed disbelief to an almost hysterical elation which swept Hindenburg and Ludendorff to fame. Meanwhile the Kaiser distributed his rewards: *Pour le Mérite* for Hindenburg and the Iron Cross Second Class for his Chief of Staff. Ludendorff in fact disagreed with the handing out of honours during war, considering the time for that to be after final victory; he agreed with Moltke, who once commented about the cheering crowds in Berlin: 'If we lose the war those same people will sneer, "There he goes, the old donkey." '[2] Nevertheless the Iron Cross Second Class made Ludendorff 'exceedingly proud'. Hoffmann received similar honour, much to his surprise, and his reaction was typically caustic. 'I had never thought that this finest of all military decorations could be won by sitting at the end of a telephone line. However, I realise that there must be someone who keeps his nerve, and by brute determination and the will to victory overcomes difficulties, panics, and such-like nonsense.'[3]

Now nerves must be steeled again. Troops began to move from the Tannenberg area even before the final destruction of Samsonov's 2nd Army. One day Ludendorff stood outside the Osterode HQ watching soldiers marching past: uniforms were filthy, faces gaunt. Ludendorff wore his Iron Cross in his button-hole. Less than a week before he would have been unrecognised, but now the depleted military band at the front of the tramping men struck up his favourite march, the *Höhenfriedberger*, and some of the soldiers managed a ragged cheer. Ludendorff's face, normally so stern, softened and he turned aside to hide his emotion.[4]

Those troops and thousands more were marching to face Rennenkampf's 1st Russian Army in the north. Ludendorff's initial orders on 28 August had been left vague: the 1st and 20th Corps should continue the pursuit of the enemy 2nd Army, while all *Landwehr* and garrison units reorganised at their present positions; Below's 1st Reserve Corps should concentrate on Allenstein in the north-west prior to a move towards Rennenkampf. At that time no orders could be sent to Mackensen because the exact whereabouts of his 17th Corps remained unknown.

As for the enemy, on 28 August it was believed that elements of Rennenkampf's 2nd Corps were in Rastenburg, while the main body of this Russian 1st Army was understood to have reached the line Schippebeil-Friedland. The nearest enemy detachments were probably about 60 miles north-east of Below's corps at Allenstein.

Time was extremely short. Rennenkampf's dilatory movements could hardly be expected to continue; moreover the situation further south in Galicia had deteriorated. The Austrian advance into Russian Poland had begun in the third week of August with Conrad, the Chief of Staff, attempting to co-ordinate four armies. Initial successes were followed by the defeat of the Austrian 3rd Army in the battle of Gnilia

Lipa, 26–30 August, when the Austrians were forced to fall back; the Russians attacked again at Rava Ruska on 3 September, and news from this theatre would soon become ominous.

Ludendorff's actions at the beginning of September displayed his abilities to best advantage. Despite his weariness he undertook complicated staff work with brilliant success: hundreds of disorganised units had to be regrouped, resupplied and redirected to a fresh front; ammunition stocks had to be replenished, new men and materials rushed forward, scores of train and road convoys arranged. The whole army had to be rebuilt and pushed into battle again.

In early September the 8th Army comprised 18.5 infantry divisions and two cavalry divisions, amounting to 232 battalions and 1,212 guns. Of these, 184 battalions and 1,074 guns were reorganised to move against Rennenkampf, with the remainder being switched to protect the southern border.[5] Latest intelligence reports indicated that Rennenkampf intended to make a stand between the river Pregel and Lake Mauer, on a line about 50 miles south-east of Königsberg. German dispositions were made accordingly: the two corps sent by Moltke from the west disembarked into positions stretching from Allenstein to Elbing, while the rest of the 8th Army concentrated ready to advance between Willenburg and Allenstein. Ludendorff's plans were simple. 'We intended to attack Rennenkampf on a wide front between the river Pregel and Lake Mauer, while enveloping his left wing beyond Lötzen and further south.'

The concentrated 8th Army would fight in three groups: one thrusting from the river Pregel towards Lake Mauer, comprising the Guards Corps, 1st Reserve, 11th and part of 20th Corps, the second east of Lötzen, comprising the remainder of 20th Corps, the 8th and 1st Cavalry Divisions, and 17th Corps, and the third in the direction of Lyck. This town lay on the Russian left flank: a German attack in this region, undertaken by François's crack 1st Corps and the 3rd Reserve Division, might allow an encircling movement.[6]

On 2 September Rennenkampf ordered his army to take up defensive positions. Three days earlier Zhilinsky had told him: 'General Samsonov has suffered a complete defeat and the enemy now has full liberty to turn against you. Keep this in view ... Be careful that the enemy does not operate against you through Lötzen.'[7] Rennenkampf therefore allotted a full corps to the defence of Lötzen, which, lying in the midst of the Masurian Lake region between Lakes Mauer and Lowentin, guarded a 10-mile gap between almost impassable stretches of swamp and water.

By 4 September, after intense efforts by Ludendorff and his staff, the 8th Army was in a position to advance. 'Now we are preparing for something new,' wrote Hoffmann in his diary. He added: 'Ludendorff is a first-class fellow to work with. He is the right man for this business – ruthless and hard. We get on admirably, and I am proud that some of my ideas have been considered for his new plan.'⁸

Within twenty-four hours the first 8th Army units began to move forward. Immediately, Ludendorff's nervousness began to increase. 'This operation ... was extraordinarily daring,' he wrote. The 8th Army would be heavily outnumbered. 'Immense superiority could be concentrated against us at any moment and at any chosen point. Our right wing, in particular, was in danger to the east of the Lakes. It might be overwhelmed.'⁹ François, whose corps comprised the bulk of this right wing, demanded extra strength; Ludendorff initially placed a division of 20th Corps at his disposal, but soon this had to be returned to the German centre.

The Battle of the Masurian Lakes began on 7 September. By this day the German left wing and centre had reached the planned positions between the Pregel and Lake Mauer, and skirmishing began immediately. German units opposite Lötzen – the 17th Corps and 1st and 8th Cavalry Divisions – took longer to reach their sector. Meanwhile the right wing advanced on both shores of Lake Spirding, with François capturing the village of Bialla on the 7th, south-west of Lyck.

Fighting gained rapidly in intensity on 8 September, and reports reaching the 8th Army HQ caused Ludendorff renewed depression: the Russians, firmly entrenched, maintained their positions, and the advancing German lines were slaughtered by machine-gun fire. Repeated attacks by Mackensen's 17th Corps against Lötzen – at 5 am, noon and 8 pm – failed to make progress and resulted in fearful casualties; the situation in this area deteriorated still further when the narrow land between the swamps became clogged with vehicles, waggons and men.

Only François continued to make progress. On 8 September he wheeled north aiming to cut behind the Russian lines, leaving the 3rd Reserve Division to deal with Lyck. He enjoyed strong local superiority – 40 battalions and 200 guns against 16 battalions and 30 guns – and his enemy comprised troops fresh from the reserve: these weak, second-line units began to scatter; frantic appeals were made to the Russian 10th Army now being formed further east, but no help arrived.¹⁰ Farnçois continued to push north. At dawn on 9 September his leading division managed to reach a position behind the Russian 2nd Corps defending Lötzen, and four divisions from this corps retreated after fierce fighting. François seized 5,000 prisoners and 60 guns, and continued to strike north-west in an attempt to prevent Rennenkampf's full withdrawal; Mackensen, finding Russian defences in front of him at Lötzen suddenly weakened, pushed forward to tear a gap in the Russian centre.

Ludendorff received this excellent news on the morning of the 10th. 'The rejoicing at Headquarters can be imagined. A great success had once more been achieved.' But Ludendorff added: 'Still nothing de-cisive. The Russian army was not yet beaten.'[11]

Rennenkampf panicked, and thereby saved his army. Unlike Sam-sonov who had retained his optimism and continued to push into the German trap, Rennenkampf ordered precipitate retreat. Ludendorff, on the other hand, felt he had to guard against a counter-attack such as Samsonov might have attempted in Rennenkampf's position. 'Ren-nenkampf, who was now co-operating with reinforcements arriving further south, would be able to make a vigorous attack in any direc-tion. Our lines were very thin everywhere ... The situation was still extremely critical, and the tension was great.'[12]

This cautious attitude was reflected amongst corps commanders. On 11 September the 11th Corps believed, mistakenly, that it was being attacked by a superior force; Ludendorff therefore shifted the line of march of the 17th and 1st Corps to enable support to be pro-vided, and this brought François in a more northerly direction away from the Russian retreat route. The decision was soon reversed, but by then at least half a day had been lost. Meanwhile the Russians streamed back, force-marching night and day in increasing confusion. Insufficient time was given for François to reach the vital junctions of Stallupönen and Vilkoviski, and the Russians repulsed cavalry en-circling attempts.

By nightfall on the 11th Ludendorff realised that the chance of annihilating the Russian 1st Army had been lost. Nor did the condi-tions of the latest 8th Army HQ help to lift his depression: by now the staff had moved to Bordenburg, recently occupied by the Russians, and the state of the place offended Ludendorff's passion for cleanli-ness. 'The dirt there was incredible. The market was full of filth. The rooms were disgustingly unclean.'[13]

By 13 September the Russian 1st Army had almost completed its retreat back over the border. The bulk of the German 8th Army re-mained on the Niemen. Ludendorff and Hindenburg reached Inster-burg, fifty miles from the frontier. Immediately upon arrival at this town on the 14th staff engineers hurried to establish a communica-tions link both with Moltke's Supreme HQ and the Austrian HQ. Ludendorff waited impatiently in the Hotel Dessauer, where once again the stench provided evidence of recent Russian occupation; as Hindenburg wrote: 'The heady odours of scent, leather and cigarettes were not able to cover the odour of other things.'[14]

Contact was established with the Austro-Hungarian Supreme HQ at Neu Sandec. Conrad spoke calmly, but his words revealed disaster. The battle of Rava Ruska had been raging for eight days; defeat had been inflicted when the Russian 5th Army cut the hinge between the Austrian 3rd and 4th. Withdrawal was taking place; Lemberg must now be in Russian hands, and another Austrian stand might not be possible until the Carpathian mountains over 100 miles to the west.

'A Russian invasion of Moravia and then Upper Silesia seemed possible,' wrote Ludendorff. 'The Austro-Hungarian Army would have to be supported if it were not to be annihilated.' The deplorable situation nullified any chances of the 8th Army invading Russia to reap the rewards of Tannenberg and the Masurian Lakes – 'help must be sent immediately and could not be too powerful'. Nor would the 8th Army be able to send reinforcements to the Western Front.[15]

Ludendorff put in an urgent telephone call to Moltke. Almost immediately he heard that Germany's position in the West had also suffered a severe setback; the Schlieffen Plan had failed. The French counter-attacked on 5 September, almost enveloping the right flank of Kluck's 1st Army. Kluck still tried to block this assault on 7 September south of the Marne, but French reinforcements were rushed to the area, and further along the line the French 5th and 9th Armies turned on Bülow's 2nd. German withdrawal began on 9 September, by which date the Allies had gained a clear strategic victory.

Moltke's voice wavered over the telephone line. He bore ultimate responsibility – and indeed, his indecision had contributed a great deal to the defeat. The Chief of General Staff informed Ludendorff that a new army, the 10th, was being created at Breslau to support the Austrians. The commander would be General von Schubert. And, continued Moltke, Ludendorff would be the Chief of Staff. Ludendorff immediately suggested stronger measures: the entire 8th Army should be sent to Upper Silesia and Posen under Hindenburg, since the Russians in the north were too battered to attempt renewed invasion. Moltke would only say that consideration would be given to this proposal.

'General von Moltke was deeply moved by the state of affairs in the West,' commented Ludendorff afterwards. The two men, associates for many years, would never again have an official conversation: within twenty-four hours Moltke would leave the Supreme HQ.

Ludendorff's bags were packed during the evening of the 14th in anticipation of an early start for Breslau next morning. 'I did not find it easy to leave the Commander-in-Chief and the staff after two victorious battles. A fine sense of confidence had grown up between us, the confidence of men who think alike.' The future looked extremely unsettled. 'I knew absolutely nothing about my new sphere of action . . . The journey to Breslau was not exactly cheerful.'[16]

CHAPTER EIGHT

To the Gates of Warsaw

UNKNOWN TO LUDENDORFF, THE DAY HE LEARNT OF THE DISASTERS ON both the Austrian and Western Fronts contained additional misery of a far more personal kind. Also on 14 September his eldest stepson Franz fell critically wounded near Bouconville. This teenager had only reached the front from cadet school at the beginning of the month: now he lay in a military hospital with fearful head wounds from grenade splinters.[1]

Clouds hung low over the Prussian landscape as Ludendorff drove southwards on the 15th. Rain spattered the windscreen of the staff car, and the dreary weather matched Ludendorff's mood. Darkness fell and still the car drove on. Late at night he reached Posen, his birthplace, and his thoughts remained gloomy: soon the Russians might smash through this countryside which he knew so well. 'With deep grief I saw my native province faced with a period of much difficulty and sorrow.' Ludendorff also commented: 'It was obvious that the war would now be a long one and required enormous sacrifices of the Fatherland. The hour had come when everything, literally everything, would have to be staked on the war ... Germany had to become an armed camp.'[2]

Also on the 15th the Kaiser took one of his last major military decisions. On his own initiative he sacked Moltke, and with only scant consultation he appointed General Erich von Falkenhayn, Prussian Minister of War, to his place. Ludendorff had lost someone upon whom he could count as a friend, and in his place had to deal with a man who would soon become an enemy. Falkenhayn, debonair and dapper, would have a strong influence over the Kaiser, with serious results: soon Hoffmann described the new Chief of General Staff as 'the criminal', and Ludendorff agreed.[3]

Yet even Ludendorff realised that Moltke had been unsuitable. He described his superior as a 'remarkable man' and declared: 'He had a keen grip on military affairs, and could handle big situations with extraordinary mastery.' But Ludendorff added: 'His temperament was not really resolute and his inclinations were more pacific than warlike.'[4]

Ludendorff reached Breslau on the morning of 16 September. A telegram was handed to him immediately he arrived, before he had even time to contact his new superior. The content gave him much pleasure: Supreme HQ had agreed to the proposal made by him to Moltke on the evening of the 14th, that the bulk of the 8th Army should move directly to the support of the Austrian Army in Upper Silesia; the army would be renumbered the 9th; Hindenburg would retain command, with Ludendorff once more his Chief of Staff. The new 9th Army would comprise the 11th, 17th, 20th and Guard Reserve Corps, plus three separate divisions. Hoffmann would still be Chief of Operations.

Ludendorff immediately took the initiative and began to plan for the coming campaign even before Hindenburg's arrival. The Chief of Staff drove to Neu Sandec on the 18th to discuss the situation with Archduke Frederick, Austrian C-in-C, and with Conrad. The latter retained his strength of character and his optimism, and almost immediately found himself in complete agreement with Ludendorff's proposals. The Austrian retreat had continued in appalling conditions until safety was reached on the west bank of the Wisloka river. Nearly a quarter of a million Austrian troops had been killed or wounded since mid-August, plus over 100,000 captured; clearly the German 9th Army would have only a frail ally to lend support. Nor were Russian dispositions clear.

But from this murky, depressing situation Ludendorff and Conrad found positive signs of hope. In all probability a gap still remained between Russian forces facing East Prussia, shattered at Tannenberg and the Masurian Lakes, and those facing the Austrians. The latter would be extended following the advance from Lemberg; supplies would be short; the same foul weather which had made the Austrian retreat so wretched would dislocate Russian communications. Ludendorff and Conrad therefore agreed that the German 9th Army should advance into the space between the Russians in north and south, and supporting the Germans on the right flank would be General von Dankl's 1st Austrian Army. The direction of advance would be across the Vistula towards Warsaw itself.

Ludendorff returned to Breslau; Hindenburg and Hoffmann had reached the town on the evening of the 19th. Staff work began immediately and progressed well, although difficulties of working with the Austrians were soon experienced. 'Yesterday was our first row with the Austrians,' wrote Hoffmann in his diary on 23 September. 'They aren't out for business as we are.' The Chief of Operations added: 'I am terribly on the stretch to see how the operations will work out. I think it will be all right.'[5]

Once again the Ludendorff-Hoffmann teamwork brought extremely rapid and efficient results. About 750 train convoys were organised to regroup the four corps making up the 9th Army; supplies were rushed forward; and the advance began on 28 September – just two weeks after Ludendorff had received his orders to move to Breslau. The Russians fell back. Hoffmann scribbled in his diary on the 29th: 'We are on the point of a brilliant success: from the moment of our advance the Russian Army ceased to press the Austrians and is now in retreat behind the Vistula. The direction our attack will take cannot yet be foreseen, and depends entirely on the news we get.'[6]

The administration of an army making forced marches involved colossal work, and conditions were deplorable. Autumn weather had closed in, bringing thick curtains of rain to sweep the desolate Polish countryside. 'Each day presented the Headquarters Staff with some fresh, difficult decision,' wrote Ludendorff. 'The subordinate commanders had to act on their own initiative. It was a bold plunge into the unknown.' Daily, the supply problems became greater. Roads were virtually impassable, having already been used by the Austrians in retreat, the Russians in advance, and lately the Russians in retreat. 'Even the great high road from Cracow to Warsaw was knee-deep – it had a layer of mud a foot high.'[7]

Headquarters shifted from one wretched location to another – Wolbrom, Miechow, Jedrzejów ... 'Wolbrom was only a factory; and the two others had all the characteristics of the small, dirty, Polish towns. Bugs were all in the day's work.' And as Hindenburg commented: 'As soon as we crossed the frontier it was as if we had entered another world.'[8]

Leading units reached the Vistula south of Warsaw on 6 October. But now the Russians were regrouping under the able command of the Grand Duke Nicholas Nicholaievitch, and threatened to push down from the Warsaw area with about 60 divisions against 18 German. Hoffmann noted in his diary on 8 October: 'Here everything is in excellent order, except for the Austrians! If only the brutes would move!' Both sides drew up along the wide Vistula; each attempted to cross and to prevent the other and sudden, vicious actions broke out throughout the next week, especially to the north of the line where Mackensen's 17th Corps attempted to drive directly on Warsaw; eventually this corps, five depleted divisions, had to withstand violent pressure from 14 Russian divisions operating on far shorter supply routes.

Hoffmann's diary provided evidence of the strain suffered by Ludendorff and his staff. 'Ludendorff and I stand by and support each other,' he wrote on 12 October, 'and the Chief says: "God be with us, I can do no more!" ' On 18 October Hoffmann commented: 'Here we are in the midst of heavy fighting, and more to come: and what will be the end of it, God knows. We have done all that human wills and powers could do ...'[9]

An enemy Caucasian corps managed to establish a bridgehead on the German bank of the Vistula at Kosjenice; more enemy troops pushed over, together with artillery which initially fired with their trails half in the river through lack of room. Ludendorff detached four German brigades to help contain this Russian pocket, but increasingly feared these units might be subjected to a flank attack. 'I shall never forget the battle near Kosjenice,' he wrote, and added: 'All the troops who participated in these engagements look back on them with horror.'[10]

'I still count on victory,' declared Hoffmann in his journal on the 18th. 'Ludendorff does so no longer.' And three days later: 'Ludendorff has become frightfully nervous, and the chief burden lies on me.'

German withdrawal began on 27 October. Such a decision had become inevitable: appeals for extra help from the Austrians had met with no response, and suspicions had arisen that their units might soon pull away; winter weather made supply difficulties even more acute. Once again, despite his nerves, Ludendorff organised retreat in superb fashion: instructions had already been sent to units that all spare stores and equipment should be sent to the rear, and the regiments now moved comparatively unencumbered. General lines of retirement had previously been laid down, with these heading in a westerly direction to avoid a Russian enveloping movement. Road and rail demolitions were undertaken systematically, and the Russian pursuit soon slowed.

By the end of October the 9th Army had almost returned to its original line. The campaign was far from being a total failure: time had been gained to allow the Austrians to recover, and the imminent threat of Russian invasion had been removed; Ludendorff's staff functioned with awesome precision, enabling the Germans to keep the initiative even in withdrawal. The 9th Army would be ready to advance again within 10 days.

During the final days of retreat Ludendorff received an urgent summons to Berlin. He arrived on 31 October and was shown into Falkenhayn's room at the General Staff HQ in the Königsplatz – the red-brick building which Ludendorff had known so well before the war. But now, instead of the friendly Moltke at the other side of the table, Ludendorff was confronted by the handsome, self-centred Falkenhayn. The two men formed a complete contrast: Ludendorff's bull-like, unimaginative character against Falkenhayn's suave and somewhat devious nature. Probably they distrusted each other from the beginning. Ludendorff, with a lifetime of steady soldiering, probably suspected the other man's qualifications – Falkenhayn had left the army in 1896 through debts and had gone to China, returning to Germany after the Boxer Rebellion and becoming War Minister in 1913. No definite reasons seemed to exist for Falkenhayn's summons to Ludendorff; nor did either appear to benefit from the discussion. Ludendorff was subjected to a long discourse concerning the Western Front, and although the Chief of General Staff displayed optimism, his words failed to remove his listener's fears. Falkenhayn intended to smash through the Allied line at Ypres; battle had begun the previous day.

Ludendorff, on the other hand, believed a decisive victory had to be achieved in the East before the Russians became too strong. Conrad had already suggested to Falkenhayn that reinforcements should be moved from the West to the East Fronts, and Ludendorff now made a similar appeal. The Chief of General Staff replied by stressing his hopes for the Ypres offensive, for which all possible strength would be required.

Discussion also touched on another point. Ludendorff believed the command structure in the East should be clarified. At present Hindenburg commanded the 9th Army while von Schubert had taken over the depleted 8th Army further north: Ludendorff now suggested that Hindenburg should be made overall commander for German forces on this front, including garrison troops. Falkenhayn deferred a decision.[11]

Ludendorff emerged from the General Staff HQ feeling dispirited and dissatisfied. The atmosphere in Berlin failed to improve his mood. 'I felt that I was in another world. The difference between the immense strain under which I had been living since the beginning of the war and the way of life in Berlin was too great. The passion for amusement and pleasure reigned supreme. People did not seem to realise the seriousness of our position in the war. I was unpleasantly impressed and felt like a stranger.'[12]

Nor could he find comfort with his wife: Margarethe had left the capital to take rooms in Düsseldorf. At least Ludendorff had recently received better family news: Franz was recovering from his head wound and would soon be awarded the Iron Cross – only the seventh to be given to his brigade. But the injury would prevent him from rejoining his unit – doctors had declared him unfit for infantry service. Soon he would begin to pester Ludendorff for permission to join the Flying Corps instead.[13]

On 1 November Ludendorff returned to the 9th Army HQ, now at Czestochova, 100 miles south-east of Breslau. On the same day he heard that at least one of his requests to Falkenhayn had been granted: Hindenburg was appointed C-in-C East, with Ludendorff his Chief of Staff and Hoffmann Chief of Operations, controlling the 8th and 9th Armies and all other forces in East and West Prussia, Pomerania, Posen and Silesia, plus frontier garrisons. Mackensen would command the 9th Army with General Grünert his Chief of Staff. Ludendorff was delighted with the news, and also with the immediate shift of the new Eastern Headquarters to Posen. Ludendorff and the rest of the staff took up quarters in the luxurious royal castle, only completed in 1910.

Plans must now be prepared and executed for the renewed offensive: pressure had to be maintained, even if forces were insufficient. Ludendorff was convinced that action should be taken before the Russian armies along the Vistula had chance to regain strength. And he increasingly believed that the 9th Army must again seize the opportunity offered by the gap between the northern and southern army groups. The target would be the Lódz region, about 120 miles southeast of Posen: a strike in this direction would hit the exposed Russian right flank.

But the movement would be extremely difficult, involving another shift in the 9th Army front: troops would have to be taken round to the nearest railheads at Hoensalza and Thorn, almost 100 miles north of Lódz. Staff problems would be immense, surprise would be essential, and the movement would leave the present front acutely exposed. Ludendorff's fears for the operation delayed his final decision, then on 3 November he came to the conclusion that the manoeuvre must be attempted despite the massive risks. He immediately approached Hindenburg, who provided full backing as always: senior officers were summoned to the Operations Room during the evening of the 3rd. Hindenburg walked over to the map and said nothing, merely pointing to Lódz. 'The raising of my left hand explained what I meant.' Orders were issued immediately.[14]

'This was a particularly harassing and busy time,' wrote Ludendorff. Planning had to be perfect. 'The more I thought about the problem ahead of us, and realised the position and our fearful peril, the firmer was my resolution, if possible, to turn the operation ... into an overwhelming and annihilating blow. That alone could definitely save us.'[15]

Falkenhayn continued to believe that the answer lay in the trenches of Ypres. His Chief of Operations, the overbearing Colonel Tappen, visited Posen; Hoffmann met him at the station and begged 'almost on my knees' to persuade Falkenhayn to send two extra corps. Tappen barely listened.[16]

By 10 November, one week after Ludendorff and Hindenburg had decided that the daring operation should be attempted, the transfer of the German divisions had been completed in total secrecy. In the south, General Böhm-Ermolli's 2nd Austrian Army filled the gap caused by the shift north of the German 9th. Further appeals were made to Supreme HQ for more troops, but these requests met with only limited response – two cavalry divisions plus other troops who 'arrived too late and at odd times', according to Ludendorff. German strength would remain at about 250,000 men against over 500,000 Russians.

Mackensen's 9th Army struck south-east from Thorn on 11 November. The target was the joint between Rennenkampf's 1st and General Scheidemann's 2nd Russian Armies defended by the 5th Siberian Corps. Within 36 hours this corps had been shattered; within four days the two Russian armies had been pushed apart with the loss of over 25,000 prisoners. Speed and surprise had been totally successfull allowing the German 1st Reserve Corps into open country before wheeling to pierce the flank of the 1st Army.

Rennenkampf was thrust north-east and the breach between the two Russian armies gaped wider still. Through this opening flooded the other four corps of the German 9th Army – the 20th, 25th Reserve, the 17th and the 11th, inclining south to encircle Lódz by 18 November. Hoffmann noted on the 19th: 'By all human calculations we must win, but waiting is nervous work.'[17]

Suddenly the situation changed. An intercepted signal revealed that the Grand Duke Nicholas was refusing to flee: his orders to the 2nd Army at Lódz were for maximum defence. Powerful Russian counter-attacks, undertaken with superior numbers, caused the 25th Reserve Corps to lose contact with the 20th; the latter found itself pressed further back, and Russian troops thrust between the two. At the same time Russian forces approached from the south, having been rallied west of Warsaw. The 25th Reserve Corps became isolated and surrounded.

Ludendorff and Hoffmann remained at Posen, and fretted for fresh information, spending over eighteen hours each day in the Great Hall of the castle which had been turned into the Operations Room. Strain began to damage nerves again, with Hoffmann this time suffering perhaps even more cruelly than Ludendorff. 'Our left wing is defeated,' he wrote on 22 November. 'How we can get them out and put things straight again, I don't know – but perhaps something will occur to me. We are on a razor-edge.' Hoffmann added: 'We have too few men. My nerves are worn out. Five nights' suspense is too much – one cannot keep it up . . .'[18]

'We learnt from enemy wireless messages,' wrote Ludendorff, 'how hopefully the Russians regarded the situation, how they planned the various battles, how they already exulted at the thought of capturing various German corps. They were preparing trains in readiness for the transport of prisoners. I cannot describe what I felt then. What was at stake? . . . Nothing less than a lost campaign . . .'[19]

Too few men in the East – while in the West valuable troops advanced to senseless slaughter at Ypres. But the outnumbered German troops near Lódz fought magnificently in foul, freezing conditions, and none struggled more bravely than those in the trapped 25th Reserve Corps commanded by General Reinhard von Scheffer-Boyadel. For nine days they battled in sub-zero weather, and not until the evening of 22 November did they cease their offensive and try to escape. During the night of the 22nd they filtered through the forests to strike the 6th Siberian Division north-east of Lódz. Battle continued throughout the 23rd; during the late afternoon Scheffer's troops broke through. They brought with them their wounded – 2,800 men – and even 16,000 Russian prisoners and 64 captured guns. Now this corps marched into line between the 20th and the 1st Reserve, and a German front had been reformed capable of withstanding subsequent assaults.

The German campaign therefore failed, but disaster had been averted. Both Ludendorff and Hoffmann criticised the Supreme Command bitterly for lack of effective support; Falkenhayn's offensive had failed in the First Battle of Ypres, with about 130,000 German casualties, and the race to the sea had ended with neither side obtaining supremacy.

'I am horrified at the way the war is being carried out in the West,' declared Hoffmann in his diary on 1 December. 'Falkenhayn is the evil genius of our Fatherland, and, unfortunately, he has the Kaiser in his pocket.'[20]

Russian troops evacuated Lódz on 6 December and retired in good order towards Warsaw. Elements of the 9th Army advanced to occupy the battered town and to push further east. Then winter clamped down and the opposing forces attempted to consolidate their positions amidst the mud and sleet showers.

The Hindenburg-Ludendorff partnership had functioned superbly in 1914. Frequently Ludendorff's nerves had shown signs of acute strain, but each time he managed to pull himself together helped by the stoical Hindenburg and the urbane Hoffmann. The achievements were colossal even if total victory had been denied: the victory of Tannenberg less than a week after the new commander had arrived on the Eastern Front; the switch to the Masurian Lakes only four days later; the offensive to the Vistula less than a fortnight after arriving in southern Poland; the advance from Thorn less than a week after deciding to switch an entire army to a new front; the subsequent successes with a quarter of a million Germans thrown against over half a million Russians. The sheer planning and organisation involved throughout these complex stages, often in terrible conditions, revealed Ludendorff as nothing less than a genius as a staff officer, no matter how much help he may have received from Hindenburg and Hoffmann.

Some recognition had already been forthcoming. On 27 November Hindenburg received his elevation to Field-Marshal; Ludendorff became a Lieutenant-General. The Kaiser visited the Posen HQ on 29 November to express his personal congratulations; adulation increased throughout Germany for the 'Great Twin Brethren', whose successes were in striking contrast to the continuing grim news from the Western Front.

Ludendorff acknowledged 'the almost crushing work of those four months of war' but he viewed the results with 'proud satisfaction'. He wrote: 'Our troops, who had been constantly fighting or on the move since the beginning of August, had shown themselves beyond all praise.' And he added: 'Honour and perpetual remembrance to the Germany Army of 1914!'

F

CHAPTER NINE

The Winter Battle

FIGHTING REMAINED SPORADIC DURING DECEMBER AND INTO JANUARY 1915. Work continued in the freezing conditions – often 10 degrees below zero – to improve conditions and to restore communications: railways were repaired as far as possible, though ice hindered progress. 'The troops,' wrote Ludendorff, 'who were everywhere exhausted, suffered much on account of this. It was particularly regrettable that we were not able to get their Christmas parcels delivered in time.'

Life at Posen Castle proved more comfortable, especially the long winter evenings spent sitting round the polished table beneath the chandeliers; above the officers hung the heads of deer and elk decorating the panelling, and on the centre of the table stood a potted palm, the gift of the Kaiserin. Officers talked deep into the night – 'common cares and common glory united us' – and newcomers were impressed by the relaxed atmosphere. One such new member of the staff arriving in December was Wilhelm Breucker, who sat between Ludendorff and Hindenburg at table during his first evening. 'Ludendorff did not mention one single word about the operations at Tannenberg ... but he proudly told the story of how his old brigade had impressed the divisional commander at the last parade.'[1]

Ludendorff's stepson Franz received a delighted welcome when he came to Headquarters: Franz had now recovered from his head wounds and was stationed in the nearby Air Division after his successful pleas to be allowed to join the Air Corps; he passed his examinations both as an observer and a pilot in minimum time and his brother Heinz was attempting to follow his lead. Margarethe visited her son and husband at Posen during the winter for two or three extremely happy days. She later remembered vividly her impressions of the old city, with its Gothic spires, tumbling roof-tops and strange languages, all such a contrast to Berlin.[2]

Planning intensified for the opening of the 1915 campaign. Ludendorff and Hindenburg agreed this should begin as soon as possible, even if weather conditions remained harsh: the side which advanced first might gain the critical advantage. Once again the *Ober-Ost* HQ began to press for further reinforcements, especially from four new corps which were being formed in Germany. At the same time the Austrians also requested help: Conrad suggested to Berlin that an offensive should be launched through the Carpathians supported by German forces, and linked with a German attack from East Prussia. Ludendorff and Hindenburg sent their approval from Posen, and were especially anxious that the Carpathian offensive should be strong enough – and early enough – to prevent the fall of Przemyśl: this besieged town lay in the centre of the Austro-Russian front about 150 miles south-east from Cracow.

Falkenhayn disagreed, and relations between the Supreme and *Ober-Ost* commands suddenly deteriorated sharply. 'No pressing emergency from which Austria-Hungary had to be relieved existed at the moment,' wrote Falkenhayn. 'A relief of Przemyśl would certainly have been valuable. But no such great importance with regard to the general conduct of the war could be attached to it as to make it repay the expenditure of German reserves.'[3] A deeper issue existed based on the fundamental question of priorities between the East and West Fronts. Ludendorff still believed that Supreme Command should take 'the great decision to stake everything against Russia': with stalemate in the West, Germany's wisest plan would be to throw everything possible against Russia; victory in the East would free German forces for a renewed onslaught in the West. Hindenburg agreed: 'The decisive battle in the West, a battle which would have meant final victory, was the *ultima ratio*, but an *ultima ratio* which could only be reached over the body of a Russia stricken to the ground.'[4]

After the war Falkenhayn continued to insist that the *Ober-Ost* command believed that final victory could be obtained against the Russians: in fact both Ludendorff and Hindenburg were fully aware that the war would only be won by defeating France and Britain after the destruction of the Tsar's armies. Thus Falkenhayn wrote: 'The assumption that a final decision in the East could be obtained was, of course ... unfounded ... No decision in the East, even though it were as thorough as it is possible to imagine, could spare us from fighting to a conclusion in the West. For this Germany had to be prepared at all costs.'[5]

Early in January 1915, Hindenburg and Ludendorff agreed that if Falkenhayn denied support to the Austrians, then this should be despatched from their 9th Army regardless of the weakening which would result in their own line. A number of units were therefore released for the Austrian front, including the HQ staff of the 2nd Corps, nearly three infantry divisions and a cavalry division. These troops, plus Austrian elements, would be named the German South Army and would fight alongside the Austrian main army in the Przemyśl region.[6] This *Ober-Ost* initiative gained the Kaiser's approval on 8 January:

Hindenburg and Ludendorff, with their immense public prestige, could not be denied the despatch of limited support to Germany's struggling ally.

Within twenty-four hours Falkenhayn retaliated with a sudden order to the *Ober-Ost* HQ: Hindenburg and Ludendorff would be separated. 'I was surprised by a telegram from our General Headquarters,' wrote Ludendorff, 'stating that I had been made Chief of Staff of the Southern Army.' Commander of this new force would be General von Linsingen – who already had an excellent staff. Moreover Ludendorff's transfer represented demotion. The command of which he had been Chief of Staff comprised two large armies plus supporting elements, his new one a small single army.

Hindenburg answered by petitioning direct to the Kaiser for the partnership to remain intact. His words, even if composed with Ludendorff's collusion, revealed the close relationship between the two men.

> I have grown into close union with my Chief of Staff; he has come to be a true helper and friend, irreplaceable by any other, one on whom I bestow my fullest confidence. Your Majesty knows from the history of war how important such a happy relationship is for the conduct of affairs and the well-being of the troops. In addition, his new and so much smaller sphere of action does not do justice to the General's comprehensive ability and great capacity ... On these grounds I venture most respectfully to beg that my war comrade may graciously be restored to me.[7]

The Field-Marshal sent another message to the Kaiser, again bypassing the Chief of General Staff. Hindenburg pleaded that the four new corps should be sent to the Russian front, and his argument revealed the basic stance adopted by *Ober-Ost* command against Falkenhayn.

> Their employment in the West will only lead to a strengthening of our defence, or – as at Ypres – to a costly and not very promising frontal push. Our army in the West ought to be able to hold well-protected positions sited in successive lines and to maintain itself without being reinforced by the new corps until decisive success in the East has been attained.[8]

Ludendorff left Posen on 10 January, hoping that he would be allowed to return when the Kaiser received Hindenburg's letter. Next day he reached Breslau for talks with Conrad, Linsingen – and Falkenhayn. Ludendorff put his point of view; the response seemed frigid. 'It was all unsatisfactory and pointless,' commented Ludendorff, 'a contest of opinions settled beforehand.' On 12 January Falkenhayn travelled to Posen for talks with Hindenburg, during which the *Ober-Ost* commander displayed his usual courtesy but also his stubbornness.

Both Hindenburg's letters achieved their aims. By the end of the month Ludendorff had repacked his military baggage and left his latest quarters in Munkacs to return north. His fortnight with the Austrians was instructive: troops were insufficiently trained and provided for, and the army suffered from a mixture of nationalities. Ludendorff commented: 'A Jew in Radom once said to one of my officers that he could not understand why so strong and vital a body as Germany should ally itself with a corpse. He was right.'[9] Offensives to relieve Przemyśl eventually failed dismally in early spring; the fortress fell to famine with the loss of 100,000 men and many guns: Falkenhayn pointed out that he had predicted such a disaster.

Meanwhile Ludendorff's welcome return to Posen coincided with the second victory over Falkenhayn resulting from Hindenburg's letters: the Kaiser now approved the despatch of the four new corps to the Russian front. Planning could proceed for a fresh offensive in East Prussia. But then Falkenhayn made another move: discussions at the *Ober-Ost* HQ were threatened with disruption when Falkenhayn began to insist on supervising operations. He wrote: '[I] therefore began to familiarise [myself] with the idea of taking the conduct of operations in the East into [my] own hands. The translation of this idea into fact was prevented at the moment by gigantic preparations on the part of the enemy for an offensive in the West.' Added to this threat of an Allied attack – realised by the Anglo-French thrusts in Artois and Champagne from mid-January into March – was the Kaiser's disapproval of any direct move by Falkenhayn to eclipse Hindenburg and Ludendorff.[10]

Preparations intensified at the *Ober-Ost* HQ, all the more urgently when intelligence reports revealed that the Russians themselves planned a decisive offensive in early spring 1915, entailing two large-scale attacks against East and West Prussia. The arrival of the new corps from Germany allowed the creation of three armies under *Ober-Ost* command: the 8th on the Angerapp Line and among the Masurian Lakes; the 9th further south opposite Warsaw; and the 10th now being formed behind the lines.

Once again Ludendorff, Hoffmann and their staffs worked long hours at maximum pressure. Scores of intelligence assessment were studied, facts collated, diagrams traced over maps, figures compiled for railway rolling-stock and road transports. From this staff-work emerged three salient points. First, enemy plans apparently envisaged the main Russian thrust being launched against the northern wing of the German 8th Army, between the Niemen and the Gumbinnen–Insterburg road – reinforcement of the Russian front opposite this wing had been noticed during recent days. Second, these reinforcements had been used to bolster the centre of the Russian 10th Army facing the German 8th, and the flanks remained comparatively weak. Third, the railway system and provision of rolling-stock would allow the secret deployment of the new German 10th Army in the far north, between Memel and Tilsit. An attack could therefore be launched from this area directly south into the weak right flank of the Russian 10th while the enemy was preoccupied with his own plans. This thrust, combined with a push by the German 8th further south against the enemy left, could crush the Russians in the Masurian Lakes region: the German 8th would be strengthened by the 20th Corps from the 9th Army, to counter reinforcements which had been sent to the enemy centre. Even further south, the remainder of the 9th Army would provide a distraction by beginning a supposed attack towards Warsaw.[11]

This clear and deadly assessment of enemy frailties and German potential was translated into rapid action: orders were issued on 28 January, less than a week after Ludendorff's return to Posen. Once again troops were rushed to railways sidings and crammed into carriages which clattered north over the misty, icy Baltic countryside – 120 trains in non-stop progression. Some halted to the west and some to the north of Tilsit. This town had special significance for those like Ludendorff who studied the Fatherland's military history: here, on a swaying raft moored in the middle of the Niemen, Napoleon Bonaparte had met Tsar Alexander I in June 1807 to discuss peace; waiting on the bank had been Friedrich Wilhelm, king of crushed Prussia, lonely and largely ignored. 'A nasty king, a nasty nation, a nasty army,' the French leader had confided to his new-found Russian friend. Now the humiliation of Tilsit could be revenged by Ludendorff's army.

Moreover, this army would employ a new weapon – gas: Ludendorff intended to use chemical weapons with artillery for the first time in military history, and thus to open a new and even more deadly era of warfare. He showed no signs of scruples, and in this respect he displayed the paradox so often evident in the character of military leaders – a mixture of the brutal with the humane. Ludendorff always seized the opportunities offered by modern technology, whether these took the form of mass killings through machine guns, monstrous artillery pieces, or gas shells. His attitude was clearly that he must make use of all possible means to win his battles, regardless of the indiscriminate suffering which might be caused. As far as weapons were concerned, Ludendorff was an extreme progressive. Yet in other ways he could also be a military conservative, for example with his condemnation of guerrilla warfare: war must be fought according to the rules, including with a certain amount of chivalry – but not including any avoidance of modern weapons of mass destruction.

Battle preliminaries opened far to the south near Bolimov on 30 January, when units of the 9th Army launched their feint towards Warsaw. Bombardment of Bolimov began early in the morning, supported by 18,000 gas shells. Results were less than expected since the freezing temperature prevented the full explosion of the deadly xylyl bromide contained in the shells. The attack nevertheless succeeded in distracting enemy attention from the build-up in the north, and by

5 February these preparations had been completed. Also on the 5th, as Hindenburg's HQ moved forward to Insterburg, the weather deteriorated rapidly. Blizzards swept across East Prussia for the next forty-eight hours, snapping the frozen pines in the forests and piling snow six feet deep in the ditches and trenches; temperatures dropped to an unprecedented 40 degrees below zero, and men found it almost impossible to walk in the gale. Troops huddled beneath their greatcoats; Hindenburg and Ludendorff waited impatiently in the Hotel Dessauer, Insterburg.

On 6 February the *Ober-Ost* command decided that the attack must proceed despite the weather. Conditions might even help surprise. Orders were issued over the telephone to corps commanders, and soon after the freezing dawn on 7 February German troops left their trenches and began to wade forward across the wastes.

This initial attack was launched by the German right wing in General von Litzmann's 8th Army area: the remainder of the 8th Army and the 10th Army would move twenty-four hours later. By nightfall on the 7th, troops in the 40th Reserve had almost reached Johannisburg and further south had crossed the frozen Pissa. Johannisburg fell next day, and at the same time the general German advance began.

The feats performed by man and horse during the following days are beyond description [wrote Ludendorff]. The heads of the marching columns worked their way laboriously through snow-drifts. Waggons got stuck in the snow. The columns stopped and got longer and longer. The infantry edged their way past the waggons and guns, and tried to catch up with those in front. Ten to twelve horses were harnessed to guns and ammunition waggons. So the roads were gradually covered with long marching columns, infantry pushing ahead, interspersed with only a few guns and still fewer ammunition waggons.[12]

The weather multiplied staff problems – the delays in bringing up reinforcements to a particular point, failure of communications, difficulties of supply. Ludendorff's face revealed the strain: his complexion, already pale, now appeared waxen. But on 13 February the Russian commander General Sievers ordered full retreat; German troops entered Lyck on the 14th, and next day elements of the 8th Army seized Marggrabova to the north-east which had been abandoned by the Russian HQ staff only a few hours before. Also on the 15th the weather changed again, with milder winds blowing from the south to thaw the drifts and to turn the icy roads into slush and slime. Both sides struggled through the morass, infantrymen covered with mud and floundering through the mire. Hundreds more Russian stragglers fell to the advancing Germans, but pursuit was obliged to slow down; by darkness on the 15th the Russian 3rd and 26th Corps had managed to reach the Grodno region and comparative safety.

Behind them lay the Russian 20th Corps still in the Augustovo Forest, and the German ring tightened round this gallant rearguard. Terrible fighting continued for the next five days, until the trapped Russians surrendered late on the 21st with 30,000 men filing through the German lines into captivity, among them 11 generals. The remainder of the Russian army retreated further west and perhaps the most horrible of all the battles on the Russian front came to an end.

'The Winter Battle in Masuria,' wrote Hindenburg; 'the name charms like an icy wind or the stillness of death. As men look back on the course of this battle they will only stand and ask themselves: "Have earthly beings really done these things, or is it all but a fable and a phantom?" '[13] Casualty figures for the battle are unreliable, but probably at least 60,000 Russian prisoners were taken. The Grand Duke's plans for offensives into Prussia had been shattered, and from this point of view the result was tactically important. On a more immediate strategic level, the battle was perhaps indecisive, with weather and lack of strength robbing the Germans of final victory, and the advance of the German flank into Russian territory to the east could not be secured whilst the situation further south remained uncertain. Moreover, although the Russian 10th Army had been decimated, almost immediately the newly-formed Russian 12th under General von Plehve opposed the German southern wing to prevent further advance.

The front line swayed to and fro, with casualties remaining heavy for both sides and yet without significant results. It seemed that Ludendorff's spectacular successes had ended for the moment, and even that Falkenhayn had been correct in arguing against the winter offensives. With the closing of these large-scale attacks and counter-attacks, a phase had finished in the war on the Eastern Front, although of course this aspect could not be identified at the time. The phase covered Tannenberg, the Masurian Lakes and the Winter Battle in Masuria – the massive clashes which earned Ludendorff his reputation. They had also revealed tendencies in the fighting – some peculiar to the Eastern Front and some common to the whole war – which would steadily become more pronounced. These features included the importance of the road and rail systems, upon which Ludendorff relied so heavily, and also the destructiveness of modern weapons which so often precluded frontal attacks against prepared positions: even Ludendorff, who appreciated this factor more than most First World War commanders, was sometimes obliged to accept terrible casualties in attempting to force the enemy in a direct assault. As far as the features peculiar to the East were concerned, the most important was the apparent ability of the Russians to withstand defeat by withdrawing deep into their own territory, obliging the advancing Germans to expose the flanks to counter-attack. This Russian advantage had defeated Napoleon in 1812 and would lead to the collapse of Hitler's

armies in the Second World War. Now, in 1914–15, Ludendorff realised that German moves forward had to be cautious, which allowed
the Russians some respite.

Hence the Russian recovery after Ludendorff's initial victories: he
lacked sufficient strength to exploit his success. Yet Tannenberg remains one of the most important battles of the First World War: it
played a fundamental part in the ultimate German victory in the East,
even though Russian resources and Russia's geographical advantage
meant that this final victory would only be obtained after many more
months of bloody, confusing and exhausting campaigns. A German
defeat at Tannenberg would almost inevitably have meant the defeat
of the Fatherland within the first six months of war; instead Ludendorff's success led the way to Brest-Litovsk, the Russian Revolution,
and also to European upheaval and tragedy from which the world has
still to recover.

Russia's ability to pull back and summon fresh armies meant that
stalemate continued: there would be no easy path to complete German victory and instead the enemy must be bled to death. And in
March 1915 the way ahead seemed unclear. At the beginning of the
month Hindenburg and Ludendorff moved their HQ forward to
Lötzen; spring gradually touched the nearby lakes and forests. In the
West, the Allied offensives were maintained in the Artois-Champagne
region followed by German counter-attacks; neither made decisive
headway despite ghastly casualties. Falkenhayn believed that the four
additional corps which had been sent to the Russian front might have
made a considerable difference to his western forces, and once again
relations between the *Ober-Ost* and Supreme Command became dangerously strained.

'Really, the whole of Berlin seems to have gone mad,' wrote Hoffmann in his diary. 'We are winning the greatest victory known to
history, and three days later they all behave as if we had been defeated,
because the pursuit comes to a stop after 200 kilometres . . . Our whole
army stands on Russian soil.'[14] Ludendorff wrote: 'It is simply impossible to put it all on paper, the proud hopes, the despondence, the
disappointments, the heart-searching before a decision, the annoyance
caused by one thing and another . . .'[15]

Ludendorff managed to find some relaxation in the pleasant town
of Lötzen, despite the continuing tension. During these weeks he sent
a telegram to Margarethe: he would expect her at 10 o'clock next
evening at Thorn station. Margarethe rushed to be ready for the sudden journey. 'This could only be done if everything went like clock-
work, and no unforeseen obstacles arose.' She managed to arrive on
schedule, to find Ludendorff waiting impatiently for her. He himself
had almost been late since his car had broken down on the way from
Lötzen; Margarethe wrote: 'With an angry gleam in his eye he ex-

claimed, "I should have had that chauffeur hanged if I had not got here in time to meet you at the station." '

Margarethe, after a happy few hours, a sad parting and a lonely journey home, experienced some of the glory which now hung over Ludendorff. A stranger's child was introduced to her and stared with wide eyes before whispering: 'I thought you would wear a little golden crown.'[16]

Ludendorff's fame also resulted in a succession of painters applying for permission to visit HQ and paint his portrait. The General was an unwilling subject. According to Wilhelm Breucker he refused one artist, Professor Reusing from Düsseldorf, with the words: 'Give Reusing my compliments. Leaders of armies should be painted. I, as Chief of Staff, should stay in the background.'[17] Another painter, Professor Vogel, managed more success but emerged from the sessions rather shaken: Ludendorff seemed 'positively alarming' with his constant stern expression. 'Your husband,' Vogel told Margarethe, 'gives me cold shivers down my back.' Margarethe wrote: 'Even in his family we knew that grim countenance. They used to say, "Be careful! Look out! Today father looks like a glacier." '[18]

The struggle with Falkenhayn took a new and even more serious form. During March and April forces had to be detached from the north to assist the Austrians further south, where a new army was created, the 11th; an offensive beginning on 3 May between Gorlice and Tarnow obtained considerable success. Przemyśl was retaken on 3 June, and on the 23rd the Austro-German troops crossed the Dniester. Falkenhayn had given this campaign full support, and now attempted to obtain rewards by extending his influence over Hindenburg and Ludendorff.

Already, a conference at Pless on 3 June had revealed strong divergences of opinion, and these soon became more acute. During June the *Ober-Ost* HQ began to plan for their own next offensive in the north, with Hindenburg, Ludendorff and Hoffmann in full agreement that Austrian successes in the south could not be decisive since the Russians were merely retreating further west: the Russian armies remained in being. After a meeting with corps commanders on 29 June, Ludendorff accepted Hoffmann's scheme for another encircling movement which promised dramatic opportunities for the last, conclusive victory. This plan entailed a vigorous assault by the 10th Army westwards, combined with a thrust from the north by the Niemen Army. The immediate target would be Kovno. 'Once this fortress had fallen,' wrote Ludendorff later, 'the corner-stone of the Russian defence on the Niemen, the road to Vilna and to the rear of the Russian forces, would be open.'

Ludendorff issued orders for necessary troop movements.[19] But signs of Falkenhayn's interference had already become apparent. Hoffmann had noted in his diary on 30 May: 'HM is entirely under Falkenhayn's influence and does not love us ... Of course we are intentionally rather thrust into the background.' And on 16 June: 'GHQ goes on stripping us, so that we are glad if we can hold on and stick to what we have ... There is certainly some dirty work about it.'[20]

Hindenburg and Ludendorff were summoned to an Imperial Conference at Posen on 1 July. Hindenburg detailed the proposed offensive; Falkenhayn immediately rejected another attempt to encircle the enemy. 'A fact had become clearly evident,' he declared. 'With the comparatively modest forces at Germany's disposal for offensive action, the continuation of the operations against flank or wing of the Russian front could no longer offer prospects of important successes. The enemy had long been watching for them.'[21]

The Chief of General Staff therefore proposed a direct attack launched further south in the Warsaw sector. The Kaiser supported Falkenhayn. Ludendorff damned the whole decision and his anger was further roused by the attitude of Tappen, Falkenhayn's Chief of Operations, who sneered: 'These people only want to attack where nobody opposes them.'[22] Ludendorff agreed that a flank attack would not succeed unless sufficient troops were available to exploit the initial success – hence his constant demands for more troops. On the other hand a frontal offensive could never obtain complete victory, since the Russians would merely retreat, and German soldiers would have to advance directly against prepared enemy positions – resulting in the horrendous casualties which were so much a feature of the Western Front. Ludendorff's whole nature rebelled against the idea. A telephone call to Lötzen revealed the Kaiser's choice, and Hoffmann commented: 'The Chief is coming back at 11 o'clock this evening. He will be furious.'[23]

'Ludendorff came back from Posen in a savage temper,' wrote Hoffmann next day. For the next week the *Ober-Ost* staff were subjected to Ludendorff's violent rages: he seemed unapproachable, bawling out anyone who attempted to discuss matters with him, behaving in a completely irrational and unjust manner to his subordinates. 'I'm sick of Headquarters,' confided Hoffmann to his diary. 'The fellow is not satisfied until he can abuse us every day.'[24] Ludendorff's rage increased even further on 10 July. A special train arrived at Lötzen carrying the GHQ Chief of Operations Section; Tappen put forward official reasons for his unexpected visit, but nobody believed him, and Hindenburg, Ludendorff and Hoffmann realised that this arrogant officer had been sent to check whether GHQ instructions were being obeyed. 'Hindenburg's and Ludendorff's fury can be imagined,' wrote Hoffmann. 'I endured it with the utmost self-control.'[25]

German units advanced on 13 July in the direction of Warsaw as ordered by Falkenhayn. Ludendorff's fears of heavy casualties proved over-pessimistic, since the Russians were taken partially by surprise. Resistance stiffened before Warsaw, but the enemy evacuated the city on 4 August and fell back behind the Vistula, as Ludendorff had expected. Large areas of territory were gained, but the Russian forces remained intact. General retirement spread, with Brest-Litovsk being occupied by German units on 25 August, Grodno on 2 September and Vilna on 19 September.

> The Russian armies were certainly kept on the move [commented Ludendorff], but they escaped ... The strain on our troops was tremendous, owing to the continuous movement for many weeks on bad roads and, generally speaking, in bad weather. Clothing and boots were in rags and tatters. Supply was difficult ... As the distance increased, the difficulty in bringing up ammunition increased proportionately. Thus the advance slowed down and lost its impetus.[26]

But the offensive did bring one development which might be to Germany's advantage: the Tsar dismissed Grand Duke Nicholas, despite his undoubted skills, and assumed personal command himself with Mikhail Alekseyev as his Chief of Staff. In the German GHQ, Falkenhayn believed he had won a great victory, one which eclipsed the previous efforts by Hindenburg and Ludendorff, and during August he asserted further authority by taking over direct control of the 9th Army.

Hoffmann described *Ober-Ost*'s counter-action in a diary entry on 5 August. 'We forced the Field-Marshal to the point of threatening resignation – he refused, until Ludendorff threatened to resign.' Next day Hoffmann added:

> As a result of Hindenburg's threat of course we had two slimy telegrams from GHQ to the effect that no one had meant to hurt his feelings, that a division from the West would be sent to us, etc. Falkenhayn is so powerful with HM that no other opinion has any weight. The great victory that could have been won has not yet been won, and now it cannot be won ...[27]

In the third week of August preparations were made by GHQ for a triumphant celebration at Novo-Georgievsk, expected to fall at any moment. It was arranged for the Kaiser to review his troops, Falkenhayn beside him. A telegram reach the *Ober-Ost* HQ in the evening of 19 August giving details of this event, but without including an invitation for Hindenburg even though the troops were officially under his command. *Ober-Ost* retaliated by organising a special train which took Hindenburg and Ludendorff to the function. Hoffmann, back at Lötzen, had delighted visions of Falkenhayn's expression when he saw the uninvited guests. The Chief of the General Staff in fact said to Ludendorff: 'Now, are you at last convinced that my operation was right?' 'On the contrary,' snapped Ludendorff.

Rows continued into autumn. Falkenhayn now sought to transfer forces from East to West, believing he had pushed the Russians out of the reckoning for a considerable period. In the West the Allies renewed their offensives in Artois and Champagne on 25 September, with the battles reaching new heights of carnage at Vimy Ridge and Loos. On 6 October Hindenburg refused to allow more troops to leave the East for this slaughter; Falkenhayn's reply emphasised the support which he believed he enjoyed from the Kaiser. 'Whether Your Excellency agrees with the views of GHQ does not matter, once a decision has been made by his Majesty.'[28]

'I can still well remember Ludendorff's letters at that time,' wrote Margarethe. 'They were nothing but one long complaint against Falkenhayn.'[29]

Autumn rains brought an end to campaigning for another year. In the East, the front now ran from Mitau on the Baltic to the eastern end of the Carpathians; in the West, minor gains made by the Allies were utterly out of proportion to casualties suffered. During the year about 612,000 Germans had been lost, 1,292,000 French, 279,000 British, without any appreciable shift in the trench pattern. To the south, the Austrians were having to face a new enemy: Italy had declared war on 23 May and the repeated battles of Isonzo continued in dreary, bloody succession. British attempts to open a new front in the Dardanelles against the Turks were failing. On all fronts, the war entered a period of terrible stalemate as 1915 drew to a close. And, with the lull in hostilities, Ludendorff undertook new tasks in complete contrast to any he had hitherto attempted; in doing so he revealed fresh, unmilitary abilities.

CHAPTER TEN

'With Heart and with Hand'

Ober-Ost HQ MOVED BY RAIL ON 20 OCTOBER 1915 ACROSS THE NEWLY acquired territory to Kovno, where Hindenburg, Ludendorff and Hoffmann established living quarters in a villa belonging to an expatriate German. The Russian retreat had enabled vast areas of Polish-Russia to be occupied; now these had to be administered, and the task would fall mainly on Ludendorff despite his total lack of experience in civil affairs.

'I determined to resume in the occupied territory that work of civilisation at which the Germans had laboured in those lands for many centuries. The population, made up as it is of such a mixture of races, has never produced a culture of its own and, left to itself, would succumb to a Polish domination.' Rather than allow this to happen, Ludendorff intended to place German authority firmly, yet fairly, over the lives of the people: only in Germany would they find a future.[1]

Kovno itself lacked elegance befitting Ludendorff's lofty aims. He described the town as typically Russian – 'with low, mean wooden houses and comparatively wide streets'. But the area had strong historical connections which appealed to him. Close by, over the Niemen, stood a memorial to mark the spot where Napoleon had watched his troops flood into the Russian homeland in 1812; not far away could be seen another memorial, 'the tower of an old German castle of the Teutonic Knights, a symbol of German civilisation'.

Soon after his arrival at Kovno, Ludendorff attended a service in a former Russian Orthodox church; there, on foreign soil, he heard the strong voices of German troops as they sang one of his favourite hymns:

> I have given myself with heart and with hand,
> To thee, land of love and life, my German Fatherland ...

Ludendorff commented: 'I was deeply moved. This hymn ought to be sung every Sunday in all the churches, and should be engraved on the hearts of all Germans.'[2]

Ludendorff's administrative region covered the Baltic provinces, Lithuania, Latvia, Russian Poland and parts of West Prussia previously encroached upon by the enemy, an area almost as large as France, and containing a jumble of nationalities among whom the Jewish population was especially strong. Ludendorff had still to develop his hatred of the Jews, and at this time he worked closely with them to ensure Yiddish rights were respected.

The region had been devastated by war, with communications destroyed, villages and towns battered, citizens scattered, livestock slaughtered. Ludendorff set about restoring the district to a semblance of peaceful normality, whilst attempting to lead the people into the sphere of the Fatherland. His high and romantic notions were backed by acute administrative skill: he approached the problems in Chief of Staff fashion. Moreover, he acted on his own: Hindenburg largely preferred to spend his time hunting on local estates; Hoffmann showed no interest and rapidly became bored. 'Ludendorff . . . keeps everyone on the run from morning till night,' complained the Chief of Operations on 2 November. 'This restlessness – work for work's sake – is extremely uncomfortable for everybody.'[3]

Ludendorff's enthusiasm grew even though the magnitude of the problems expanded at an impossible pace. Railways had to be repaired and enlarged, river bridges rebuilt, factories put into operation, agriculture restored. Above all, Ludendorff believed that the German voice had to be heard, comprising a unifying factor to bind together the various elements which had been confused by war. He despatched squads of men with wall posters, printed in five different languages, and nineteen newspapers throughout the area were organised to give support. These journals included those in Yiddish, for example *Letzte Nais,* and a significant number of journalists specially invited into the area were Jews.[4]

In general, Ludendorff made a point of attempting to see that Germans were not given undue privileges: all nationalities were to be treated the same. At the same time he tried to instil into the varying nationalities a sense of their own identity, despite his ideals about the Fatherland: he believed every man had the right to his own nationality, which provided him with his identity, and this conviction clearly lay behind his later belief regarding German aspirations for a German Fatherland pure from outside 'pollution'.

Armed with these ideals and principles, Ludendorff divided each province into districts; he created a police force and established lawcourts with provincial courts of appeal and a High Court in Kovno; a civil service bureaucracy was developed, a standardised system of finance was introduced, and taxes and customs duties imposed; industries were often nationalised.[5]

But Ludendorff's efforts were far from totally successful. The task was too great. He relied on a multitude of officers and civil servants acting beneath him, and very often these individuals proved to be inept and even corrupt. Above all, Ludendorff's vision of a benevolent Fatherland supervising the various nationalities in the region was virtually unworkable, especially in the continuing chaos and tension of war. Whatever Ludendorff's personal convictions, German rule appeared to be that of a conqueror; German troops marched through the streets; a German dictatorship had been imposed, and opposition to the Fatherland remained strong.

Nevertheless, these weeks revealed a new facet of Ludendorff's character. He displayed a sensitive attitude to the aspirations of the differing nationalities which marked a complete contrast to the image of Ludendorff as a stiff-necked and unfeeling Prussian officer. He showed a genuine desire to institute a civilian administration, even though his attitude continued to be that of a staff officer; he concerned himself as much with industrial matters as he did with institution of law and order – once again, this preceded his later policy in Germany, when he attempted to put into practice his belief that all elements, whether industrial, economic, political as well as military, must be combined for the common struggle. The military must have the final word in time of war, but allied to the fighting effort must be all the other factors which constituted the state. Moreover, Ludendorff now employed very unmilitary people to help him. Artists were gathered, and the 'Artists' Corner' at the HQ became famous; writers arrived from the German homeland, some with highly extrovert natures. Ludendorff's help was sought by the poet Herbert Eulenberg, who had tried to enlist as a soldier but had been turned down as militarily useless. Ludendorff spent one night reading his book, *Der Morgen nach Kunersdorf,* and then invited the poet to his office. Eulenberg entered the General's room: his sideburns were so long that one had become entangled round the button of his coat, giving him a lop-sided appearance, but Ludendorff uncharacteristically overlooked the man's untidiness, and took him on to his staff. Eulenberg was ordered to write essays on the area, describing the different cultures and regional aspects but avoiding politics.[6]

Ludendorff continued his military duties alongside his civilian undertakings. And, during this winter of 1915–16, he became increasingly convinced that insufficient support for the armies in the field was being provided by those back in the Fatherland, not through the fault of the people themselves, but through the incompetence and corruption of the politicians. This belief would soon become an obsession.

Ludendorff wrote to the Bavarian General Ritter von Wenninger on 16 December:

Twice the chance to hit the Russians decisively has been denied to us. Well, bitter hate brews in me, so I'll have to keep quiet. What has been left undone in this war, missed opportunities, to the detriment of the

Fatherland, is too much to prevent the perceptive man being oppressed. I am not a carping critic, Excellency, but a German who sees with sadness how the strength of the people is squandered, how the war profiteers cannot be restrained, how so many have climbed to the top who belong at the bottom.[7]

Personal pleasures helped to give brief relaxation. All three of his stepsons were now in the Flying Corps, and all were stationed on the Eastern Front. During the winter they spent some weeks at Kovno airfield and often visited Ludendorff. As always, he found their company extremely enjoyable, and the teenage boys responded to his affection. 'I think those must have been the happiest hours of their lives,' wrote Margarethe.

The hours were too short. The eldest boy, Franz, already a victim of head splinters whilst an infantryman, narrowly escaped death again. The struts of his bi-plane snapped as he flew a reconnaissance mission over the Russian lines; somehow he managed to keep the machine in the air until he reached German territory and then the frail craft hurtled from 2,000 feet to smash into a small coppice. He suffered concussion, a complicated fracture of the hip and severe bruising, but once again recovered and returned to the fight. His mother commented: 'He considered it indecent to worm himself into a sheltered job'; he even managed to join one of the crack squadrons as a pilot officer, no doubt with some help from Ludendorff.[8]

Throughout these winter weeks the simmering conflict with Falkenhayn became stronger and more bitter. Both the Supreme HQ and the *Ober-Ost* HQ began to plan for their 1916 spring offensives, and it soon appeared that neither could undertake a decisive campaign without sacrifices by the other. Falkenhayn submitted a report to the Kaiser in December which declared that the French General Staff would defend the Verdun region with all possible strength, and that advantage should be taken of this: 'The forces of France will bleed to death – as there can be no question of a voluntary withdrawal – whether we reach our goal or not.' Capture of Verdun would break the heart of France and 'England's sword would be knocked out of her hand'. Falkenhayn's optimism persuaded Wilhelm to continue his support, and almost immediately demands were made for manpower from the Russian front – where Ludendorff believed resources to be insufficient already.[9]

'The times when Hindenburg could get his way against Falkenhayn are long past,' despaired Hoffmann on 7 January 1916. 'Time has taken the trumps out of his hand. The times have changed, the times of our Great Deeds are long past, and also the times of Falkenhayn's grosser blunders – viz. Ypres etc. I do not see how the situation can possibly change under the present Emperor.'[10]

Late in January, Falkenhayn summoned Ludendorff to talks at

Lida, where the *Ober-Ost* Chief of Staff arrived with plans for an offensive across the Dvina. Falkenhayn seemed conciliatory but blinded by his prospects for Verdun. 'We thought something was going to happen, but we were mistaken,' wrote Hoffmann on 29 January. 'However, there was no quarrel – just nothing at all.'[11]

Soon after dawn on 21 February troops of the German 5th Army advanced on an eight-mile front against the French at Verdun. The defenders were already shaken by a massive artillery bombardment and gave ground through the hilly, wooded countryside. Then the French Supreme Commander, Marshal Joseph Joffre, prohibited further retreat: General Henri Pétain took local command, and on 26 February the initial German advance was halted; French reinforcements were rushed to the front and battle continued into March.

Rumours were growing in the East that the Russians intended an offensive against Vilna. Meanwhile Ludendorff left Kovno on 10 March to visit Berlin, where he attended the wedding of Prince Joachim of Prussia, and where he learnt details of an extremely controversial issue causing deep division amongst the decision-makers. Admiral von Tirpitz, highly respected State Secretary for the Navy, had tendered his resignation on 6 March; the sixty-seven-year-old Admiral had offered to resign before, and for the same reason, but this time it had been accepted. Tirpitz had long believed that the war could only be won by resuming unrestricted submarine warfare, regardless of the danger of sinking neutral US vessels and hence precipitating America's entry into the war. From the outset, Chancellor Bethmann Hollweg insisted that political considerations must be paramount, and that conflict with the US must be avoided at all costs – hence the cessation of such warfare in September 1915. So far the Chancellor had emerged victorious from the arguments, enjoying the support of the Kaiser.

Recently, however, Falkenhayn had interfered in the debate, supporting Tirpitz. The matter received Cabinet discussion on 6 March, to which Tirpitz had not been invited; once again the reintroduction of unrestricted U-boat war had been deferred, and the Admiral immediately resigned. Soon, Ludendorff would voice his opinion – and his words would help put him into power. Meanwhile Falkenhayn's support of Tirpitz, in opposition to the Kaiser, threatened to bring him disapproval from Wilhelm.[12]

Reports of Russian plans for an offensive suddenly multiplied; Ludendorff had still to return from Berlin. On 14 March Hoffmann considered bringing up reserves but hesitated since such a movement might cause anxiety. Then, on 19 March, the Russians attacked at a number of points north and south of Lake Narotch, clearly aimed at breaking through towards Vilna and Kovno. Ludendorff hurried back from Berlin, to find the German lines still holding. The battle marked his first defensive conflict – and few reserves were available either in

Prussia or in the German homeland. All were needed for the blood-bath of Verdun.

For three days the situation on the 10th Army front remained critical, especially in the area of slushy, water-logged ground held by the 21st Corps. Thaw conditions provided especial horror for both defenders and attackers, with men fighting waist-deep in icy water, wounded soldiers drowning as they slipped beneath the slush, troops struggling to keep their positions with their fingers and clothing always frozen and saturated. 'The roads were literally bottomless,' commented Ludendorff. 'The reserves ... could only make slow progress from the Vilna–Dvinsk railway by wading through the swamps. Everyone was strung up to the highest pitch of anxiety, wondering what would happen next.'[13]

But Russian troops exhausted themselves in the slog forward across the open countryside, and gradually the fighting ebbed again during late March and April 1916 as men collapsed from sheer exhaustion, without adequate supplies either of food or ammunition. On 28 April elements of the German 10th Army counter-attacked under heavy artillery cover and managed to recover lost ground between Lakes Narotch and Vishnevskoye. Fighting since 19 March cost the Russians between 70,000 and 100,000 casualties and 10,000 prisoners, compared with about 20,000 Germans. Yet Hindenburg and Ludendorff could ill afford any reduction of strength: moreover they lacked forces for a full-scale counter-offensive. The fearful struggle at Verdun continued to bleed not only the French but also the German forces engaged. And signs were growing stronger that the British intended an assault in the Somme sector.

'From the West we hear of various changes in the commands,' noted Hoffmann on 12 May. 'Among others, some Chiefs of Staff are to be superseded. Falkenhayn is apparently looking for scapegoats.'[14] Other reports reached the *Ober-Ost* HQ: these provided evidence that the Russians might be shifting forces away from the Prussian front, probably to the south against the Austrians.

During this tense, uneasy period an official communication informed the *Ober-Ost* HQ that the Kaiser intended to honour Hindenburg and Ludendorff with a visit; with him would travel Falkenhayn. The Imperial party arrived on 29 May. Both Ludendorff and Hoffmann hoped to use the occasion to press for more forces, but both knew their efforts were hopeless. The Kaiser appeared in one of his best moods: convivial, hearty and theatrical; Falkenhayn seemed strained, but as opinionated as ever. 'A very pleasant visit,' commented Hoffmann, 'which went off excellently, but from a military and political point of view quite futile.'

Stirring news reached Kovno of a brilliant naval victory over the British at Skagerrack, believed to be a severe blow to enemy claims to naval superiority. Almost immediately, doubts arose over the results of this Battle of Jutland. And, within days, further reports reached the HQ which caused intense depression: Russian forces had launched a massive attack on the Austrians with apparent total success. On 4 June the Russian South-West Group commanded by General Alexei Brusilov advanced over a 300-mile front and achieved complete surprise through the absence of a preliminary bombardment. Plans for this offensive had been carefully prepared by Brusilov, whose five armies faced five Austro-Hungarian armies southwards from the Pripet Marshes. Troops had steadily tunnelled forward, and in some sectors had even dug beneath the Austrian wire; preparations were made for a sudden surprise bombardment, to be followed by a massive infantry assault.

Russian guns opened fire early on 4 June. The result proved especially devastating opposite the Russian 8th Army in the vicinity of Lutsk, front-line trenches, into which the Austrian command had placed two-thirds of the available troops, were either demolished or isolated, and were made relatively easy targets for the infantry assaults which began on 5 June. Further south the Russian 11th Army drove forward after a short bombardment, drawing away Austro-Hungarian reserves from other threatened areas. And at the most southern end of the line the Russian 9th achieved even greater success, seizing the enemy salient near Okna together with 11,000 prisoners.

Reports reaching Ludendorff became increasingly depressing. And the result of this Brusilov offensive would have dire effect on Ludendorff's own position, even though he himself was not directly involved in the huge, swirling battle to the south. Brusilov's victory would strike an irreparable blow to Austrian morale, to such an extent that henceforth Austrian troops would only prove useful if bolstered by German elements. Austria's value as an ally suddenly diminished; Ludendorff's problems increased correspondingly.

CHAPTER ELEVEN

Move to the West

'WAILS FOR HELP, OF COURSE,' COMMENTED HOFFMANN. IN FACT LUDEN-dorff could spare only limited numbers of troops – even if time were available for their transfer to the Austro-Hungarian front. Threats were building up in his own sector; in the south, Brusilov's success proved too rapid for assistance to arrive. Confused orders helped the Russian victory, with Falkenhayn instructing the Austro-Hungarian high command to retreat westwards, and the local commander, Pflanzer-Baltin, deeming it more advisable to take his decimated 7th Army south-west into the Bukovina.[1]

By mid-June 1916, the 7th Army had almost disintegrated, and Brusilov reported total enemy captives as being nearly 193,000 men along the whole front – the actual number was perhaps even higher. At the same time Brusilov found himself unable to take full advantage of his victory, mainly through supply problems; instead the Russian commander urged a renewed offensive in the north, against the Germans, under plans already prepared.

In the midst of this strained, expectant atmosphere the Kaiser summoned Hindenburg and Ludendorff to a conference at Pless, where they arrived at the end of June. Ludendorff managed to snatch a few private words with Bethmann Hollweg, who appeared very distressed by the general situation and by Falkenhayn's handling of affairs, especially at Verdun. Forces were stretched in both the East and West, and, in the latter, the British attack in the Somme region was still expected daily. In the East, the Austro-Hungarian defeat now prompted Hindenburg and his Chief of Staff to demand increased authority. Both had long believed that only unity of command on the Russian front, over both German and Austrian forces, could stabilise the situation; such a supreme command now seemed even more imperative, in view of the deteriorating Austro-Hungarian position. But opposition to the idea from Falkenhayn was inevitable, and for the moment Hindenburg and Ludendorff were refused their plea; to Ludendorff the journey to Pless seemed a waste of valuable time.[2]

Yet the atmosphere at Pless had a strong effect on the *Ober-Ost* partnership. It appeared highly likely that personnel changes might soon be made; the Field-Marshal and Ludendorff confided in Hoffmann, who in turn revealed his thoughts in his diary on 2 July. 'It seems that the Chancellor has made a fresh attack on Falkenhayn. Whether he will pull it off seems to me, however, still doubtful . . . It is all rather exciting. Ludendorff, of course, is very much up in the air. The only person who truly preserves an Olympian calm is the Field-Marshal.'[3]

The relationship between Falkenhayn and Ludendorff had almost reached breaking point, with the situation aggravated by the effect of the Brusilov offensive. Clearly, the Austrians needed help. Falkenhayn insisted he could spare only minimum numbers from the Western Front, where the Allied bombardment in the Somme region had begun on 24 June, obviously heralding the expected offensive. Ludendorff, however, was reluctant to part with men from his own north-east theatre. His reasons were twofold: undoubtedly he was reluctant to help Falkenhayn, and sought to embarrass the German Chief-of-Staff; yet he also had a more straightforward motive – he himself felt threatened, especially as reports indicated an increasing likelihood of a Russian switch in his direction.

Reserves sent to the Austrians in the south were therefore inadequate and late in arriving. A counter-offensive on the Stokhod was attempted on 20 June, and failed within two days with heavy losses. Only Russian supply difficulties prevented further defeat. And the failure of the Austro-German counter-attack led to renewed bitterness between Falkenhayn and Ludendorff, with the former accusing the latter of refusing to provide full assistance.

Then, at the beginning of July, both Falkenhayn and Ludendorff became heavily involved in dealing with offensives launched against them. On 1 July the British 4th and 3rd Armies began their advance north of the Somme. By nightfall on 1 July, the British had lost about 60,000 men, 19,000 of them dead, and had made only minimal gains, but battle would continue until autumn. Falkenhayn felt obliged to draw reinforcements from Verdun, yet the Verdun fighting also continued, and the drain on German manpower in the West became increasingly desperate.

Twenty-four hours after the start of the Somme holocaust, the Russians opened their offensive in the northern sector of their front, aiming at the German salient in the Baranovitchi area. The attack failed, partly due to lack of adequate Russian preparations: the Russian army commander, Ragoza, had been making ready for an attack on Vilna, and was now allowed just two weeks to change the entire scheme; moreover the terrain favoured the defenders, who as it happened comprised two Austrian divisions. Ludendorff rushed in two German divisions as reserves just before the attack commenced, and he believed the availability of these units justified his refusal to send further help to the Austrians in the south. The Russians opened the battle with a colossal bombardment, which expended about one million shells over several days; on 4 July one of the two Austrian divisions collapsed, but the reserve Germans held the line; Russian activity dwindled slightly until 7 July, then faded once more twenty-four hours later after Russian losses had risen to about 80,000 men compared with the Austro-German total of around 16,000.[4]

Pressure remained intense. On 16 July the Russians launched a heavy assault in the far north, advancing from the Riga bridgehead west of the Dvina and only being checked after desperate last-ditch fighting by the 8th Army reserves. Intelligence reports reaching Ludendorff indicated a resumption of the enemy attacks at Barano-vitchi and along the Stokhod. Never had the situation seemed so fraught, manpower so short. 'We awaited these [attacks] with a sinking heart,' wrote Ludendorff, 'for our troops were exhausted by constant fighting and had long fronts to defend ... It was clear that the Russians were gathering strength for another mighty blow, while we were still bleeding from many wounds on the Somme ... Storms were threatening, and our nerves were strung to the highest pitch.'[5]

On 20 July another sudden summons took Ludendorff to Berlin for discussions with Falkenhayn. Once again Ludendorff pressed for a unified command in the East, arguing that this would allow better use of resources and a more co-ordinated policy along the whole threatened front; Falkenhayn appeared amiable, but apparently took no notice of Ludendorff's statements and instead monopolised the conversation with confident accounts of his plans for the West. Ludendorff considered the whole trip to have been completely useless and he returned to Kovno 'in a pretty savage temper'.

Only one week later the Kaiser called Hindenburg and Ludendorff to a further conference at Pless, and this time the atmosphere seemed different. Falkenhayn had lost some of his self-confidence and appeared on the defensive; the Kaiser acted in a strained and impatient manner. The background to the talks was indeed dismal. The slaughter at the Somme continued in the West; in the East, Brusilov had resumed his offensive, pushing towards Kowel north-east from the Stokhod positions in an attempt to turn the German line further north – and Brusilov now enjoyed almost double numerical superiority over the battered Austrian divisions facing him.[6] During the Pless talks another report arrived which caused fresh anxiety: Russian forces had seized Brody, 70 miles east of Lemberg on the Austrian front.

Hindenburg and Ludendorff immediately repeated their proposal for a unified command in the East. Falkenhayn again tried to avoid a definite answer, but this time the Kaiser snapped: 'I tell you I'm not leaving here until this matter is settled.'[7] Agreement was therefore reached with the Austrians that Hindenburg should assume command of the whole front as far south as Brody, stretching almost 500 miles south from Riga. This development, while not going as far as the *Ober-Ost* HQ would have liked, nevertheless gave Hindenburg greater power than ever before, and with him Ludendorff. Above all it represented victory over the Chief of the General Staff, whose authority had been severely questioned. 'Falkenhayn's position much shaken, ours much strengthened,' gloated Hoffmann.[8]

Enlargement of command necessitated a different headquarters. On 1 August Hindenburg, Ludendorff and their staffs therefore left Kovno to journey south, initially with no idea where they would set up camp. Finally they settled on Brest-Litovsk. To begin with, the headquarters functioned in a special train drawn up in the station siding: immediately the personnel suffered from lack of room, with the huge maps consuming much of the space, and from the heat caused by the sun scorching through the metal roof. Ludendorff searched for an alternative. 'Desolation reigned,' he wrote. 'The ugly but highly important railway junction and the gutted town offered few attractions.'

Above the town stood the citadel, which at first glance also seemed unsuitable. 'The whole place was neglected and overgrown ... Nettles had grown to a tremendous height and the air was damp and musty.' But Ludendorff set to work to clear the place: despite his other activities, including the need to organise the despatch of German reinforcements to help the Austrians to block Brusilov in the Kowel region, Ludendorff still managed to find time to supervise repairs and restoration of the citadel building. 'I had the barracks cleared of the invading creepers, so that the air could get to the walls and dry out the damp; trees were also felled and branches lopped to allow the sun and air to get in. I took pleasure in putting things to rights ...'[9]

Ludendorff seemed in excellent spirits. Both physically and mentally he apparently flourished during these difficult months, regardless of the military problems on the one hand and the continuing struggle with Falkenhayn on the other; his complexion was healthy, although inclined as always to be florid; his paunch had begun to sag even more over his tight uniform trousers; his temper seemed reasonably steady, although occasional outbursts of rage still shook headquarters. He studied the flow of reports from the fighting front with relative calm, and found reason for some optimism even though Russian strength was proving greater than any yet experienced on the Eastern Front, with Brusilov still attempting to batter towards Kowel. Russian thrusts had so far been blocked or at least had been confined, for example at Trysten on 28 July, and the marshy terrain in the Stokhod region favoured the defenders. Brusilov's offensive would be maintained until early October, but by the beginning of August it had become apparent that initial German apprehension might be unfounded.

Further south the situation seemed more dangerous. On 7 August the Russian 8th Army was ordered to resume its drive westwards against the weakened Austro-Hungarian forces at the end of the Allied line, and Ludendorff had to despatch a steady flow of reinforcements, eventually amounting to over four German divisions. Already, by late July, the southernmost Russian commander Lechitski had penetrated the Carpathian passes leading into Hungary; only the harsh Carpathian terrain prevented a more rapid advance. Moreover, it seemed increasingly likely that fighting in this sector might at last bring nearby Rumania out of her position of neutrality: Russia might soon gain a new ally.[10]

At the Somme, the Allies launched a succession of attempts to gain ground, and although British and French advances were only minor, German casualties rose to a terrifying new level. At Verdun, the French fought with renewed tenacity; already, German losses had risen above 280,000 men. These casualties, added to perhaps 450,000 already suffered on the Somme and the continuing drain on the Eastern Front, caused fresh waves of depression in Germany itself. Ludendorff may have worked on unperturbed, but others lacked his equanimity.

Discontent in the Fatherland had soared sharply in 1916, leading to a succession of strikes and the emergence of strong left-wing opposition to the war. In turn, the right-wing elements had already increased their demands for military control which would keep the working-class in its place and introduce firm, even ruthless policies for winning the war. Inflation had driven the middle class to urge sterner measures than those provided by the existing, relatively moderate, leadership of Bethmann Hollweg and Falkenhayn. War aims should be vigorously pursued, no matter how ambitious; all weapons should be employed, no matter how barbaric – including unrestricted submarine warfare.[11]

This political struggle inside the Fatherland inevitably affected Hindenburg and Ludendorff. Falkenhayn advocated total U-boat war and his support for this popular policy threatened Bethmann Hollweg's position. The Chancellor had no real faith in the U-boat war, knowing it would bring America into the conflict, but rather than risk his own political demise by stating this view too openly, he counter-attacked by proposing another measure, equally popular: greater power for the two heroes Hindenburg and Ludendorff. Already, he had helped the partnership to assume wider authority in the East; now the Chancellor saw the two men as a substitute to Falkenhayn himself.

Behind this power struggle on the economic and political levels lay the basic differences in military policy between Falkenhayn and Ludendorff. Falkenhayn had always insisted that not only should Germany concentrate her efforts on the Western Front, as opposed to the East, but also that she should fight a planned war of attrition rather than adopt the Schlieffen concept of annihilation to which Ludendorff had remained true. Falkenhayn believed the Allies could only be persuaded to sue for peace through limited operations designed to wear down the enemy's will to resist. Forces must not therefore be squandered in large-scale offensives in the East, since such plans would merely diminish Germany's capacity for the strategy of attrition in the West.

By early 1916 it had become clear to Falkenhayn that the Allied determination to continue the struggle was far greater than he had estimated. He therefore altered his policy and increased the pressure. Thus the offensive at Verdun was aimed at drawing in French forces, bleeding France to such an extent that Britain herself – weakened by the U-boat war – would realise the uselessness of the continued struggle. By August 1916 this plan had clearly failed: German losses were almost as great as those of the French. Discontent inside Germany, and opposition both to the war and to Falkenhayn, spiralled still higher. The military initiative seemed in the hands of the enemy.

Falkenhayn had never been popular either in the army or amongst Germans as a whole. Many army officers believed him to be a careerist and opportunist – especially those commanders who had been superseded by this younger man. Politicians had found him supercilious as War Minister; civilians remembered the brutal manner in which the army had put down civil disturbances in Germany in 1913, and Falkenhayn's close involvement with these excesses. Hindenburg and Ludendorff were still regarded as the heroes of Tannenberg; Falkenhayn as responsible for the losses at Verdun.[12]

A crisis was clearly approaching. During August Falkenhayn, previously so calm and arrogantly confident, visibly lost all his assurance and began to waver in his decision-making. A situation of near mutiny arose among subordinate officers at the Supreme HQ: many started to murmur that Falkenhayn must be replaced, and that duty dictated they should present their views to higher authority. The difficulty lay in deciding where that authority rested: Tappen, Chief of Operations, remained as aloof as ever.

'The rest of us witness these events with dismay,' remembered Colonel Max Bauer, then working in the Operations Section. He himself approached the Minister of War, Wild von Hohenborn, but without result; then he contacted von Plessen, the Adjutant-General. 'At first General Plessen was indignant at this peculiar step, and it took some time for me to explain that it was only as a last resort that we had undertaken this unsoldierly measure. Finally I seemed to have convinced General von Plessen; the latter, however, first sent for Colonel von der Schulenburg, who had been Chief of Staff before Verdun...'[13]

Ludendorff increased his pressure for more reinforcements to help block Brusilov's continuing offensive; Falkenhayn refused to grant them. On 12 August Hindenburg was persuaded to send a telegram to the Kaiser which stressed his objections to Falkenhayn's interference; Wilhelm sent a prickly reply. Hoffmann then took the liberty

of urging Hindenburg to issue a direct challenge – Falkenhayn or himself – but the Field-Marshal shied away from this drastic step. Hoffmann noted: 'One needs nerves like ropes. The other day I was so
sick of the whole thing that I asked Ludendorff to let me go ... He
over-persuaded me kindly, and I am still here.'[14]

Further talks were suddenly arranged at Pless for 16 August. The
united front presented by Hindenburg and Ludendorff seemed to
achieve results: Falkenhayn failed to appear at dinner and the rumour
spread that he intended to resign – yet, after the departure of Hindenburg and Ludendorff he closeted himself with the Kaiser again, with
apparent success. On 17 August a telegram reached Brest-Litovsk
from Wilhelm, to the effect that the Eastern Command should confine
its attention to the Russian front and not pass comments on the Western situation; the Kaiser also upheld a recent decision by Falkenhayn
to transfer a division from the East.

Ludendorff reacted violently, despatching an orderly to Hindenburg
with a request that he should be allowed to resign. Hindenburg,
alarmed by the prospect of losing his Chief of Staff, asked Wilhelm
for an interview. The Kaiser refused. Hindenburg, Ludendorff and
Hoffmann therefore composed a long letter setting out their grievances,
despatched on 20 August. Wilhelm's reply arrived three days later.
'It consists,' sneered Hoffmann, 'of a very gracious autograph letter
to the Field-Marshal; no grasp of our difficulties ... We might again
have saved ourselves the bother.'[15]

Falkenhayn's final removal from power came about for a totally
different reason than might have been expected. It came not as a result
of his advocacy of a war of attrition, or the U-boat controversy or Verdun – however important these issues might have been – but through
Rumania's intervention in the war. This small nation had long
coveted areas of Austria-Hungary; now, in August 1916, the Rumanian
decision-makers felt sufficiently protected by Russia's recent successes
to throw aside the mantle of neutrality. On 17 August a military convention was signed with the Entente, providing for extensive Allied
assistance in return for the employment of Rumania's twenty divisions on the Eastern Front. On 27 August Rumania declared war
on Austro-Hungary, thereby embarking on hostilities with the Central
Powers as a whole.

The Fatherland would now be faced with fighting on yet another
front, and one which linked enemy efforts in Italy and Serbia with the
Russian theatre in the Carpathians. The actual decision took Berlin
and the GHQ completely by surprise; Falkenhayn had ruled out such
a possibility in discussions with the Kaiser. Earlier on 27 August
Colonel Bauer met Wilhelm walking in the castle grounds at Pless.
'He was calm and cheerful and told us that Rumania would certainly
not declare war ... A few moments later we received news in our
office that Rumania had already declared war.' Next morning Bauer

again approached von Plessen. 'I . . . represented to him that the only man who could help us was Ludendorff, and begged him to assist us.'[16]

Falkenhayn's incorrect assessment proved to be the final mistake which convinced senior officers at GHQ to move against him. Nor could the Kaiser continue his attempts to retain him. Whatever his own feelings – and even at this stage he still held a high opinion of Falkenhayn – the pressure had become too great. The Chief of the General Staff must go. Yet Wilhelm acted unwillingly: he feared he was yielding to 'democratic' forces which themselves threatened the power of the crown. The whole episode was extremely distasteful to him, and increased the possibilities of early friction between himself and Falkenhayn's successors.[17]

Ironically, Germany had less to fear from Rumania's intervention than was thought at the time. Indeed, Rumania's entry into the war proved more of a disadvantage to the Entente powers. The country was virtually indefensible; the German offensive would soon place the Rumanians in a highly dangerous position, leading to the withdrawal of Russian divisions from further north until eventually almost a third of the Russian army had to be diverted to the south. Thus Rumania's entry should have been seen as a cause for celebration in Germany, rather than as the reason for ousting Falkenhayn. Equally ironically, Falkenhayn himself was to play a large part in the successful invasion of Rumania, in his capacity as a field commander.

But now Hindenburg and Ludendorff took the next, and most decisive, step towards their military dictatorship. At 1 pm on 28 August, 1916, the telephone rang in Ludendorff's office. General von Lyncker, Chief of the Military Cabinet at GHQ, informed Ludendorff that the Kaiser demanded his immediate presence at Pless, together with Hindenburg. Lyncker refused to supply more details, except to say that Falkenhayn knew nothing of the affair and would be informed only after they had arrived; he added: 'The position is serious.'

It needed only minimum perception to realise the implications. Hindenburg wrote: 'I thought of Verdun and Italy, Brusilov and the Austrian Eastern Front; then of the news "Rumania has declared war on us!" Strong nerves would be required.'[18] Hindenburg and Ludendorff boarded their train at 4 pm that same afternoon. 'We left Brest,' wrote Ludendorff, 'never again to return to the Eastern Front. Behind us lay two years of strenuous, united work and mighty victories.'[19] In front lay unprecedented power and extremes of glory and misery.

CHAPTER TWELVE

Supreme Command

CONTRARY TO LYNCKER'S STATEMENT, FALKENHAYN WAS INFORMED ON 28 August 1916 that Hindenburg and Ludendorff had been summoned and would be arriving next morning: the Kaiser wished to discuss the Rumanian situation with them. Falkenhayn replied that 'he could only regard this summoning of a subordinate commander, without previous reference to him, for a consultation on a question the solution of which lay in his province alone, as a breach of his authority that he could not accept, and as a sign that he no longer possessed the absolute confidence of the Supreme War Lord'. He therefore begged to be relieved of his appointment; his request was granted early next morning just before Hindenburg and Ludendorff arrived.[1]

Meanwhile the Military Cabinet discussed the difficult question of the titles to be given to Hindenburg and Ludendorff. A solution was reached early on the 28th: the Field-Marshal was to be described as First Chief of Staff of the Armies in the Field, and Ludendorff as Second Chief. The Kaiser approved, but he had considerable misgivings about the whole changeover. He apparently wept when taking the decision to replace Falkenhayn, and he lacked any regard for the two newcomers at GHQ: he dubbed Ludendorff as 'that sergeant-major'. The choice had been forced upon him, and he would always resent this fact.

The train from Brest-Litovsk pulled into the station at Pless at 10 am, 29 August, 1916. Waiting on the platform was General von Lyncker, who immediately informed Hindenburg and Ludendorff of their elevation and their new titles. Hindenburg affected surprise at the announcement, and indeed he only brought a small amount of kit with him since he said he had expected to be away from Brest-Litovsk for only two or three nights. The party climbed into cars and drove to the castle. There, on the steps, stood the Kaiser awaiting the arrival of his wife from Berlin. Wilhelm immediately greeted Hindenburg by his new title, much to the surprise of Bethmann Hollweg who was standing nearby and who had not heard of the latest development.

Falkenhayn, also on the steps, had neglected to tell the Chancellor despite the fact that they had just been talking together.

Transfer of power took place extremely quickly. Falkenhayn was already about to depart for his new post as army commander against the Rumanians; he shook hands with Hindenburg and left with a curt, ambiguous farewell: 'God help you and our Fatherland.'[2]

Hindenburg and Ludendorff had both been virtually unknown twenty-four months before. Now Germany's future lay in their hands and gradually their authority would erode other traditional areas of power. The Military Cabinet declined in importance; the Kaiser's main role came to be that of mediator between the Hindenburg-Ludendorff partnership and the politicians, and the latter stood almost no chance of success in any dispute should the military leaders decide to be stubborn. These gradually filled influential posts with men who would give them their full support and potential opposition became increasingly frustrated.

Two factors lay behind this new situation. First, the acute threats which faced Germany; secondly, the characters of Hindenburg and Ludendorff themselves. Apparently only these two men could save the country. Yet it is doubtful if they could have obtained their eventual power if their personalities had not been as they were: Hindenburg, the official leader, never appeared to be a dictator – his gentleness and charm brought him affection instead. Ludendorff, the real leader, remained in the background; probably he would never have been allowed to become a dictator in his own right, and instead he worked behind the cover provided by the other.

But now, in late August 1916, Ludendorff made clear that, while content to remain officially subordinate to Hindenburg, this outwardly secondary role must be on his own terms. He rejected the title of Second Chief, and insisted instead on 'First Quartermaster-General'. He wrote: 'In my opinion there could only be one Chief of the General Staff; but in any case, I had been expressly assured that I should have joint responsibility in all decisions and measures that might be taken.'[3]

Ludendorff had never acted through motives of personal ambition, and from this moment onwards he had an even greater feeling than before of conducting a crusade to save the Fatherland: he believed that he was acting for an almost holy, and quite unselfish, purpose.

> My position was a thankless one ... I entered on my duties with a sacred desire to do and think of nothing that did not contribute to bringing the war to a victorious end. For this purpose alone had the Field-Marshal and I been called upon. The task was perfectly enormous. The awful feeling of responsibility did not leave me for a single instant ... Never before has Fate placed so heavy a burden on human shoulders. With bowed head I prayed God the All-Knowing to give me strength for my new office ...[4]

Ludendorff turned easily and quickly from such intensely religious thoughts to practical measures. Within hours he had established his office in Pless. He gathered his personal staff around him at the castle and immediately turned to the basic mechanics of command: the choice of key personnel. Tappen was dismissed as Head of the Operations Section and his place taken by Lieutenant-Colonel Wetzell, previously Senior Staff Officer and Chief of Staff of the 3rd Corps on the Western Front, who had distinguished himself at Verdun. 'He proved an excellent and valued assistant,' wrote Ludendorff, 'with his enterprising and fertile mind and the care he put into his work.' Colonel Bauer, who remained at Pless, was of a different opinion. 'Although there was continual friction between him and the rest we kept it to ourselves, because we wished to save Ludendorff annoyance.'[5] Another major appointment was that of von Vollard-Bockelberg as head of the organisational section: Bockelberg had served with Ludendorff at the General Staff HQ in Berlin before the war, and had been employed in the operations section in the East.

Bockelberg was in fact the only senior staff officer brought by Ludendorff from the Russian front. Hoffmann remained behind. Ludendorff's decision in this respect has been held as evidence that he did not want to be eclipsed by his brilliant subordinate; it is far more likely that he realised that Hoffmann's abilities and knowledge would be most valuable in the continuing struggle against the Russians. He therefore had him appointed Chief of Staff to Prince Leopold of Bavaria, the new C-in-C East, against considerable opposition, since Hoffmann was only a Colonel. 'It is a big jump for me,' wrote Hoffmann. The two men would maintain close contact, especially as Hoffmann – like Ludendorff with Hindenburg – became the guiding force in the Eastern Command.[6]

Simultaneously with these personnel changes, Ludendorff hurriedly briefed himself on the broad strategic issues. Within a week he had reached one fundamental decision, for which he obtained Hindenburg's approval: German forces must cease the Verdun struggle. 'That offensive should have been broken off immediately it assumed the character of a battle of attrition,' wrote Ludendorff. 'The gain no longer justified the losses.'[7]

Another strategic issue had to be considered, carrying with it immense implications – the decision whether or not to resume unrestricted U-boat war. A conference on this subject took place at Pless on 31 August, attended by the military chiefs, the Chancellor and the Kaiser. Hindenburg and Ludendorff displayed caution: they refused to make the same mistake as Falkenhayn, whose advocacy of such a course had aroused Wilhelm's anger, yet on the other hand they revealed an awareness of public feeling – which, contrary to the Kaiser's position, favoured a ruthless U-boat war. Bethmann Hollweg and Wilhelm still argued at Pless that indiscriminate sinkings would bring America's entry into the conflict. Hindenburg and Ludendorff said that on the other hand unrestricted submarine attacks were 'the only means of bringing the war to a successful conclusion within a reasonable time'. Yet they added that these attacks should not be started immediately. Ludendorff would continue to mobilise public opinion in his favour, and at the same time would seek to pass the final decision to another authority – the navy.[8]

On 5 September Hindenburg and Ludendorff embarked on their first inspection tour of the Western Front. Their special command train carried all latest devices to keep them in touch with operations, including radio telephones and the Hughes Patent Machine. Among the messages received were situation reports on the new Rumanian front, and these soon brought excellent news to counteract the gloom which had surrounded Rumania's entry into the war. The new enemy had invaded Transylvania immediately after the declaration of hostilities, meeting minimal opposition, since the German 9th Army, now under Falkenhayn, had still to arrive. Ludendorff had already made plans for one of his typical encircling moves. While the Rumanians continued their cautious advance, Mackensen prepared to strike from the east with the German-reinforced Bulgarian Danube Army: Mackensen, moving up from Salonika, crossed into the Dobrogea on 4 September; on the 6th he destroyed the fortress of Tutracaia on the Danube, even though his force was smaller than the garrison; Mackensen then headed by forced marches towards the fortress of Silistria 70 miles south-east of Bucharest. The Rumanians, while they stumbled north, were being threatened from the south; their commanders revealed extreme incompetence and their relations with the Russians proved abysmal, each partner holding the other in contempt.

News from Mackensen heartened Ludendorff during his tour and helped to reinforce his popularity at home. He himself was already making full use of an instrument which would later be known as 'public relations'. His skill in assessing and employing public opinion for his own ends, whether on military, political, social or economic levels, was indeed to prove remarkable, and confirmed the Kaiser's worst fears about the undermining of his own position. Meanwhile Ludendorff gained another, personal pleasure, to add to the enjoyment he derived from the Rumanian reports. Margarethe joined the train at Frankfurt, and she sat enthralled by the activity around her in the command carriage. For the first time she witnessed Ludendorff at work, at the centre of the huge and complex command system which had arisen through the needs of modern war and which he handled so superbly. The teleprinter clacked; Morse code operators worked continuously; messengers milled round the train at each stop; complicated maps and diagrams were constantly altered.

'I was at the very heart of the amazing machinery of the war,' wrote Margarethe. 'You cannot conceive the perpetual stir and bustle . . .

Reports, orders and the allotment of troops had to be worked out in the train and sent off. Conferences took place and the officers were up to their eyes in work, bending over maps and papers.'[9]

Margarethe left the train reluctantly at Metz; Ludendorff proceeded via Charleville to Cambrai, HQ of the Army group commander Prince Rupprecht of Bavaria. Reports reaching Cambrai revealed fresh fighting on the Somme – 'we were all obsessed by thoughts of that terrible conflict.' Talks only lasted a few hours at Cambrai but were extremely far-reaching: Ludendorff alternated between listening intently and asking a quick succession of incisive questions in his clipped, rather harsh voice; Hindenburg sat silent for most of the time. And from the meeting emerged a number of salient points, which Ludendorff seized upon as the basis of his military philosophy for the remainder of the war. This philosophy showed a strong contrast to that of previous commanders – and in some respects pointed far into the future.

Regarding the Somme,

> the loss of ground up to date appeared to me of little importance in itself. We could stand that; but the question how this, and the progressive falling-off of our fighting power of which it was symptomatic, was to be prevented, was of immense importance. It was just as necessary to have a clear idea of our fighting capacity as to know whether our tactical views were still sound. The first was an easy matter, the second of extreme difficulty.

German infantry defence had become 'flabby', said Ludendorff. Men relied too much on artillery barrages, and at the same time depended upon deep dugouts for their own protection. Artillery should be more specifically employed against enemy guns, and the deep trenches should be abandoned since they bred a defensive mentality and were often death-traps in the face of an enemy advance. Lines should not be held regardless of cost.

Men could only fight properly if they could see their enemy. The practice had become increasingly common for hand-grenades to be preferred to rifles, since men could throw these weapons from behind cover. 'The infantry soldier had forgotten his shooting through the use of grenades. He had to relearn it.' Machine guns should be used more intelligently, for example through the accelerated development of special machine-gun companies.

New offensive ideas must be studied. The emphasis should be on flexibility and on encirclement. Here, Ludendorff called upon his experience at Liège and of the larger-scale enveloping operation on the Eastern Front. Frontal attacks were usually suicidal against well-prepared defences; instead these positions should be isolated. A proper training manual should be prepared for the use of 'storm troops' and infiltration tactics, with these special units filtering between the main

H

enemy defensive posts – as the infantry had done between the Liège fortresses – so that these could be encircled.

Ludendorff's handling of the Cambrai conference emphasised his ability to cram a multitude of details into his mind: nothing seemed too trivial; he could range from discussion of body-armour to more efficient systems for rotating divisions, from the reliance on hand-grenades to the question of supply trains. He slotted each detail into the whole, all within five hours: Hindenburg and Ludendorff left Cambrai during the afternoon of 7 September for the journey back to Pless. Ludendorff left some excellent impressions: his manner had been probing, but not domineering, and he listened as well as talked. And on his side he respected the men he had met. 'The quiet dignity of the assembled Army Commanders and Chiefs of Staff ... made a deep impression on me.'

One lesson above all became paramount. 'I was strengthened in my determination to make the Government put into war what war requires. Men, war material and moral resolution were matters of life and death.'[10] This opinion would soon grow stronger, and with it the convenient belief, already half-formed, that military mistakes could often be attributed to lack of support from the home front. Ludendorff touched on this subject in a conversation with Hoffmann, who visited Pless soon after the return from Cambrai. According to Hoffmann: 'He said that GHQ and the War Office had not exerted sufficient pressure on the working capacity of our industries for the production of the necessary war material, especially of ammunition, and that, in general, there had been a complete failure of a united effort of GHQ and the Civil Administration.'[11]

By the second week in September, Ludendorff could list his main tasks, and together they amounted to a colossal burden: the introduction of a revised strategy for the Western Front; improved tactics; maintenance of the offensive in Rumania and on the Eastern Front as a whole; the organisation of the home front in such a way that the Fatherland supported the fighting fronts to the maximum extent possible. Added to these broad issues were the multitude of day-to-day administrative details. Hovering above them all was the controversial question of U-boat warfare.

In the background lurked another subject, the most important one of all: Ludendorff's attitude to the possibility of a peace by settlement. This issue also he mentioned to Hoffmann in his conversation with him early in September. He believed Germany should not accept peace terms which failed to provide territory essential for defence; this specifically applied to Belgium. Recently he had written to a friend that 'Belgium's dependence [on Germany] must be an economic, military and political one.'[12] As with the question of unrestricted submarine warfare, and indeed with that of lack of military support from the homeland, Ludendorff's attitude opened up the possibility of future controversy and factional conflict.

'I was now at home in my position and understood my sphere of work. It was an enormous field of labour that suddenly opened before me ...'[13] First Ludendorff had to find better offices. The existing GHQ rooms were considered too small, and only a few days later Ludendorff and his staff moved out of the royal castle at Pless and into the larger municipal buildings; Ludendorff himself lived in an estate agent's house. He slipped easily into his arduous routine, and as always he used time in the most efficient way possible.

By 8 am each day he was behind his desk in his spacious office. During the morning he telephoned army commanders or their chiefs of staff, heard the latest reports and held staff conferences. He consulted Hindenburg, but this only took a few minutes. 'We knew each other's thoughts,' wrote Hindenburg. 'The decisions were, therefore, usually a matter of a few sentences; indeed, very often a few words were all that were required to establish that mutual understanding which served the General as a basis for his further working-out of the plans.'[14] After this conference Ludendorff drafted orders, whilst Hindenburg often went for a 60-minute walk before being received by the Kaiser at noon. Ludendorff usually stayed away from these Imperial meetings. If events were pressing, he telephoned army chiefs of staff again during the afternoon; further staff conferences were held; more orders drafted for Hindenburg's signature. All the staff gathered for dinner at 8 pm, which usually took about 40 minutes and was followed by general conversation. At 9.30 precisely Ludendorff stood, nodded his goodnight to Hindenburg, and returned to his office. He continued working until between 1 and 2 am, sometimes later. Nothing mattered but work: he refused to have Margarethe at GHQ, even though many officers enjoyed the company and comfort of their wives.

German divisions were now on the defensive at Verdun. Fighting ceased north of the Somme during September, but the battle continued elsewhere in this theatre and daily the casualty figures rose. Relief arrangements discussed at Cambrai had to be abandoned. 'Divisions and other formations had to be thrown in on the Somme front in quicker succession and had to stay in the line longer,' stated Ludendorff. 'The time for recuperation and training on quiet sectors became shorter and shorter. Everything was cut as fine as possible. The strain on our nerves at Pless was terrible ...'[15]

Renewed Allied attacks on the Italian front were beaten off; the Eastern Front was quieter but might soon explode again with another Russian offensive before winter. News from Rumania continued to be excellent: Falkenhayn began to move forward with his 9th Army while Mackensen maintained his pressure from the south-east: on 8 September Falkenhayn struck from the north, driving the Rumanians before him, and co-operation between the forces opposing the German advance splintered still further.

Despite this excellent news, Hindenburg and Ludendorff had already decided to make a critical change in German strategy. Within days of assuming Supreme Command, they came to the conclusion that the armies must move on to the defensive in the West. Such a situation had already been forced upon the German forces; now Ludendorff believed it must be formally recognised and steps taken accordingly regardless of possible consequences to morale – indeed, he maintained that morale would sag even further, both on the fighting front in the West and at home, if the slaughter was allowed to continue. As early as September, therefore, orders were given for construction to start on the powerful defensive positions later to be famous as the Hindenburg Line. The plan was for certain withdrawals to straighten out a number of salients along the existing front, which were costly to defend and which lacked sufficient military value. Defences would therefore run along the Siegfried Line stretching from Arras, west of Cambrai, St Quentin, La Fère and Vailly-sur-Aisne, and along the Michel line south of Verdun. A decision would be made later over the timing and extent of retirement to these positions.

Ludendorff fully realised the shortcomings of such defensive lines. 'They were sufficient to postpone the decision, if the Government once succeeded in bringing the people whole-heartedly to support the war, but they could never lead to victory.' The strategy could therefore be used in three ways: as a means of forming a basis for an eventual land offensive, as a strong foundation from which discussions for peace could begin, or as a background to the adoption of unrestricted U-boat warfare. The second of these alternatives brought with it tacit recognition that there might not be military victory; the third raised again the spectre of American involvement, with all the dire results which might follow.

CHAPTER THIRTEEN

Perseverance and Power

CONSIDERATION OF GERMANY'S FUTURE MILITARY STRATEGY BROUGHT into added prominence the political and diplomatic hopes entertained in the country for a successful conclusion to the war. Ludendorff's own war aims can easily be exaggerated; indeed, he has been blamed for an extremism equalling that of Hitler in his demands for territorial expansion. In fact Ludendorff linked his aims with what he considered to be military necessity: Germany must gain territory which would protect her in the future. This especially applied to the two-front question which had plagued Schlieffen and which had been a constant source of anxiety to Ludendorff himself: the danger of simultaneous attack from both France and Russia must be avoided, and barrier or buffer regions created; at the same time France, and especially Russia, must be weakened as much as possible.

There is insufficient evidence to show that Ludendorff supported more extreme war aims, such as that proposed by the German agent Wesendonck who reported from the Caucasus that 'even the idea of a German land-route to China is not to be ruled out altogether'. Yet Ludendorff's demands were sufficient to arouse fierce opposition from more moderate German politicians: he viewed the situation strictly as a soldier, whilst the politicians were fearful of the diplomatic consequences – and with every justification.

At the same time, Ludendorff the soldier, himself began to enter the world of diplomacy, for which he was inadequately equipped. Supreme command in total war inevitably led to involvement with other than purely military affairs. Especially important were the link between strategic alternatives and possible peace proposals, and the continuing question of unrestricted U-boat war.

During September 1916 debate took place on an approach to the US President, Woodrow Wilson, to discover if he would act as a peace mediator. Bethmann Hollweg supported such a man; almost inevitably Ludendorff had doubts, fearing that the politicians might reveal Germany's weakness, but he wrote afterwards: 'I was fully in agreement, and inwardly very pleased that it was made, although I was sceptical of success owing to my view of the enemy's desire for our destruction. Their prospects for 1917 were so much more favourable than ours.'[1] Above all Ludendorff insisted that the requisite war aims must be accomplished. First, these aims had to be set out in detail, and discussion would soon begin on this controversial issue.

Meanwhile Germany had still one more weapon to use: unrestricted U-boat warfare. Ludendorff now pushed forward another party in the debate – the navy spokesman. The latter could be relied upon to give support for such an offensive, and perhaps could take the blame off Ludendorff's shoulders should events prove disastrous. As Ludendorff wrote: 'The Chief of the Naval Staff, Admiral von Holtzendorff, an eager champion of unrestricted submarine warfare, declared positively that such a policy would suffice to decide the issue within six months.'[2] Bethmann Hollweg, still opposed to this policy, apparently attempted to prevent Ludendorff from shuffling off the responsibility: the Chancellor told the Reichstag on 28 September that Hindenburg and Ludendorff must be allowed the greatest voice. The Field-Marshal and the General immediately objected to this statement on the grounds that it involved GHQ in political controversy: 'GHQ had consistently held aloof from all political activity, and had no wish to alter its policy in this respect.' The Reichstag nevertheless agreed on 7 October that the Chancellor would have to base his decisions 'largely upon those of General Headquarters'.[3]

This Reichstag motion had far-reaching implications. As Bethmann Hollweg later declared: 'By the decision of 7 October 1916 the Reichstag surrendered political power to the military commanders.' Another crucial step had been taken towards the Hindenburg-Ludendorff dictatorship: unrestricted submarine warfare would be reintroduced whenever these two officers believed it to be desirable, regardless of diplomatic consequences.

Ludendorff involved himself with other diplomatic matters during these autumn weeks of 1916, also with serious effects. In July, Germany and Austria had agreed to establish an independent kingdom of Poland, but the scheme met with opposition from both the Kaiser and Falkenhayn. The suggestion was revived again in October when von Beseler, Governor-General of Poland, promised Ludendorff that an independent Poland would be able to supply a minimum of five divisions for the war against the Allies. Ludendorff now urged Polish independence, and this was proclaimed on 5 November. His motives were a mixture of the attempt to gain military support, the attempt to create a buffer between the Fatherland and Russia after the war, and also the effect of his experiences in the Upper East. The immediate result was to extinguish faint glimmers of hope for peace with Russia. Unofficial talks had already begun in Sweden, prompted by a policy of separate peace with Germany proposed by Boris Stürmer, the

Russian Prime Minister. These now ended, since the Tsar was unable to accept the loss of Russian territory in Poland, and the affair served as a warning of the difficulties to be faced in obtaining any settlement compatible with Ludendorff's war aims.[4]

In fact, despite Ludendorff's claims that GHQ wished to remain separate from political matters, such an attitude was quite clearly no longer feasible. Military, diplomatic and political factors were so closely interwoven that they could not be disentangled even if Ludendorff had so wished. The same applied to domestic questions such as industrial output and the organisation of labour. Ludendorff complained to Wilhelm, the Crown Prince: 'All this is really no business of mine but something must be done, and if I don't do it nothing will be done.'[5] The closing months of 1916 therefore saw Ludendorff's power spreading widely throughout Germany into all aspects of life. Non-military matters began to take up increasing amounts of his time, despite the huge amount of military work which he had to undertake. His incredible energy and his capacity for covering a multitude of subjects had never before been so much in demand. He approached domestic items in a meticulous fashion: plans ranged from raising the birthrate, improving housing, reducing venereal disease, to the introduction of better propaganda, improving morale and rural resettlement.[6] In particular Ludendorff turned his attention to the question of manpower, later admitting his measures were 'ruthless'.

The position of power which Ludendorff sought, and largely obtained although in the name of Hindenburg, was of the utmost importance in the history of Germany. It emphasised the requirements of total war: everyone was involved in the conflict; all energies had to be concentrated, and, as Ludendorff declared, nations not armies waged modern war. Ludendorff therefore attempted to create a new kind of dictatorship – and his methods would be closely studied by Adolf Hitler. These methods differed sharply from those hitherto employed in Germany. Until 1916 interference in industry by either the political or military chiefs had been relatively restricted: the war seemed to be going reasonably satisfactorily and materials continued to be in relative abundant supply. This attitude changed dramatically after Falkenhayn's dismissal.

Two days after his appointment to the Supreme Command Hindenburg outlined his plans in a letter to the War Minister, clearly drafted by Ludendorff. Already the two men had been in close touch with leading German industrialists, including Hugo Stinnes. Now Hindenburg proposed tight control of the economy by General Headquarters and by the chief monopolies, giving preference to the large concerns at the expense of the small companies, and aiming at rigid supervision of labour forces and the supply of raw materials. Hindenburg urged a 100 per cent increase in the production of ammunition, to be achieved by spring 1917, and a threefold increase in the production of artillery and machine guns; at the same time manpower would be rigidly combed to find fighting men, hence the need for better use of available manpower resources in the factories.[7]

Hindenburg justified his 'Programme' by reference to the powers given to the army under the law of the state of siege. But the implications were enormous: Bethmann Hollweg, amongst other politicians, was fully aware of the dangers of curtailment in civil authority should the proposals be accepted. Political dissent and labour unrest seemed inevitable, and, as expected, heated discussion now broke out.

By autumn 1916 a number of compromise solutions had apparently been found. A new institution, the war office – *Kriegsamt* – was established under General Groener which would implement the Hindenburg programme, although this body would be controlled by the War Ministry rather than by GHQ. Hindenburg and Ludendorff immediately sought to gain further ground. In return for their agreement to the so-called compromise they insisted that Stein should be appointed to the War Ministry, since this individual was likely to be more co-operative with GHQ than his predecessor Wild. Bethmann Hollweg agreed. Hindenburg and Ludendorff then turned their attention to the controversial manpower issue.

Already, on 30 October, the Chancellor had been requested to take urgent steps towards full conscription of men and women in the 15–60 age group, but the Reichstag hesitated to take this extreme measure. GHQ therefore pressed for an Auxiliary Labour Bill – *Hilfsdienstgesetz*. This became law on 2 December, but only after amendment by the politicians from the harsher proposals urged by the GHQ partnership. From now onwards all male Germans aged between 17 and 60 were obliged to perform 'auxiliary labour' essential to the war effort; a worker was not allowed to leave a job without permission; fines and prison sentences could be given to those who refused offers of employment. Under the terms of the Bill, Workers' Councils were established in any firm which employed more than 50 people, and their function was to 'promote a good understanding among the workers and between the workers and their employers'.[8]

In practice the law was heavily weighted on the side of the industrialists and the bourgeoisie, rather than the working class, though the trade unions celebrated the creation of the Councils as a triumph for 'war socialism'. The Councils, in fact, were far from being a significant step towards industrial democracy – so would be the similar types of body created by the Nazis. While Hindenburg and Ludendorff remained in power, the Councils amounted to little more than tokens, in return for which industrial workers lost considerable freedom of movement. The law strengthened the position of the industrialists; the bourgeoisie found it relatively easy to claim that whatever activity they engaged in was 'essential to the war effort'.

The Auxiliary Labour Bill failed to please Ludendorff, even though

Ludendorff as a young lieutenant.

Margarethe, Ludendorff's first wife, whom he married in 1909 and divorced in 1926.

Dr. Mathilde von Kemnitz, Ludendorff's second wife and literary collaborator.

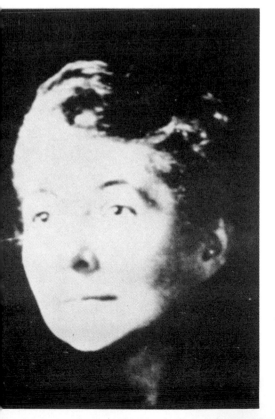

Ludendorff with Field-Marshal Hindenburg,
victors on the Eastern Front.

The Kaiser, using periscope binoculars, at the
battle HQ on the Western Front, in June 1918.
To his right is Prince Henry of Prussia.

Theobald von Bethmann-Hollweg, the German Chancellor.

Major-General Max Hoffmann.

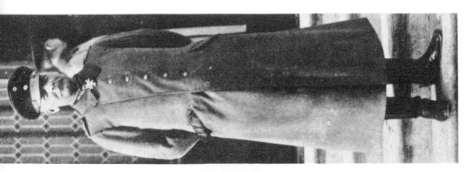

General Erich von Falkenhayn.

Ludendorff strides forth on the occassion of his 70th birthday.

Ludendorff with Adolf Hitler in 1923.

initially he gave the law a warm welcome simply because both industrialists and trade unions had co-operated in its formation. One of its
biggest failings was the vagueness surrounding the definition of work
essential to the war effort. Ludendorff's demands for simple conscription had been rejected; he wrote later: 'The Bill departed from the
principal of universal liability to service ... and gave no security that
the labour power obtained would be so employed as to produce the
maximum results.' Ludendorff noted that it was particularly irritating
to the troops to find 'auxiliary' workers being far better paid – for the
same work and in the same positions – than men who had been called
up for service under previous legislation and who were now soldiers.
'On the lines of communication there were still greater contrasts.
Troops withdrawn from the heavy fighting at the Front saw auxiliary
workers and women workers in peace and safety, working for wages
far higher than their own pay. This was bound to embitter the men ...
There was something fundamentally unsound in such a situation.'[9]

In general, Ludendorff condemned the law as

neither fish nor fowl. We wanted something wholesale ... It soon became clear that the Auxiliary [Labour] Law was not merely insufficient,
but positively harmful in operation ... In practice the law, largely owing
to the manner in which it was administered, was but a shadow of the
reality we desired, a reality which would have devoted the whole strength
of the nation to the nation's service.[10]

Ludendorff's fears were soon realised. The ultra-ambitious target
figures for industrial production under the Hindenburg programme
had to be reduced; industry claimed that the Auxiliary Labour Bill
created more problems than it solved; complaints about the Bill by
GHQ steadily increased, together with allegations that Groener's activities at the *Kriegsamt* were pro-labour. A steadily widening split
appeared between GHQ and the trade unions, together with a similar
divergence between GHQ and Social Democrat politicians.

Already, autumn 1916 had brought more gloom. The French
launched their expected offensive at Verdun, gaining ground in the
last week of October and first week of November; fighting at the
Somme subsided in mid-November, but about 650,000 German casualties had been suffered. Especially serious was the acute lack of experienced small-unit leaders resulting from the Somme losses; as a whole
the German army had changed radically since the highly professional
force which invaded Belgium in August 1914, and no one appreciated
this more than the highly professional Ludendorff.

Further serious news reached Ludendorff's office late on 21 November: Franz Joseph, eighty-six-year-old Austrian Emperor, had died a
few hours before and with him had departed the symbol of the former
mighty Austro-Hungarian Empire. Franz Joseph's great-nephew, the
Archduke Charles, came to power and the new ruler immediately

sought to shift away from Germany's influence: the Austrian GHQ was moved from Teschen to Baden near Vienna, so that a safe distance lay between the Austrian command and the pressures from the German HQ at Pless. Archduke Frederick was dismissed as Austrian C-in-C, and the Emperor himself took over. Conrad, the able and courageous Austrian Chief of Staff, went soon afterwards: his successor, General von Arz, lacked fire and independence. Hoffmann also noted that the young Austrian monarch was 'encouraged by an ambitious wife whose whole sympathies were on the side of the enemy, and who hated Germany'.[11]

But the weeks before Christmas brought one dramatic success. By November it had become clear to the Russians that their new Rumanian ally was crumbling, and during the month the southerly movement began of thirty-six infantry and eleven cavalry divisions.[12] The reinforcements would arrive too late. Early in November German troops penetrated the mountains into western Wallachia and a cavalry corps soon began to move rapidly east towards Bucharest. On 23–24 November Mackensen's forces crossed the Danube, with his forty battalions only opposed by eighteen Rumanian, and within twenty-four hours Mackensen's cavalry had contacted Falkenhayn's advance units. By 29 November the two armies of the Central Powers were threatening Bucharest, and Mackensen rode in triumph into the Rumanian capital on 6 December. Remnants of the Rumanian army were driven north into Moldavia and German troops advanced to seize the vital oil wells and grainfields, although with progress slowed both by the arrival of the Russians and by supply difficulties in the appalling winter conditions.

News of the victory against Rumania brought an almost hysterical reaction in depressed Berlin and boosted Ludendorff's spirits. He declared: 'With the termination of the campaign in Rumania, the fighting of the autumn of 1916 was decidely to our advantage.'[13] He made use of his newly-realised skill in propaganda to elevate his position in the struggle against politicians and trade unionists. Moreover the advantage to which Ludendorff referred, however superficial it might actually have been, might be put to good use on the international level: victory over the Rumanians could prevent any peace initiatives by Germany appearing as a sign of weakness. Bethmann Hollweg immediately prepared to make the first move.

Unfortunately for Germany, the triumphant seizure of Bucharest came just too late: twenty-four hours before Mackensen's entry into Bucharest, David Lloyd George succeeded Asquith as British Prime Minister, and Germany would now have to deal with a British leader who believed that war should be pursued to total Allied victory. Moreover, Lloyd George seemed likely to introduce radical new ideas: the Prime Minister profoundly mistrusted orthodox military opinion which seemed to have no solution to the problem of winning the war, other than a continuous slaughter – even though this itself, eventually, would bring victory for the Allies.[14]

On 12 December Bethmann Hollweg formally proposed to President Wilson that he should mediate between the belligerents. The Chancellor made no mention of German terms – these had still to be decided upon formally, with Ludendorff yet to set out his position in rigid detail. The Chancellor and the Kaiser nevertheless hoped that by avoiding reference to German terms, the Allies would be obliged to declare their position first. Thus Wilhelm confided to his American dentist: 'We've got the English and French Governments in a nice predicament, trying to explain to their people why they don't make peace. They're wild with rage at us for surprising them in this way.'[15] Wilson's reply, sent on 18 December, turned the tables on the Emperor and his Chancellor. He agreed to act as mediator, but asked each of the belligerents to declare their terms. The Kaiser's reaction was explosive: he believed that Wilson had discussed the reply beforehand with the Entente Powers. 'They began the war, they have been beaten, all along the line, they must state their intentions first.' Moreover Wilhelm rejected the idea mentioned in the US answer that President Wilson should preside over a conference – 'I go to no conference. Certainly not to one presided over by him.' On 26 December the American President was therefore informed that Germany preferred to deal directly with her enemy; four days later the Allies condemned the German 'peace' suggestions as insincere and insignificant.

Failure of this attempt prompted Ludendorff to increase his efforts for the introduction of the ultimate weapon. Already, on 26 December, he had despatched a telegram to Bethmann Hollweg; this declared that the submarine was 'the only means of carrying the war to a rapid conclusion . . . The military position does not allow us to postpone this measure.' The Kaiser summoned a conference to take the final decision; Wilhelm, the Chancellor, Hindenburg and Ludendorff and the Chief of Naval Staff therefore assembled at Pless on 9 January 1917. The atmosphere proved as sharp and frosty as the weather.

Ludendorff ordered the Chief of Naval Staff to present his case for all-out submarine warfare; the naval leader expressed his confidence that such a campaign would be decisive within a few months. Hindenburg reported that the GHQ urged the adoption of the policy, especially in view of the naval opinions. Bethmann Hollweg could do little against such expert opinion. He deplored the effect that the indiscriminate use of this weapon might have upon neutrals, especially America, but at the same time admitted his lack of qualifications for discussing the military aspects. As he wrote later: 'The decision had already *de facto* been taken . . . I could not advise His Majesty to do other than to accept the opinion of his military advisers.' This decision was approved by the Kaiser during the evening: notes would be delivered to neutral countries explaining Germany's policy of introducing a blockade around French and British shores.

Hindenburg and Ludendorff relished their victory. They declined to offer Bethmann Hollweg dinner after the conference, and the Chancellor left Pless in deep despair convinced that America's entry into the war would now be inevitable.[16] Later that night Bethmann Hollweg was urged to resign by Valentini, Chief of the Civil Cabinet, but he thought it his duty to remain; next day, 10 January, Hindenburg submitted a request to the Kaiser that the Chancellor should be replaced, urging the fact of GHQ's increasing apprehension over Bethmann Hollweg's attitude to the war, but the Kaiser hesitated to take this step: removal of Bethmann Hollweg would serve to reinforce the victory of the military leaders over the civilian power, and would in turn further undermine Wilhelm's own frail authority.

Also on 10 January 1917 the Allies informed President Wilson of their war aims, all of which must be obtained before peace could be concluded. These, in which the influence of Lloyd George could clearly be seen, were described as being the restoration of Belgium, Serbia and Montenegro, and the liberation of the Italians, Czechs, Serbs, Slovenes, Rumanians and Slovaks from alien domination.[17] The firm allied attitude confirmed Ludendorff's belief that the end of the war was far away, and that 1917 would be bloody and brutal. 'By the will of the Entente the war had to continue and to be decided by force of arms. It was to be Victory or Defeat.'[18]

CHAPTER FOURTEEN

Withdrawal

'THE OUTLOOK FOR THE COMING YEAR WAS EXCEEDINGLY GRAVE,' commented Ludendorff. His gloomy assessment continued: 'Our position was uncommonly difficult, and a way out hard to find. We could not contemplate an offensive ourselves, having to keep our reserves available for defence. There was no hope of a collapse of any of the Entente Powers. If the war lasted our defeat seemed inevitable.'[1]

So much depended upon the submarine offensive. After last-minute delaying attempts by the Foreign Office, Germany announced on 31 January 1917 that unrestricted submarine warfare should be resumed after 1 February. American reaction was immediate. On 3 February diplomatic relations with Germany were severed, and other nations followed suit during the next weeks – Brazil, Bolivia, Peru, other Latin American countries, and China.

Spring would soon be approaching and with it a resumption of land warfare. At the end of February the GHQ moved to Kreuznach, nearer to the Western Front. Offices were established in the Oranienhof, and Hindenburg and Ludendorff moved their private quarters into an elegant villa once owned by Emperor Wilhelm I; around the building spread magnificent gardens, still bare with winter but with buds beginning to swell on the multitude of exotic shrubs. During these weeks, whilst the fighting fronts lay shrouded with fog and soldiers shivered in the muddy trenches, and while military activity remained relatively low, Ludendorff worked over sixteen hours a day in his attempt to prepare army and country for another year of war. The next Allied attacks might be stronger than ever before. 'GHQ had to bear in mind that the enemy's great superiority in men and material would be even more painfully felt in 1917 than in 1916. They had to face the danger that "Somme fighting" would soon break out at various points on our fronts . . .'[2]

At the same time, Ludendorff's non-military work steadily increased. His stature amongst Germans as a whole was immense, offering as he did the greatest hope of salvation. His authority remained unquestioned – and would do so as long as success surrounded him. Yet Ludendorff knew very well that his military victories were far from being sufficient; even greater accomplishments must follow, and these could not be obtained in the military sphere without a firm economic background upon which they could be based. And, as Ludendorff had expected, the Auxiliary Labour Bill had clearly failed to cure Germany's economic ills. GHQ began to press for sterner measures, proposing the use of force to settle any labour disputes and to keep the workers under control. Bethmann Hollweg continued to urge co-operation with the unions rather than coercion; meanwhile industrial unrest simmered more strongly.

Ludendorff's energetic efforts to settle the host of problems surrounding him became almost frenzied. He launched a widespread campaign to eradicate war profiteering, hoping to appease the unions, but he admitted later that this attempt largely failed; rail and road transport was reorganised and an Inland Water Transport Department established; new coal mines were found in North-East Serbia, and at Ludendorff's suggestion a special Coal Controller was appointed; supplies of iron and oil were reorganised together with stocks of timber and rubble required for the trenches; GHQ secured supplies of artificial manures to increase phosphates being brought from occupied areas of north France and Belgium. The list appeared endless. As always, Ludendorff involved himself in details of work given to subordinates: he seemed to find it impossible to delegate and he explained: 'I had to keep myself constantly *au courant* if I was to decide rightly on many difficult problems.'[3]

Above all this lay military planning. And by now Ludendorff and Hindenburg had completed preparations for their next move. Discussions had recently intensified concerning a highly-secret and dramatic operation code-named 'Alberich'; final troop movements had taken place, apparently undetected by the enemy. By midnight, 23 February, 'Alberich' was ready.

Early in the morning, 24 February, German guns began to fire opposite Allied lines between Arras and Noyon, and British troops huddled in their trenches waiting for the salvoes to land around them. None came. Instead the explosions thundered to the front, across the other side of the desolate No Man's Land. The Germans were firing on their own trenches.

British patrols filtered through the barbed wire entanglements and found enemy lines deserted. Further to the east smoke gushed in enormous clouds, and during the night fires could be seen blazing across the fields. The British moved cautiously forward during the next few days: the Germans had mysteriously – and extremely efficiently – retired from the Arras-Soissons salient and were now established twenty miles back in the Siegfried Line. Advancing British units discovered the whole area to be an empty wilderness, with nothing left which could have been of use to them – roads were ripped up, wells ruined, villages and hamlets razed, walls levelled. Trees had been felled and carted away. Even the majority of the local inhabitants had disappeared.

Ludendorff had organised this 'Operation Alberich' with his usual meticulous care. Responsible for the actual withdrawal was Crown Prince Rupprecht of Bavaria, but this army group commander objected to the withdrawal plan and involved himself to the minimum extent possible. Instead Ludendorff supervised the removal of the local population eastwards – only small groups were left behind, provided with scanty rations; he took a detailed interest in the transfer of works of art from the district and in all the measures taken to deny the enemy sustenance and defence. At the same time the Siegfried Line was made as strong as possible: each successive defence line was spaced in depth; machine-gun positions were carefully sited; supply roads to the front were extended and improved.

'The decision to retreat was not reached without a painful struggle,' observed Ludendorff in his memoirs. 'It implied a confession of weakness bound to raise the morale of the enemy and lower our own. But as it was necessary for military reasons, we had no choice.' The order to carry out Alberich was issued on 4 February, and complete secrecy was maintained. Withdrawal was initially intended to begin on 16 March, then intelligence reports indicated an early Allied attack – in fact the offensive being prepared by General Robert Nivelle, hero of Verdun, who had succeeded Joffre as French C-in-C in December. Nivelle's assault, to be carried out with 'violence, brutality and rapidity', was thwarted by the sudden German move; by 5 April 'Operation Alberich' had been completed. Ludendorff had succeeded in shortening the German line and hence freeing 14 divisions; moreover an excellent base had been established from which a German offensive could eventually be launched.

But Ludendorff's fears for necessary economic support from the Fatherland for such an offensive remained strong. The troops had to be supplied with equipment, weapons and ammunition from the German industrial centres, yet economic problems appeared immense and even the modified Hindenburg programme for industrial output now seemed hopelessly over-ambitious. Opposition to the war, or at least to wartime conditions, became increasingly vocal among the workers: the food situation was critical after the bad winter of 1916–17, and the miserable living standards at home seemed a stark contrast to the optimistic announcements by the politicians. Industrial unrest festered further into a multitude of strikes.

Ludendorff advocated a mixture of honesty and almost brutal repression. He believed right-wing politicians were mistaken in glossing over domestic difficulties, and he urged instead that the workers should be told the true position – and at the same time should be persuaded to join in the common struggle against the enemy. If persuasion failed, as seemed likely, then rigorous coercion would be necessary, and Ludendorff had no hesitation in demanding even greater GHQ interference in industrial relations.

But another problem had now arisen – the February Revolution in Russia, which provided tremendous encouragement for the radical left in Germany and at the same time opened the possibility of an end to the war in the East. Rasputin, hated adviser at the Russian court, had been murdered on Boxing Day; strikes erupted with ever-increasing frequency, reaching a peak at the beginning of March. On 10 March the military garrison in the Russian capital mutinied to join the workers in revolt. Tsar Nicholas was obliged to abdicate. For the moment the 'Establishment' managed to retain frail power and a Provisional Government, soon dominated by Alexander Kerensky, was formed from the generals, existing politicians and leading industrialists. The new regime pledged itself to continue the war, but opposition surged again, led by the revolutionary masses in Petersburg who formed their own Council, the Soviet, dominated by the Bolsheviks.

Contacts had been maintained throughout the war with Russian dissidents, among them the Bolshevik leader Vladimir Lenin in his Swiss exile. In mid-March Ludendorff received a visit from Alexander Helphand, a Russian employed by the German Foreign Office as an agent with the code-name 'Parvus'. Helphand had been sent by the Centre party politician Matthias Erzberger, who believed with increasing fervour that peace must be made as soon as possible, for the sake of the Fatherland. Helphand declared to Ludendorff that Lenin's return to Russia would ferment further revolution; Ludendorff gave his approval for the Bolshevik to travel through Germany. Not until 4 April could this be arranged, and Lenin left Zürich on the 9th to arrive in Petersburg on the 16th.[4]

By then Ludendorff had even more important matters to deal with. On 6 April news reached Kreuznach that America had declared war on Germany, with Congress voting 373 to 50. President Wilson lamented: 'It means that we shall lose our heads along with the rest and stop weighing right and wrong.' Such a decision had been feared and even expected. But now, more than before, time hung in the balance with the outcome of the war depending on which came first, destruction of the Allies through the U-boat war, or decisive American intervention at the land battle front. Ludendorff remained optimistic: the submarine war seemed to be progressing well with the strangulation of Allied supplies. In fact the results were probably better than even Ludendorff dared to believe. Allied ships lost rose from 181 in January to 259 in February, and during February the British First Sea Lord, Jellicoe, warned that the country would run out of food and some raw materials by July. Ship casualties continued to rise – 325 in March, 423 in April. Britain attempted to retaliate with accelerated mine development, depth charges and detection devices such as the hydrophone; argument continued over the introduction of another anti-submarine measure, the convoy.

America could offer minimal practical support on the Western Front: the army had still to be expanded and properly equipped for a European role. At the time of the US declaration of war the number of troops stood at about 200,000 men, the same size as Serbia's in 1914; in May only about 1,300 US soldiers had reached the Western Front and the first complete units did not disembark in France until June.[5] Time might still therefore be in Germany's favour, but the margin would be slim.

On 9 April 1917, Ludendorff's fifty-second birthday, vigorous assaults were launched by the British 1st and 3rd Armies north and south of Arras. Trenches of the German 6th Army were first subjected to a heavy artillery bombardment and gas attack, and some sections of the line gave way; Canadian troops stormed and took Vimy Ridge during this first day, fighting forward in driving sleet and seizing German battery positions. Ludendorff remained in his office at the Kreuznach GHQ, neglecting the dinner party which had been arranged for him. His gloom grew steadily. 'I had looked forward to the expected offensive with confidence, and was now deeply depressed. Was this to be the result of all our care and trouble during the past half-year?'

Hindenburg came to find Ludendorff and to remind him of the dinner-party. The Field-Marshal had also read the news of the initial Allied success. 'The evening report of this 9 April revealed rather a dark picture. Many shadows – little light. In such cases more light must be sought.' Hindenburg therefore searched for some reason for optimism. 'A ray appeared, though a tiny flickering ray' – the enemy advance had apparently slowed. Hindenburg made a characteristic gesture to comfort his Quartermaster-General: he took Ludendorff's hand in both his own and declared: 'We've lived through worse times than this!' He wrote afterwards: 'My confidence was unshaken. I knew that reinforcements were marching to the battlefield and that trains were hastening that way. The crisis was over.'[6]

But not for Ludendorff. The separate reactions of Hindenburg and his colleague reveal the differences between them: the immediate crisis might indeed be ended, but for Ludendorff this was insufficient. He had to probe and dissect until he found the reasons for the British and Canadian success. He sent immediately for officers from the front, and until they arrived he made repeated telephone calls aimed at finding the exact details of the day's battle. He finished his examination somewhat reassured: the principles laid down by GHQ for tactical defence seemed sound, although they had been wrongly applied by some local commanders.

A gap had been torn into the German line about 10 miles wide and 4 deep, and now this must be plugged. 'It was the business of GHQ to provide reserves on a large scale,' wrote Ludendorff. 'But it was absolutely impossible, with the troops at our disposal and in view of the military situation, to have a second division immediately behind every division that might possibly fall out. A day like 9 April threw all calculations to the winds.'[7]

Reserves were scraped together and by 15 April the battle had ended – Allied losses were about 84,000, German around 75,000. The fighting provided a grim warning for the future. Moreover this battle of Arras had only been intended by the Allied High Command as a preliminary and a distraction for a far greater offensive by the French. On 16 April, even before the guns at Arras subsided, Nivelle launched his attack.

Frenchmen in the Reserve Army Group battered forward on a 40-mile front between Soissons and Reims – 1,200,000 men backed by 7,000 guns. Nivelle aimed to outflank the Siegfried Line by penetrating the Chemin des Dames south of Soissons. German defences had been well prepared; artillery fire destroyed the French tanks moving forward *en masse,* and the lines of infantry were cut down by pre-planned artillery and machine-gun fire. The French managed to gain the first German line on the Chemin des Dames, but were then stopped; further frenzied assaults made little ground, and in five days the French had lost nearly 120,000 men. On 29 April mutinies broke out in 54 French divisions, unknown to Ludendorff at the time even though French combat troops on the Western Front ceased to be effective for almost two weeks.

Hoffmann visited Ludendorff during this battle, and he wrote afterwards: 'General Ludendorff made no secret of his uneasiness caused by the internal conditions, and especially by the entire want of decision by the Chancellor.'[8] Within a very short time another fear would arise: the British had found means of combating the U-boat menace.

On 10 May a trial convoy put to sea. Results were dramatic, and by the end of October over 1,500 vessels in 99 homeward Atlantic convoys would have reached safety, with only 10 ships lost in convoy formation. Britain was also developing better offensive measures, including hunter packs and wider mine distribution: figures for U-boats destroyed began to creep steadily higher. On the Western Front the British resumed their attacks, attempting to divert attention from the French mutinies: General Sir Herbert Plumer's 2nd Army advanced at Messines on 7 June after a 17-day bombardment and after mines packed with one million pounds HE had ripped a gap in the German lines. Ludendorff rushed forward precious reserves. The British made no attempt to press forward after their initial success, and Ludendorff guessed correctly that Messines merely formed the prelude to some larger offensive.[9]

Meanwhile Ludendorff increasingly believed that he must fight the war on two fronts: inside and outside Germany. The Fatherland seemed to be lacking in spirit; armies were receiving insufficient support; a defeatist attitude seemed prevalent. For all this Ludendorff blamed the politicians, and especially the Chancellor. On 26 June Bethmann Hollweg received a visit from the Nuncio Pacelli, who delivered a letter addressed to the Kaiser from the Pope offering his services as a mediator. Pacelli attempted to discover from the Chancellor the type of peace terms which Germany would be prepared to negotiate. Bethmann Hollweg's reply was non-committal, but Ludendorff's suspicions were nevertheless aroused and he began to move more actively against the Chancellor. Next day Hindenburg wrote a letter to the Kaiser, presumably prompted by Ludendorff, in which the Field-Marshal declared: 'Our greatest anxiety at this moment ... is the decline in the national spirit ... The question arises whether the Chancellor is capable of solving these problems – and they must be solved, or we are lost!'[10]

Ludendorff maintained his attitude that peace must only be obtained from a position of strength: Germany must only accept favourable terms, and a return to the status quo would be unacceptable; among the necessary terms was the need to obtain suitable control over Belgium. The debate now became more heated in Germany, with opinions split between the 'annexationists', to whom Ludendorff was allied, and those who desired 'peace with understanding'. The latter included not only Bethmann Hollweg, but Ludendorff's previous principal associate Hoffmann. As long ago as December 1914 Hoffmann had confided to Bethmann Hollweg that he believed Germany must avoid making claims over Belgium, and recently this officer had been in close touch with the politician Erzberger, who sought peace more desperately than perhaps any other Reichstag member.[11]

On 3 July a strong attack on the Government was launched in the Reichstag by Friedrick Ebert, Chairman of the Social Democrat party, who demanded more positive peace moves. Next day Erzberger rose to make a major speech in which he urged a return to defensive war since the U-boat campaign had failed to match expectations. Two days later, 6 July, Erzberger cited specific figures on the U-boat offensive, and pointed out that such results would never succeed in defeating Britain: the Reichstag should take the initiative by setting up a committee to draft the terms of a compromise peace.

Erzberger's speech caused a sensation, both in the Reichstag Main Committee and amongst the population as a whole. Bethmann Hollweg also spoke on the 6th, insisting that Germany had always waged a defensive war, and that to make another declaration of peace now would be detrimental to the interests of the Fatherland. Nevertheless, the Reichstag began to discuss a draft Peace Resolution, which declared: 'The Reichstag strives for a peace of understanding and the permanent reconciliation of peoples. Forced territorial acquisitions and political, economic or financial oppressions are irreconcilable with such a peace . . .'[12]

Ludendorff's belief that he must fight an internal political war was confirmed. He immediately increased his attacks on Bethmann Hollweg for his ineffectual handling of the Reichstag debate. On 7 July Ludendorff and Hindenburg hurried to Berlin to voice their protests to the Kaiser; Wilhelm made a show of strength against the military leaders by replying that the Reichstag events fell outside the scope of GHQ, and he instructed Hindenburg and Ludendorff to return to Kreuznach immediately.

But the Kaiser's defiance would rapidly diminish, and political opposition to Bethmann Hollweg suddenly increased with the Chancellor being attacked by a wide variety of Reichstag parties. The Conservatives declared: 'We would fight to the death in order to win, rather than to succumb like cowards' – a sentiment which Ludendorff firmly endorsed. The Centre Party, by contrast, believed that Bethmann Hollweg must go since he had led the Reich at the outbreak of war and would thus find it more difficult to negotiate an early peace. The National Liberal leader, Gustav Stresemann, made a rambling speech on 8 July in which he declared: 'The whole conduct of the nation's affairs is being carried on under the motto "We shall not succeed anyhow." ' He added: 'The prevalent defeatism is due to the fact that the nation believes it is moving from failure to failure in this greatest of all wars.'[13]

Clearly the Fatherland approached acute political fragmentation. And this had important effects on Ludendorff: political disintegration meant even less co-operation between civil and military leaders in a determined prosecution of the war; on the other hand, a weak political situation opened increased opportunity for added military power.

Bethmann Hollweg offered his resignation on 10 July but the Kaiser refused to let him go. Then came further military moves, initiated by Colonel Max Bauer on the GHQ staff: he, like many politicians, believed that a satisfactory peace could only be obtained if Bethmann Hollweg were replaced. He therefore sought royal assistance by telephoning Crown Prince Wilhelm and urging him to hurry to Berlin in order to discover the political feeling. 'I explained the position to him,' wrote Bauer, 'and convinced him of its gravity.'

Prince Wilhelm received a number of leading politicians on the morning of 12 July, with these civilians standing before him stiff to attention whilst he rapped out his question. Was it or was it not necessary to have a new Chancellor? All agreed Bethmann Hollweg must go.[14] The Crown Prince presented his findings to his father during the early afternoon, and the two men were still deep in discussion when Bethmann Hollweg arrived at the palace at 7 pm. The Chancellor now found himself under Imperial attack for his inability to overcome the crisis; Bethmann Hollweg tried to defend himself by describing the progress made with the Peace Resolution, which he read out to the Kaiser and Crown Prince. Both declared that Hindenburg should be informed of the content of this resolution, and a telephone call was made immediately to GHQ.

Thirty minutes later GHQ replied. Hindenburg demanded alterations in the document, all of them uncontroversial, and the Kaiser agreed. The problem seemed to have been settled. But at GHQ Hindenburg had fresh discussions with Ludendorff and suddenly stiffened his attitude as a result. General von Lyncker, Chief of the Military Cabinet, rushed into the Kaiser's room only a few minutes after the telephone call had come from the Field-Marshal: now Wilhelm heard that another telephone message had been received from Kreuznach. Hindenburg and Ludendorff had handed in their resignations, and those of the remainder of GHQ would follow at once.[15]

Ludendorff wrote later: 'The Government had lost the determination to win ... The army did not receive what it needed for victory. I no longer believed that a change would take place under that Chancellor ... So I wrote out my resignation. The Field-Marshal joined me.'[16]

'I needed all the resources of the Fatherland,' explained Hindenburg after the war. 'To dissipate these resources by internal friction at a time of extreme tension, instead of concentrating them, could only lead to a diminution of our political and military power ... I could not take the responsibility of standing by and saying nothing.'[17]

The resignations amounted to flagrant blackmail and to complete military interference in political affairs – and to an attempt to supersede the Kaiser's own freedom of action. Wilhelm knew very well that Ludendorff had pushed the Field-Marshal into taking such a drastic step. He declared: 'This kind of behaviour on the part of a Prussian general has never been heard of before.'[18] The military leaders were ordered to report to Berlin immediately.

But Bethmann Hollweg knew this to be the end. He declared it was of course unthinkable that the Field-Marshal and General, who enjoyed the confidence of the nation, should be allowed to resign. Next morning, 13 July, the Chancellor tendered his resignation which the Kaiser accepted: Wilhelm informed Hindenburg and Ludendorff of this development when they arrived in Berlin, and no mention was made of their own threatened departure.

The upheaval marked Ludendorff's final step to supremacy. His defiance had overcome both political and Imperial opposition. But power had arrived too late. As far as possibilities of peace were concerned, the cautious and relatively moderate influence which Bethmann Hollweg had tried to exert would be replaced by a different approach; Ludendorff had always found it extremely difficult to compromise and now, in July 1917, chances of a compromise end to the war had been drastically reduced. Those in favour of annexations and ambitious peace terms celebrated Bethmann Hollweg's departure, while those who sought understanding and a return to the status quo looked fearfully at the future.

CHAPTER FIFTEEN
Struggle for Survival

A NEW CHANCELLOR HAD TO BE FOUND, AND THE SEARCH BROUGHT fresh confusion. 'I was surprised to find,' declared Ludendorff, 'that the authorities concerned did not have a successor to the Imperial Chancellor always in readiness, and that in a matter of such decisive importance for its destiny, Germany had to live from hand to mouth.'[1]

Conservative politicians held a celebration party on the evening of 17 July 1917 to rejoice in Bethmann Hollweg's fall, but the feeling of triumph ebbed almost immediately. 'The next morning,' wrote the Conservative deputy Count Kuno von Westarp, 'we had more than just a physical hangover. The fulfilment of a long-sought event often brings new disappointment and anxieties. This the politician discovers, especially when he has hopes for or worked towards the sacking of a leading statesman without making sure of his successor.'[2]

Candidates had to be acceptable to the Supreme Command, to the Kaiser, and to the politicians. Possibilities were rejected in quick succession – Prince Bülow, Tirpitz, Count von Bernstorff, Count Hertling ... Increasingly desperate, the Kaiser ordered Count von Valentini to find someone whom Hindenburg and Ludendorff would find agreeable. The Head of the Civil Cabinet searched through the political directories, with von Lyncker giving his help as GHQ representative, but their efforts failed to achieve success. Then the name Michaelis was suggested. Few people could supply further information about him – the Kaiser had never met him – but this Prussian Food Controller was said to be on good terms with GHQ, and Hindenburg sent his approval: 'He is a decent, God-fearing man, and I accept him in God's name.'[3]

Dr Georg Michaelis, very old and very deaf, was as surprised as everyone else by the sudden elevation. He accepted after consulting the daily message contained in his Moravian Brotherhood prayer-book – a means of seeking advice and encouragement which Ludendorff also used. Michaelis read the text of the day: 'Do not fear and be dismayed, for the Lord, your God, will be with you in everything you do.'[4]

The Chancellor's first task was to deal with the Reichstag Peace Resolution, under discussion since 6 July. Even before Michaelis's appointment was confirmed Hindenburg and Ludendorff took steps to influence the newcomer against this resolution. Hindenburg told the Kaiser that it would 'weaken the army's strength and power of resistance', and the Field-Marshal and Ludendorff discussed the draft with politicians during the afternoon of 13 July. They insisted that they opposed the weak tone rather than the idea of a resolution as a whole: Ludendorff suggested 'peace of adjustment' rather than 'peace of understanding' and that Michaelis undertook to influence the Reichstag.

Debate took place on the 19th, during which Michaelis attempted to appease both politicians and GHQ. 'Peace must be the foundation of a lasting reconciliation between nations,' he declared, then added: 'Peace must ensure that the alliance between our enemies does not turn into an economic ring against us.' He believed he had achieved compromise: the resolution was carried, but he told the Crown Prince: 'My interpretation took from it all its dangers. When the time comes the resolution will allow us to conclude any peace we like.'[5]

So began Michaelis's short and ill-fated pretence of being a Chancellor. Agitation for peace continued: at the end of July a movement among naval ratings in support of an early end to war flared into mutiny; in August the Pope again offered to mediate, thus resurrecting the need for Germany to declare her war aims.

But by now Ludendorff was heavily involved in military matters. Turmoil had continued inside Russia, seriously affecting Russian forces and resulting in the elimination of perhaps 50 per cent of the officer corps. Alexander Kerensky nevertheless planned a renewed offensive, under Allied pressure, and on 1 July Brusilov attacked towards Lemberg against weak German forces. The Russians managed to advance 30 miles over a 100-mile front, and further south the Austrians suffered heavily. Hoffmann remained calm. He himself had been planning an offensive towards Tarnopol and Ludendorff responded to his request for reinforcements by sending six precious divisions from the West.

Hoffmann's attack began on 19 July 1917. Preceded by an intense bombardment, German forces smashed forward in the Zloczov region, driving eastwards for 10 miles on a 15-mile front. Russian forces, now exhausted and demoralised, began to crumble: Tarnopol fell on 25 July and by the end of the month the Russians were streaming back from Galicia.

On 31 July the Western Front exploded into battle again. Ludendorff had expected an offensive in Flanders since the preliminary Allied operations at Messines early the previous month, but he had

full confidence in General Sixt von Arnim's 4th Army defending this
sector, and especially in Arnim's Chief of Staff, von Lossberg. For
several days German defences had been subjected to massive bombardments, and the effect on the troops began to cause Ludendorff some
concern. 'At some points they no longer displayed that firmness which
I, in common with the local commanders, had hoped for . . .'[6]

One German medical officer wrote:

> Again and again we had to dig ourselves and our comrades out of masses
> of blackened earth and splintered wooden beams. Often we found bodies
> crushed to pulp, or bunks full of suffocated soldiers. The 'drum-fire'
> never ceased. No food or water reached us. Down below, men became
> hysterical and their comrades had to knock them down . . . Even the rats
> panicked.[7]

Now, on 31 July, the British 5th Army advanced against the
battered enemy line beneath a clear summer sky. According to the
German medical officer, Stephen Westman:

> German machine gunners and infantrymen crawled out of their holes,
> with inflamed and sunken eyes, their faces blackened by fire and their
> uniforms splashed with the blood of their wounded comrades. It was a
> kind of relief to be able to come out, even into air still filled with smoke
> and the smell of cordite. They started firing furiously . . .[8]

Fierce counter-attacks against the British left succeeded in blocking
the advance for a number of hours, but gradually the offensive obtained additional pressure, and by evening British and French troops
had advanced two miles. The weather broke during the night: for the
preceding weeks the sun had baked the earth, and now rain sluiced
the hard-packed soil and filled the shell-craters, and further bombardment churned the earth to mud. Battle continued into August under
increasingly hellish conditions for both attacker and defender.

'The fighting on the Western Front became more severe and costly
than any the German Army had yet experienced,' stated Ludendorff.
'I myself was being put to a terrible strain. The state of affairs in the
West appeared to prevent the execution of our plans elsewhere. Our
wastage had been so high as to cause grave misgivings, and had ex-
ceeded all expectation.' Despite his anxieties, Ludendorff still believed
there should be no talk of peace until Germany could demand adequate terms. 'I was convinced that the West Front would stand even
more battering, though Fate might have even greater trials in store for
it.'[9]

The 11th Battle of the Isonzo opened on the Italian front on 18
August, with the heavily reinforced Italian 2nd and 3rd Armies pushing against the Austrians and gaining the advantage. The Austrians
despatched urgent requests for help: Ludendorff scraped together as

many units as he could and sent them hurrying south. At the same time he provided all possible support to Hoffmann for what was hoped to be the final thrust against the Russians. His nerve faltered as he fought to resist the temptation to transfer troops back from the East to Flanders. Hoffmann noted on 21 August: 'Ludendorff rang up early yesterday morning: "I'm very sorry, I must have some troops." Very well: I sent out all the orders. In the afternoon he rang up again: "Perhaps I can manage." So I cancelled all the orders. Today, we shall probably get counter-orders again. I can't blame Ludendorff . . .'

On 1 September forces in General Oscar von Hutier's 8th Army struck against the far north of the Russian front. Hutier, Ludendorff's cousin, employed important new tactics which would soon carry his name. The usual preliminary bombardment was abandoned, and instead a brief, sharp concentration of fire was directed on to a given point; the infantry assault began almost simultaneously, and both guns and men were brought into position at the last possible moment to provide added surprise. In the actual attack infantrymen by-passed the enemy strongpoints – in similar fashion to the assaults on Liège in 1914 – and these fixed enemy positions were masked by gas and smoke. These tactics therefore bore a strong resemblance to those already discussed by Ludendorff for the Western Front, and he had most probably been involved in Hutier's arrangements for the East, including schemes for encirclement once initial penetration of the enemy line had been achieved. Now, in early September, results proved excellent: the Russian 12th Army fell back eastwards in apparent panic.

'We changed their retreat into something of a rout,' wrote the delighted Hoffmann on 10 September. 'We should of course have liked to continue our advance in the direction of Petersburg, but unfortunately we had to stop, as Ludendorff, with the best will in the world, could not let us keep the necessary divisions. He needs them, and Austria needs them, so we must resign ourselves.'[10]

This startling victory caused further consternation in Russia. The Kerensky Government fled from Petersburg to Moscow; the Bolsheviks began to seize power. 'Russia seems to be all upside down again,' noted Hoffmann on 11 September. Meanwhile Ludendorff had to keep his attention fixed on the West. Foul weather continued to hamper the attackers in Flanders, enabling only limited gains to be made. But the restricted nature of these British and French advances made them easier to consolidate and defend.

In early September, amidst all his military anxieties, Ludendorff received tragic personal news. He immediately arranged to see Margarethe and travelled to Berlin on 8 September. 'I hastened to meet him with surprise and delight,' wrote Margarethe. 'He looked, however, so sad and serious that I stood aghast.' Ludendorff began to stammer a sentence: 'The boy, the child . . .' Margarethe completed the sentence for him: '... is dead.' She wrote years later: 'I must have screamed out aloud as the sound still rings in my ears and I often seem to live through the whole thing in a dream.'[11] Franz, survivor of grenade wounds and of a previous crash, had been shot down on 5 September in an encounter with a British pilot over the Channel: his body was washed up on the Dutch coast weeks later. Ludendorff had seen him recently at Lille, and he seemed 'fresh and strong and full of enthusiasm'. His mother held a different view. He wrote in one of his last letters: 'Mother, you can't imagine what a heavenly feeling it is when all the day's fighting is successfully over, to lie in bed and say to oneself before going to sleep, "Thank God! you have another 12 hours to live." '[12]

Arrangements were made with the Dutch for Franz's body to be brought back to Berlin. Pilots met the train and provided a guard of honour to the German capital. Ludendorff paid his last respects with a special private gesture: whilst dressing for the funeral he carefully pinned all his medals and stars to his service tunic; Margarethe asked why he took the trouble, since no one would be able to see the decorations beneath his greatcoat, and Ludendorff muttered: 'Leave me be. *Fränzchen* would be pleased.'[13]

British troops in Flanders began to edge forward again on 20 September. Strains became harder than ever; in addition, Ludendorff was almost killed on a journey to the front, when another train ran into the carriage in which he was dining with his officers. The carriage slewed off the track and on to its back, but Ludendorff and the others climbed out unhurt.

In Italy, the enemy advance had at last been halted but mainly through shortages of supplies, and German and Austrian troops remained over-stretched and vulnerable. Defenders in Flanders fought in the mud and swamps as autumn rains lashed the battlefield, and in early October massive artillery duels ploughed the ground into even deeper quagmires: conditions even shocked the hardened Ludendorff.

Enormous masses of ammunition, such as the human mind had never imagined before the war, were hurled upon the bodies of men who passed a miserable existence scattered about in mud-filled shell-holes. The horror of the shell-hole area of Verdun was surpassed. It was no longer life at all. It was mere unspeakable suffering. And through this world of mud the attackers dragged themselves, slowly, but steadily, and in dense masses. Caught in the advance zone by our hail of fire they often collapsed, and the lonely man in the shell-hole breathed again. Then the mass came on again. Rifle and machine gun jammed in the mud. Man fought against man, and only too often the mass was successful.[14]

Then, as dismal winter set in, better news reached Ludendorff. On 24 October the new 14th Austrian army, under the German general

Otto von Below and with seven of its divisions also German, attacked the Italians in the Battle of Caporetto. The offensive utilised the 'Hutier tactics' which had proved so successful in the Riga area early in September; this method again brought dramatic results. And on 7 November Bolsheviks under Trotsky and Lenin stormed the Winter Palace in Petersburg to seize power from the Provisional Government. Almost immediately, contacts would be made by the new Russian regime aimed at ending the war with Germany.

Meanwhile the political situation in the Fatherland had remained unsatisfactory, and Ludendorff had continued to fear that politicians might obtain overwhelming support for a 'peace at any price' policy. Initially, therefore, he welcomed the creation of a new group named the *Vaterslandspartei* – the Fatherland Party – which promised vigorous action against both defeatists and those who spread damaging propaganda within the forces. This party originated from an idea by the provincial official Herr Wolfgang Kapp; on 2 September, the anniversary of Moltke's great victory over the French at Sedan, the group issued a lengthy manifesto: 'The German *Vaterslandspartei* aims at welding together the whole energy of the Fatherland ... We will have no peace of starvation.' Head of the party was named as Tirpitz with Kapp the Vice-President.[15]

Ludendorff commented: 'There were still men in Germany who had correctly gauged the enemy's mind. They desired to strengthen the fighting spirit ... I had no connection with them. But their work was most welcome to me.'[16] Like Ludendorff, Tirpitz and Kapp believed there should be no compromise over Germany's peace terms.

These terms were discussed at a Crown Council meeting held on 11 September at the Bellevue Palace in Berlin. Michaelis described faint possibilities of a separate peace with Britain, providing Germany renounced any interest in Belgium. Both Hindenburg and Ludendorff agreed it might be possible to give up the Flanders coast, but Ludendorff insisted on maintaining Germany's hold over Liège. He went into greater detail in a long memorandum on 14 September, in which he advocated an early peace only on condition that Germany's economic and military future could be secured. 'We must push back the Anglo-French army still further. This can only be done by joining Belgium so closely to ourselves economically that she will also seek political *Anschluss*.' Next day Hindenburg sent this document to Michaelis, with a note declaring the content was 'entirely in accordance' with his own views.[17]

Michaelis attempted to walk between the 'status quo' group and hardliners such as Ludendorff. Such a policy was impossible, and the Chancellor found his position becoming untenable. During October he came under increasing Reichstag attack, mainly through his efforts to halt the spread of 'hostile propaganda' in the army, a policy urged upon him by Ludendorff. The latter held back support for the Chancellor during these political attacks: instead he complained that Michaelis had become too involved in the Reichstag dogfighting – 'He wore out his strength in this struggle and had no time to work for the war.' Ludendorff soon levelled similar criticisms at the Fatherland Party.

The Chancellor submitted his resignation on the last day of October. The Kaiser accepted it. But Michaelis's departure did not precipitate the political crisis which had surrounded the downfall of Bethmann Hollweg: it almost seemed as if it no longer mattered who occupied the Chancellorship, since the real power rested with the GHQ. On 1 November the elder Bavarian statesman Count von Hertling became Chancellor: Hertling, aged seventy-six and lately a professor of philosophy, had been suggested by Bethmann Hollweg as his successor but had declined since he felt too old. Now he took office under even more impossible circumstances, promising that he would follow policies more in keeping with the popular will. Ludendorff wrote: 'After I had come to know the Imperial Chancellor, Count von Hertling, I became convinced ... that he too was no War Chancellor ... He called himself the "Reconciliation Chancellor". I think the time was not yet ripe for reconciliation.'[18]

Instead, Ludendorff believed the time had come to prepare for another abrupt change in strategy. Plans must be readied for the following year, 1918; Ludendorff therefore summoned key staff officers to Mons for a critical conference on 11 November. Attending these discussions were the Chiefs of Staffs of the army groups commanded by Crown Prince Rupprecht and the German Crown Prince Wilhelm, respectively Generals von Kuhl and von der Schulenburg. Almost immediately Ludendorff declared that his policy of a defensive in the West would be ended: next spring the German armies would launch massive attack. Ludendorff had reached his decision despite – or even because of – shortage of German resources: the Fatherland could not afford a war of attrition.

Three sectors were considered for the spring offensive: in the north between Ypres and Lens, in the centre between Arras and St Quentin or La Fère, and in the south on both sides of Verdun. Terrain would be difficult in the north, although an attack in this region offered the possibility of pushing through Flanders to Calais and Boulogne. The south also suffered from unsuitable terrain, and gains were likely to be merely tactical. The centre promised far greater rewards; the front around St Quentin seemed weakly defended and, according to Ludendorff, 'the strategic results might indeed be enormous'. A successful offensive could split the British and French armies apart and open the road to Paris. No final decision was reached at the Mons conference, but the planners began to consider each alternative in greater detail.[19]

German forces had to withstand one more offensive before this desperate year of 1917 came to a close. At 6.20 am, 20 November, about 250 British tanks roared and whined ponderously forward southwest of Cambrai. Lack of preliminary bombardment enabled the British to obtain complete surprise; new artillery methods enabled German batteries to be pinpointed, and these came under heavy fire simultaneous with the tank advance. Soon after 8 am the telephone rang at GHQ and Ludendorff was informed that the enemy had already broken through at several places – this section of the Siegfried Line was weakly held since forces had been shifted to Flanders. Ludendorff immediately ordered up reserves, but not until the afternoon did he manage to obtain a clear view of the initial British success. 'It made me very anxious. Everything possible, however, was already being done.' It would take at least forty-eight hours for the reinforcements to entrain, travel, and disembark for deployment.[20]

German troops often found themselves helpless in the face of this first major tank engagement. According to one German participant, Surgeon Stephen Westman:

> The infantrymen almost panicked when they saw the huge steel monsters coming towards them, flattening the barbed-wire entanglements and rolling over the deep trenches. Mercilessly they overran single soldiers, pressed them to the ground, leaving behind crushed and flattened remnants of what, a few seconds before, had been human beings. All the poor footsloggers could do was to throw a bundle of hand-grenades underneath the tank and try to blow it up.[21]

Ludendorff had in fact underestimated the value of armoured vehicles, despite his constant preference for mobility. At the end of 1916 he had considered that 'the time was not yet come for us to undertake the contruction of tanks' and he believed 'the best weapons against the tanks are coolness, discipline and courage'. The first German machine had only been made ready for trials in May 1917, and by the end of the year only five German tanks were available.[22] Yet the battle for Cambrai contained valuable lessons for the future. However, the fighting also revealed that tank successes should be exploited in minimum time, and this the British failed to accomplish.

By the evening of 20 November the British 3rd Army under General Sir Julian Byng had advanced about three miles, but then progress slowed. Many leading tanks faltered through mechanical defects, and British infantry reserves were too weak to make adequate use of the armoured breakthrough. By 25 November Ludendorff's anxiety had begun to lift; by 29 November it even seemed possible that the Germans might be able to turn the initial British success to their own advantage, by striking hard at the flank of the enemy penetration.

This attempt began the following morning just after 8 o'clock. German infantry thrust into the southern edge of the bulge employing a version of the Hutier tactics: units made only limited attempts to take high ground, and instead filtered down the valleys. Within forty-eight hours the Germans had regained their original positions in the south over a three-mile frontage, and in the first week of December the British had to yield further areas.

As 1917 closed it seemed that the military position had improved on all fronts. The Germans continued to hold at Flanders; in Italy the battle of Caporetto, also called the Twelfth and final battle of the Isonzo, had finished in mid-November with resounding Austro-German success, with the Italians pushed back to a line south of the Trent to the Piave and down to the Gulf of Venice. French and British reinforcements for Italy had been drawn from France, totalling 11 divisions under Plumer, thus weakening Allied strength on the Western Front.

But the most dramatic reports reached Ludendorff from the East. Russian peace feelers had become more tangible during November. On 2 December the Russian Armistice Commission crossed the German line at Dünaburg and travelled to Brest-Litovsk; the German C-in-C East was authorised to conclude an Armistice, which was signed on 15 December to last until noon, 14 January 1918.

At last, after over three years of struggle, Germany might be able to draw forces entirely from the East to face the West. 'How often,' exclaimed Ludendorff, 'had I not hoped for a revolution in Russia in order that our military burden might be alleviated! ... Now it had come true, and as a surprise. I felt as though a weight had been removed from my chest.'[23] On 18 December the Kaiser conducted a Crown Council meeting at Kreuznach to discuss peace terms with Russia; Ludendorff advocated the annexation of Russian territory in the Baltic region, but was opposed by Foreign Secretary Richard von Kühlmann and a further conference was arranged for 2 January 1918.[24]

'A quiet period, which our exhaustion rendered so imperatively necessary, supervened at last,' wrote Ludendorff. He was able to spend Christmas 1917 with Margarethe, and although the atmosphere remained sad with the memory of Franz, the General could relax for a few hours. Then he returned to his papers and continued his planning for the great spring offensive. Despite his anxieties and weariness, Ludendorff felt reasonably content – for perhaps the last time in his life.

CHAPTER SIXTEEN

Switch to the Offensive

LUDENDORFF'S HEALTH HAD RETURNED AND TRACES OF NERVOUS TENsion were temporarily lifted: officers at GHQ found him more relaxed and amenable, although he still kept himself apart in his usual lonely manner. Each day he walked or rode in the beautiful *Rosengarten* above the houses of Kreuznach, or, if time was short, in the grounds near the Oranienhof GHQ building. In the interests of exercise, he always walked from his villa to the office. 'My regular walks to and fro afford an opportunity to many kindly disposed people who wished to please me by their greetings, at times, by gifts of flowers. Otherwise I led a secluded existence because – I know men.'[1]

His work continued on a host of topics. 'It had,' commented Ludendorff, 'become quite the usual practice, when anything wanted doing at home, to appeal to me.' The German domestic situation had deteriorated, and Ludendorff involved himself with questions of food and fuel supplies. By this winter of 1917-18 many Germans were starving; some froze to death; cloth had become so scarce that soldiers were sometimes obliged to wear second-hand uniforms, taken from the dead. Talk of peace inevitably grew louder under these conditions.

Ludendorff also realised that war must be brought to an end soon. Politically, the German people might be unable to sustain another year; militarily, the immediate future looked satisfactory but further ahead the outlook seemed ominous. Britain and America had begun to gain the definite edge in the Battle of the Atlantic, and Ludendorff complained: 'The submarine war had not up to date produced those economic results which the Chief of the Naval Staff had expected, and which I, relying on the opinions of the experts, had hoped for.'[2] By 1918 a U-boat operating from the Baltic coast could only hope for six voyages before being destroyed. Above all, American troops would soon be playing a significant part in the European conflict: by January 1918 about 225,000 US soldiers had reached the Western Front, even though they had still to be organised into efficient fighting

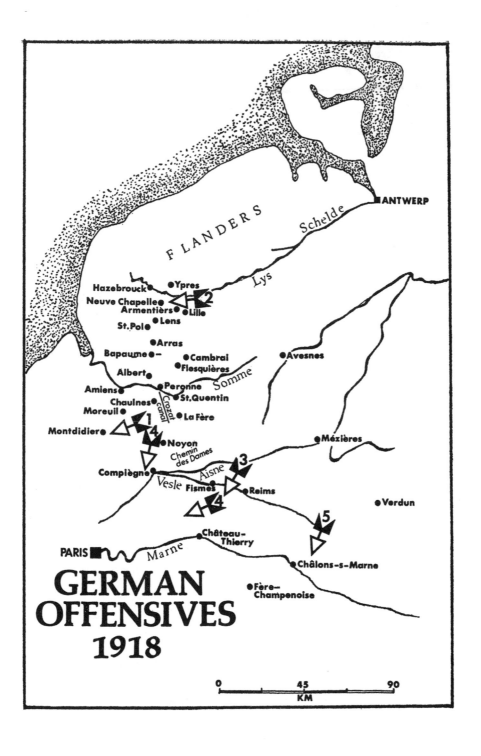

GERMAN
OFFENSIVES
1918

divisions. Ludendorff realised that Germany must strike decisively at the earliest possible moment.[3]

Staff officers assembled at Kreuznach on 27 December for further discussions on the proposed spring offensive. Ludendorff increasingly favoured the assault in the centre around St Quentin, code-named 'St Michael'. Detailed consideration was also given to questions of revised fighting methods on the lines of the Hutier system; Ludendorff in fact laid greater stress on tactics than on overall strategy. 'Tactics had to be considered before purely strategical objects which it is futile to pursue unless tactical success is possible.'[4]

At the beginning of January 1918 violent disagreement arose between Ludendorff and his most trusted assistant, Hoffmann. The episode was a tragic result of Ludendorff's prickly temper and inability to compromise. The two men had long held differing views over Germany's war aims and Hoffmann, promoted Major-General on 30 October, believed victory was by now impossible. He therefore advocated 'peace by compromise'.[5] Foreign Secretary Kühlmann, also opposed to acquisition of further territory, invited Hoffmann to talks in Berlin on New Year's Day; the Kaiser, impressed by this articulate officer, asked the Major-General to stay for lunch, during which he pressed him for his opinions. Hoffmann at first declined, fearing his remarks might be reported to Ludendorff, but Kaiser Wilhelm adopted a haughty stance: 'When Your All-Highest War Lord wishes to hear your views on any subject, it is your duty to give them to him, irrespective of whether they coincide with those of the High Command.' Hoffmann obeyed: he saw no advantage in pressing claims for Poland; Germany should only keep a small strip of Polish territory in the Bendzin-Thorn area for defensive purposes.[6]

The Kaiser's over-enthusiastic reaction to these remarks caused Hoffmann misgivings. He therefore tried to contact Ludendorff but failed – in fact Ludendorff was probably already travelling from GHQ to attend a Crown Council meeting scheduled for the following morning, 2 January. Hoffmann also attended this Bellevue Conference, and his fears were confirmed. The Kaiser repeated all the Major-General's ideas and finished by declaring: 'I base my conclusion on the judgment of an excellent and competent expert, namely, that of General Hoffmann, who is here.'

Ludendorff reacted as Hoffmann expected. The General's complexion deepened to purple, and his voice sounded as if the collar of his tunic were strangling him. He shouted that the Emperor had no right to canvass the opinions of officers over his, Ludendorff's, head; any line drawn on a map by the Emperor, resulting from this type of discussion, could most certainly not be accepted. Hindenburg muttered: 'We must certainly think this matter over carefully.' Wilhelm, appearing as uncomfortable as Hindenburg and Hoffmann, finally said: 'I will await your report.'[7]

This painful scene brought two results. First, the break between Ludendorff and Hoffmann would never be mended. As the historian Wheeler-Bennett put it: 'The symbol HLH (Hindenburg-Ludendorff-Hoffmann) was shattered. It had in fact become merely a gigantic L.'[8] Secondly, Ludendorff's outburst amounted to a direct challenge to the Kaiser, a claim that the Supreme Command could question the Emperor's right to act upon advice from whatever source. Moreover the issue could not be counted as purely military, involving as it did political and diplomatic considerations. And, with this challenge, Wilhelm had felt unable to assert Imperial authority. Nor did the Supreme Command oblige Wilhelm by sending the report which he had mentioned at the conference; instead, on 7 January he received a stiff letter from Hindenburg, clearly composed by Ludendorff:

In the Polish Question Your Majesty has chosen to place greater reliance upon the judgment of General Hoffmann than upon that of General Ludendorff and myself. General Hoffmann is my subordinate, and bears no responsibility whatsoever in the Polish Question. The events of 2 January have been the cause of pain to General Ludendorff and myself, and have shown us that Your Majesty disregards our opinion in a matter of vital importance for the existence of the German Fatherland.[9]

The Kaiser sent a hasty reply: a misunderstanding had arisen, he claimed, and no definite decision with regard to Poland had been taken. Wilhelm therefore confirmed his acquiesence to GHQ, although he refused to dismiss Hoffmann as demanded by Ludendorff. Another change did take effect, however: on 15 January Hindenburg told the Kaiser that the army had lost confidence in Rudolf von Valentini, Wilhelm's faithful Chief of the Civil Cabinet, whom GHQ believed to be 'entirely to blame for the swing to the left in the Government'. 'I don't want your paternal advice,' snapped the Kaiser, and Hindenburg hurried from the room to the sound of Wilhelm's shouts that Ludendorff was a 'malefactor with whom he would never shake hands again'. Yet Valentini still resigned, to be replaced by Friedrich von Berg, Ludendorff's nominee.[10]

One implication of the Supreme Command's dominating position would be upon the German attitude at the Brest-Litovsk peace talks with the Russian delegation. Trotsky arrived to head the Russian team during January, and appeared to be prevaricating. Ludendorff became increasingly impatient, and urged resumption of fighting at a conference held in Homburg on 13 February. Strong opposition came from Chancellor Hertling and from Kühlmann, but Ludendorff insisted that 'we should never get an honest peace from the Bolshevik leaders ... they would, as before, certainly continue to work for a revolution in Germany. This danger it was impossible to exaggerate.' Hertling eventually gave way, but the Foreign Secretary remained obdurate.

The Kaiser agreed with Ludendorff: hostilities would begin almost immediately. Ludendorff's victory reinforced his authority, and at the same time ruined all remaining chances of a satisfactory relationship with the Foreign Office.[11]

Guns began firing again on the Eastern Front during the afternoon of 18 February; German troops moved forward three hours later and by next morning were pushing deep into Russian territory. The enemy, racked by over three years of war and ruined by Revolution, offered minimal resistance. On 23 February an ultimatum was presented to the Soviets, allowing for only three days of talks; these began on 1 March, resulting in the Treaty of Brest-Litovsk on the third.

Germany dictated harsh terms, and the influence of the Supreme Command emerged in vivid fashion: the Kaiser was neither involved in, nor even informed of, all the details of the negotiations and merely agreed to the finished result. Russia was obliged to agree to the independence of Georgia and the Ukraine, to leave Poland, Estonia, Latvia and Lithuania to the disposition of Germany and Austria. Russian territory was reduced by over 1,200,000 square miles; the country lost 32 per cent of all arable land, 33 per cent of the industrial units, and as much as 75 per cent of the coal and iron mines. In addition, Russia agreed to halt all propaganda activity in Central Europe – a clause which Ludendorff considered especially important.

'The conditions of the peace of Brest were aimed at the Bolsheviks,' claimed Ludendorff, 'whose revolutionary propaganda made a chronic state of warfare against them unavoidable. It was no desire of mine to destroy Russia or to weaken her so that she could no longer exist.'[12]

This treaty was taken by the Allies – and by Ludendorff's critics in Germany – to show what the Supreme Command meant by peace: the Allies could now declare that Belgium would suffer a similar fate; it had become clear that whilst Hindenburg and Ludendorff remained in power the war would only end by rigorous defeat being inflicted on Germany. This in turn made the forthcoming spring offensives even more critical. And at dawn on 21 March, nineteen days after Germany's victory in the East, Ludendorff began his assault in the West. Only a few hours before, he had reported to the Kaiser: 'The Army is assembled and prepared to undertake the biggest task in its history.'[13]

Preparations had accelerated after the New Year. In mid-January Ludendorff toured the Western Front with the Chiefs of Staff of the 2nd and 4th Armies; on 21 January the final decision was taken to adopt plan 'St Michael' for an offensive in the St Quentin region. Three days later the first orders for the battle were issued by GHQ, and at the end of the month armies began to shuffle into position. The nature of this deployment revealed that Ludendorff intended to exert as much direct control as possible, rather than standing back and concerning himself only with broad decision. Thus the armies were divided into two army groups, one under Prince Rupprecht and the other under Crown Prince Wilhelm, whereas original discussions had only envisaged Rupprecht's forces being involved. As Ludendorff explained: 'I meant to exercise a far-reaching influence on the course of the battle. That was difficult if it was being conducted by one group only; every intervention was only too apt to become mere interference from above.'[14]

On 8 February Ludendorff fixed the provisional date for the attack as 21 March; four days later he warned the Kaiser against expecting an early decision: 'It must not be believed that we will have an offensive such as we had in Galicia or Italy; it will be a gigantic struggle beginning in one place, continuing in another, and demanding much time, which will be difficult but finally successful.'[15] The initial 'Michael' offensive might be followed by others as adjuncts, notably an assault at Arras code-named 'Mars'.

By mid-March German forces on the Western Front totalled 192 divisions, including 48 which had been moved from Italy and from the East during the previous four months. Of these, 63 divisions would be thrown forward on a 47-mile front between Arras and La Fère. The 17th Army, under General Otto von Below and forming part of Rupprecht's army group, would act as the right wing striking between Cambrai and Arras. The 2nd Army commanded by Marwitz and also in Rupprecht's group would thrust below Cambrai heading in the Péronne direction. The German left wing would comprise the 18th Army, in Crown Prince Wilhelm's group, which would be split into three main elements to strike to the north and south of St Quentin. Commanding the 18th was Hutier, newly-arrived on the Western Front from Italy.

Hutier's presence emphasised Ludendorff's preference for the tactics which bore this commander's name. As usual, Ludendorff involved himself with detailed preparations for the battle including tactical training, which he insisted must concentrate on the supreme importance of mobility: speed was more important than weight of numbers at any given point. 'The fighting line must be kept thin,' he declared, 'but must be constantly fed from behind ... It was necessary in the attack to adopt loose formations and work out infantry group tactics clearly.' Battle would begin with a brief but extremely intense artillery bombardment. 'This ... was expected to paralyse the enemy's artillery by means of gas which spread over great areas, and keep his infantry in their dug-outs. At the beginning of the infantry assault, the artillery ... was to put down a barrage in front of the infantry and then pave the way for it like a gigantic roller. The infantry had to keep close up to this wall of projectiles.' Once the first enemy lines had been breached, tactics should be as flexible as possible: 'The further the attack advanced, the more nearly its character approximated to that of open warfare.'[16]

The British C-in-C, Haig, visited the 3rd and 5th British Armies at the end of February, and he recorded on 2 March: 'I was only afraid that the enemy would find our front so very strong that he will hesitate to commit his army to the attack.'[17] Also early in March, Ludendorff left Kreuznach for new headquarters at Spa. Offices had been prepared in the Hotel Britannique, in which Ludendorff had billeted during the invasion of Belgium in 1914, and accommodation proved excellent with good meals, comfortable rooms and a pleasant atmosphere. But Ludendorff still believed GHQ to be too far from the front; almost immediately he searched for a new location further forward. Meanwhile he issued additional battle plans on 10 March: these left strategic aspects open, reflecting his attitude to tactics: much depended on circumstances as they arose, and he preferred to await the development of the battle rather than setting down rigid programmes.[18]

Preparations entered the final stages. The railway system, extended during previous weeks, worked to full capacity with most movement taking place at night. First the infantry and artillery headquarters took up position, together with the intelligence sections, followed by divisional headquarters, artillery and engineer staffs, ammunition depots, motor transport columns, then the artillery and labour companies, aircraft units and searchlight trains. Finally, during these first three weeks of March the bulk of the infantry moved forward, along with the bridge-building trains, army service corps, medical corps and field dressing stations.[19]

Ludendorff took responsibility for the whole gigantic programme. In addition he continued to supervise training, constantly introducing new elements. He devoted a great deal of attention to artillery methods, which he considered to be of critical importance. He described the problems involved: 'These masses of guns and ammunition had to be got up close to the foremost lines; only thus could they engage targets far behind the enemy's front line without having to change position as the battle progressed. At the same time, they had to be covered from view, both from the front and from the air ... Nor was it possible to register, as we used to do; this would have attracted the enemy's attention.'

New targeting techniques had therefore to be found. Ludendorff enlisted Hutier's chief gunner, Bruchmüller, as the main adviser; as far as possible this Colonel worked out everything prior to the battle, especially regarding accuracy. Thus the Artillery Meteorological Service collated balloon and aircraft findings and supplied artillery with latest wind and atmospheric densities; guns were tested behind the front for individual errors, for example alterations in the size of chamber caused by wear and other changes in the bore and carriage. Massive efforts were made to produce faultless maps.[20]

Guns and trench mortars began to move up on 11 March. By 15 March the ammunition dumps were completed. Next day the leading division for the 'Michael' offensive began the final stage of their move to the front. Bands played rousing marches, and the troops sang the favourite *Muss i denn, muss i denn*. Most of the men seemed extremely cheerful, given confidence by the massive preparations all around them. 'One can only be amazed again and again,' wrote one young lieutenant, Herbert Sulzbach, 'at the careful work done by headquarters and at the preparations being made down to the last detail – that is after all the source of our greatness.'[21]

On 18 March Ludendorff moved to new headquarters over the border into France, wanting to be in direct touch with the battle formations. He drove to Avesnes with Hindenburg during the evening, noting anxiously that the weather seemed to be changing: the last few weeks had been fine and clear, but storm-clouds had gathered during the afternoon of the 18th, and by the time Ludendorff reached Avesnes thunder was beginning to roll.

The dark weather seemed to match the austere Avesnes HQ. 'Our mess was at first very unpleasant,' remembered Ludendorff. Furniture was brought up from Spa since none could be found locally. The Kaiser arrived next day, 19 March, and declined to join the senior officers in the town; instead he lived in his sumptuous special train drawn up in a secluded siding.

Hindenburg had last visited Avesnes almost a half-century before, during the Franco-Prussian War. He seized an opportunity to walk through the streets of this quiet town embedded in the heart of peaceful woods. 'Even our presence added little to its activity . . . Compared with 1870–71 the different types I saw in the streets seemed to be so unchanged that I could easily have forgotten that there ever had been such an interval.'[22]

Ludendorff's nervous excitement began to show. On 20 March news reached him of further cause for anxiety: two German soldiers had deserted from a trench-mortar company on the 18th or 19th, and now it was believed they had betrayed details of the impending attack. And, at noon on the 20th, GHQ had to make the crucial decision as to whether the attack was to commence on schedule the following day.

'Every day must have increased the difficulties of the troops,' wrote Ludendorff, 'crowded together so close up to the enemy. Already the tension was very hard to bear. The psychological pressure of the mass was urging them forward.'[23]

On the other hand the German artillery would rely heavily on gas, in turn dependent on the direction and strength of the wind. Ludendorff's meteorologist, Lieutenant Dr Schmaus, presented his forecast at 11 am on the 20th. Previous reports indicated that strength and direction were unfavourable: this latest assessment revealed some improvement, although further storms were possible.

Ludendorff consulted Hindenburg at noon and declared the attack should go ahead; the Field-Marshal agreed, and the final and irrevocable orders were issued immediately. 'Now it could no longer be stopped,' declared Ludendorff. 'Everything must run its course ... The rest was in the hands of fate.'[24] He tried to find encouragement from his small prayer-book issued by the Moravian Brethren, which he always kept by the bed. During lunch on the 20th he turned to his neighbour, General von Tieschowitz and asked: 'Do you know tomorrow's text by the Brethren?' The puzzled officer shook his head. 'It is, "This is the day of the chosen people." ' Ludendorff added: 'Can we fail therefore to have confidence?'[25]

Remaining guns and trench mortars were positioned during the afternoon and evening of the 20th. Sights were set to prearranged figures and the weapons were swivelled to point at allotted British targets. Stormtrooper squads waited in the front trenches, ready to move forward behind the rolling barrage; slightly to the rear were massed the bulk of the German infantry – 47 divisions in the attacking forces of the 17th, 2nd and 18th Armies on a front of almost 60 miles. Mist thickened over the opposing lines at midnight, deadening noise and shrouding the trenches. At 4 am, 21 March 1918, German officers synchronised their watches three times for absolute accuracy, and the gunners moved to their posts. At 4.40 am a total of 6,473 cannon and mortars opened fire.

'Michael' represented the critical point in Ludendorff's career. Upon this battle rested his hopes for a victorious conclusion to the war. The alternative, both for Germany and for Ludendorff, was too frightening to contemplate. Four weeks earlier he had been asked by Prince Max of Baden what would be the consequence of failure; his reply was terrifying: 'Germany will just have to suffer annihilation.'

CHAPTER SEVENTEEN

Attack

GERMAN GUNS WERE DIRECTED WITH HORRIFIC EFFICIENCY FROM ONE target to another. They ranged here and there, alternating between gas and high explosive, probing and torturing the British batteries, headquarters, stores and trenches. British troops tumbled from their sleeping quarters and attempted to sort themselves out in the midst of the fog, gas and smoke.

'I awoke with a tremendous start, conscious of noise,' wrote an artillery officer in the British 3rd Army, 'incessant and almost musical, so intense that it seemed as if a hundred devils were dancing in my brain. Everything seemed to be vibrating – the ground, my dug-out, my bed . . . It was still dark.'[1]

The precise artillery programme went according to Ludendorff's plan. At 5 am the mine-throwers ceased firing; at 5.30 the main artillery switched from the British batteries to the trenches, with HE on the forward lines, mustard gas and lachrimatory shells further to the rear; at 5.40 the guns changed back to the British batteries and to communication centres; soon afterwards the trenches again became the main target. Dawn broke shortly before 6 am, but the fog still lay thick in the low ground. At about 9.35 some 3,500 mortars concentrated on the British forward zone, and then, at 9.40 am the fire came together without changing pace and formed the creeping barrage. According to the official British history: 'The German shells fell in parallel lines, five yards apart, the craters nearly touching.'

Behind this wall moved the German infantry. First rushed the small groups of shock troops. 'Suddenly,' wrote the British military historian Correlli Barnett, 'the pulse of war changed its rhythm from the slow, sluggish movement of long hibernation to the quick beat of rapid events.'[2]

Ludendorff sat behind his desk at Avesnes with telephone receivers constantly in his hands. He broke off for a moment and threw on his greatcoat, *pickelhaube* and ceremonial sword, and hurried outside to stand with Hindenburg for an official photograph, then he rushed back to his desk. Reports informed him that the rolling barrage was working excellently in the 18th Army sector to the south, satisfactorily with the 2nd Army in the centre, but less so with the 17th in the north – here, the barrage had gone too far ahead and contact had been lost with the infantry. Ludendorff also fretted over weather conditions: 'Unfavourable wind diminished the effectiveness of the gas, fog impeded and retarded our movements and prevented our superior training and leadership from reaping its full reward.'[3]

By midday the fog had dispersed; the German advance quickened, with the main lines pushing behind the shock troop spearheads. By 2 pm Hutier's 18th Army and the left wing of Marwitz's 2nd were pressing into Gough's 5th Army, and the forward groups were infiltrating down the valleys which formed tributaries of the Somme. Further north, German infantry made less progress through lack of close artillery support.

By nightfall German troops along the whole front had succeeded in ousting the British from their front line: the 17th Army, fighting against the heaviest opposition, had failed to break through the second line, but these defences had been penetrated by the 18th in the St Quentin region and Gough ordered a retreat behind the Somme and the Crozat Canal. British troops were already exhausted and many of them lacked battle experience – 19 out of the 21 divisions in the 3rd and 5th Army front lines had been engaged in the Passchendaele battles, during which they lost a large proportion of their most skilled soldiers, and replacements were inadequate both in numbers and training.[4]

Battle continued at almost the same tempo during the night of 21–22 March. Ludendorff assessed the day's results and issued orders accordingly – these instructions would later be heavily criticised. He had two choices with the limited amount of reserves at his disposal: either he could send additional forces to the northern sector, to help the stalled 17th Army, or he could direct these reinforcements to the south to increase the successes being achieved by Marwitz and especially by Hutier. Ludendorff chose the latter, with the decision reflecting his usual battlefield technique: the southern attack had clearly stabbed into the enemy's weakest point, and now he intended to attempt his favourite manoeuvre, an encirclement by the 18th and 2nd Armies while the 17th in the north acted almost as a pivot. Opportunities offered by the excellent results from the south seemed too good to be missed. 'The original idea of the battle had to be modified,' wrote Ludendorff, 'and the main weight of the attack directed vigorously on that point.'[5]

German forces advanced again on the morning of the 22nd. Fog reappeared over the undulating countryside to hamper both defenders and attackers. This time German divisions lacked both the artillery bombardment and surprise, and British reinforcements had arrived at some sections of the front. In the north the 17th Army made slow progress, taking British lines near Flesquières during the afternoon and reaching Tertry and Ytres by dusk. As on the 21st, Hutier's forces made the greatest contribution and by now Gough's 5th Army seemed on the point of collapse, with Hutier's advanced elements reaching the Crozat Canal and the Somme during the late afternoon.

The same pattern continued on the 23rd – only slow progress in the north, more spectacular success in the south. Both Below's 17th and Marwitz's 2nd were finding stubborn opposition, while Hutier's 18th had clearly torn huge holes in the British 5th. Eight out of the 11 original divisions in this British army were virtually defeated, and the Germans advanced about six miles during the day to force a gap between the British 5th and 3rd – hence rendering the latter more precarious since its wing would be increasingly exposed.

Yet 23 March also saw the beginnings of failure – for the offensive, for Germany, and for Ludendorff. Reasons stemmed from Ludendorff's handling of the battle but also from factors beyond his control. Always, Ludendorff maintained that strategic aims should be kept flexible, dependent on circumstances; this attitude, whilst undoubtedly having merits, also increased the danger of lack of cohesive step-by-step effort. The original aim of 'Michael' had been to prise the British from the French by forcing the British northwards with the 17th and 2nd Armies. Hutier's 18th had been assigned to cover this operation against French interference. This objective had been loosely drawn by Ludendorff, and, with Hutier's success, he had no hesitation in trying to exploit the southern advance.

Now, on 23 March, Ludendorff issued further orders. Hutier would swerve further south towards Noyon; the 2nd Army would push almost directly forward in the centre; in the north the 17th would wheel upwards in the Arras-St Pol direction, strengthened by elements of the 6th and 4th Armies. Ludendorff's aim seemed to be the creation of an encircling movement in the south, combined with another in the north. Such an offensive would have been catastrophic for the British, if successful: not only would they have been severed from the French, but they would also be surrounded.

Ludendorff has been criticised as revealing 'a state of mental restlessness and incoherence' with these orders.[6] Restlessness and over-ambition might be more correct. He sought a decisive victory, and he realised that another chance might never be presented. Mere severance of the British from the French may not have brought conclusive results since both armies would have remained in being, and his Eastern experience had emphasised that conquest of territory alone was insufficient. Ludendorff explained his policy at an Avesnes conference during the afternoon of the 23rd, attended by the army group Chiefs of Staff. 'The object is now to separate the French and British by a rapid advance on both sides of the Somme. The 17th and 6th Armies and

later the 4th Army will conduct the attack against the British north
of the Somme, in order to drive them into the sea. They will keep on
attacking at new places in order to bring the whole British front to
ruin.' Meanwhile the 18th would continue to cause havoc in the south,
widening the gap between the Allies.[7]

The gamble failed, since German strength was insufficient to follow
up the three lines of advance. Moreover the British fell back in retreat,
rather than allowing themselves to be surrounded, thus preventing the
Germans from reaching open country. In addition, at 4 pm on 23
March the British C-in-C Haig met the French commander Pétain
and appealed for support: two days before, Haig had asked for three
French divisions, now he sought 20 to be concentrated in the Amiens
area. Pétain also agreed to take over the British front as far as Peronne,
thus including the remnants of the 5th Army. These decisions amounted to a merger of the British line into the French – so reducing the
danger of a fatal gap between the two.

Outwardly, it still seemed the Germans were moving forward to
victory. And as if to underline German supremacy, and revive memories of the glorious victories in the Franco-Prussian War, during the
day the French had been subjected to a different form of attack. At
7.15 am an explosion blasted the Quai de Seine in the 19th *Arrondisse-
ment* of Paris; fifteen minutes later another explosion erupted, then a
third. After much speculation and considerable panic, the French
realised they were being bombarded by a massive gun able to project
its shells across the 60-mile space between the capital and the nearest
German lines. In fact the so-called Paris Gun, known to the Germans
as the *Kaiser Wilhelm Geschütz,* had been developed by Krupps and
comprised a 38-cm naval weapon lined down to a 21-cm with a pro-
jecting inner tube. The barrel had been further extended, to a length
of 130 feet, providing extra range. The bombardment would continue
at intervals until 9 August, with 183 shells landing in Paris and 120
outside; 256 people were killed, but after the first few days business
returned to normal.[8]

News of the opening shots – 23 being fired on the first day – brought
fresh exultation to many at the German GHQ. During the evening of
23 March the Kaiser rushed back to Berlin to report progress and to
reveal the existence of the gun which bore his name. 'His Majesty
returned from Avesnes bursting with news of our success,' wrote
Admiral von Müller. 'He shouted to the guard on the platform as the
train pulled in: "The battle is won! The English have been utterly
defeated." There was champagne for dinner. The communiqué was
read telling of our great victory under the personal leadership of His
Majesty.' Hindenburg received the Iron Cross with Golden Rays, last
awarded to Blücher after Waterloo.[9]

During the evening of this 23 March Ludendorff's preoccupation
with the battle suffered a painful interruption. His youngest stepson

Erich was now a pilot, following his eldest brother Franz's lead; now Ludendorff learnt that Erich had been shot down behind the British lines. 'The war has spared me nothing.' He immediately telephoned Margarethe, who wrote: 'I was alone in the room ... I felt the full force of the blow. I do not know what happened. I only know that I collapsed.' A few weeks later, after the battle line had ebbed forward, Ludendorff was informed that a rough grave had been found bearing the inscription in English: 'Here rest two German pilots'; nearby were the remains of a charred aircraft. Ludendorff immediately ordered the bodies to be exhumed and he drove to the site, where he identified Erich. He told Margarethe that her son had been wrapped in a shroud by the English, 'and his features wore a look of peace'.[10]

Progress still seemed satisfactory on 24 March. Yet although Hutier continued to drive for the line Chaulnes-Noyon, his forward units were about eight miles short of this target by nightfall, despite the absence of firm resistance. The momentum of the advance had begun to flag. In the north the 2nd and 17th Armies made some advance, and Bapaume fell, but again the specified objectives were not reached. This pattern became more pronounced on the 25th. By now the 17th Army was clearly exhausted; the 2nd Army, slightly fresher, found the going difficult since the divisions had to struggle across the old Somme battlefield, riddled with shell craters and abandoned trenches. The 18th gained more ground and Ludendorff attempted to take further advantage by directing the left wing of the 2nd Army south in support: these divisions could combine with the 18th Army for a push on Amiens.

An air of desperation surrounded these latest orders. Ludendorff commented later:

> The enemy's line was now becoming denser and in places they were even attacking, while our armies were no longer strong enough to overcome them unaided. The ammunition was not sufficient, and supply became more difficult. The repair of roads and railways was taking too long, in spite of all our preparations.[11]

By 25 March the British 5th Army had virtually disintegrated. But French and British reserves were being thrown into the line, and in the north the British 3rd Army still blocked the German advance. The Allied situation in this sector improved further on the 26th; according to the official British history: 'On this day the crisis on the front of the 3rd Army may be said to have ended.'[12] Also on the 26th the Allied commanders met in the small, red-brick town of Doullens. Haig noted that Pétain looked 'terrible' and had 'the appearance of a Commander who was in a funk and had lost his nerve'. By contrast General Ferdinand Foch, now technical adviser to the French Government, seemed aggressive and determined. 'We must fight in front of Amiens,' declared Foch. 'We must fight where we are now ... We must not retire a single inch.' Haig immediately responded to this invigorating attitude: 'If General Foch will consent to give me his advice, I will gladly follow it.'[13] In this way Foch became Allied Co-ordinator, with his title elevated to Supreme Commander on 3 April, and use of Allied resources would now be better allocated and controlled.

Ludendorff attempted to urge his exhausted forces forward, especially the 17th Army. 'He was quite beside himself,' commented Crown Prince Rupprecht after a telephone call on the 26th, 'and dissatisfied with the Chief of Staff, whom he talked of removing.'[14] At 7.30 am on 28 March forces in the Arras sector attempted to push forward in Operation 'Mars', but by afternoon this offensive had been blocked with heavy losses. German units were being fought to a standstill along the whole front. Ludendorff drove forward to see the commanders through a scene of utter desolation: 'The impression it made was great – a strip, many miles in width, bleak and devastated.'[15]

Fresh supplies were rushed forward, and on 4 April the 18th Army again began to batter towards Amiens. Almost immediately Hutier's divisions met unsurmountable opposition. 'The battle was over,' declared Ludendorff. 'It was a brilliant feat, and will be so regarded in history.' In vain he sought for encouragement from the results – 'What the English and French had not succeeded in doing we had accomplished, and that in the fourth year of the war ... Our troops had beaten the French and English and proved themselves superior ... Our tactics had proved sound ...'[16]

The new front stretched from east of Arras through Albert and round via Moreuil and Montdidier to Noyon, representing an advance at the deepest point of the salient of about 17 miles. Allied losses since 1 March amounted to about 163,000 British and 77,000 French including prisoners. But German casualties were at least as high, especially among the specially trained shock troops.

Ludendorff still hoped for decisive results from 'Michael', not in the same sector but by attacking elsewhere to take advantage of weakness caused by withdrawal of Allied troops. The next offensive would be launched in Flanders, declared Ludendorff, on both sides of the river Lys. The code-name was 'Georgette', originally intended to be 'St George' but changed to a diminutive since only 11 divisions would be available – compared to 47 in the initial attacking strength for 'Michael'.

This assault opened at 4.05 am, 9 April – Ludendorff's fifty-third birthday. Once again Colonel Bruchmüller had organised the bombardment, with similar success. Three Portuguese brigades holding the line north of Neuve Chapelle collapsed under the barrage, and by noon German units had advanced through the gap in the direction of Hazebrouck. Forty-eight hours later elements of Ferdinand von Quast's 6th Army were within five miles of this town; Armentières had fallen. Next day, 12 April, Haig issued his famous Order of the Day: 'There is no other course open to us but to fight it out. Every position must be held to the last man. There must be no retirement. With our backs to the wall and believing in the justice of our cause each one must fight to the end . . .'

Gradually the German advance slowed and halted, and for the same reasons as with 'Michael' – lack of supplies, especially since these had to be brought over countryside devastated by four years of war, lack of artillery support after the initial advance, and the steadily stiffening resistance. The struggle continued throughout April, but 'Georgette' had never obtained the same momentum as 'Michael' and by 29 April the battle was over.

Ludendorff still refused to accept the appalling alternative to victory even though this was becoming increasingly inevitable. The weariness of his troops and the rapid ebb of fighting spirit became more noticeable with each attack. So many good men had gone, and newcomers were often inadequately trained. Officers were no better, and one of Ludendorff's sentences in his memoirs was especially chilling: 'We had reached such a pitch that before an action units detailed a reserve of officers, who did not take part in the fighting, in order that there might be some leaders left at the end of it.'[17] Ludendorff also became even more convinced that the Communists were undermining his army and polluting still further the poor material being sent to the front. In turn, this belief strengthened his hostility towards politicians, especially the Independent Socialists.

Ludendorff later claimed that an opportunity for peace had existed in late March: 'Michael' had provided Germany with an excellent card to play. 'The defeat produced an overwhelming impression on the enemy. In spite of my requests we did nothing in the diplomatic sense to utilise it.'[18] Supporters and opposers of annexation had continued to argue, with the debate closely linked to other domestic political issues; Chancellor Hertling attempted to avoid clear-cut statements; Wilhelm had retreated into a policy of ambivalence and into an attitude of injured pride. 'The Kaiser is ignored by both sides,' Wilhelm complained during the spring.[19]

Suffering from the war was increasing each day – starvation, privation, denial of human rights. By now clear indications existed that the majority of the German people wanted almost immediate peace regardless of war aims. Disturbances were becoming more common and more acute: on 28 January about 400,000 workers in Berlin had gone on strike, with their first demand being: 'Speedy conclusion of peace without annexations and indemnities, on the basis of the self-determination of peoples.' In mid-February the *Frankfurter Zeitung* addressed an open letter to the Supreme Command which declared: 'The course of events might be such that considerable sections of the people will prefer any peace, peace at any price, to the continuation of the war.'[20]

Now, in May, Ludendorff prepared to continue the war. He saw no other choice. But such were the weaknesses of his armies, and so inadequate were resources arriving from the flagging Fatherland, that it took almost a month for a fresh offensive to be organised. This delay served as a telling contrast to the speed with which Ludendorff had once been able to shift forces from one offensive to another.

Since 21 March 1918 over 348,000 Germans had been lost on the Western Front. Units were becoming fewer and smaller: the average field strength of a battalion at the end of 1917 had been about 900 men; after deductions for the sick, those on leave and those seconded, the average fighting strength was about 640 men. By the end of February the official field strength had dropped to 807 men, and to 692 by the end of May representing an actual fighting strength of under 500.[21] Insufficient flow of fresh manpower meant that the only way to boost these figures was to reduce the number of battalions per regiment and the number of regiments in each brigade, and so on up the line.

Chronic shortages existed in all kinds of war material, from artillery shells to simple medical supplies. Surgeon Stephen Westman described his delight in finding a British Medical Corps depot still intact. 'For months the German doctors had had to use crêpe paper bandages, like toilet rolls, to cover wounds, and one can imagine how long these flimsy dressings lasted. Instead of cotton wool, we used a kind of cellulose paper, which in no time got soaked with blood and pus and just dissolved into a wet and stinking mass.'[22]

Yet during these weeks Germany's latest enemy was increasing rapidly in size and effectiveness. At the end of May the figure of American troops on the Western Front stood at 667,119, and the rate of arrival was accelerating, together with disembarkation of latest war equipment.[23]

Ludendorff's next assault would continue his previous policy of attempting to roll up the British front and thrust this enemy back into the sea. But conditions were changing rapidly. Strategically, the greatest rewards were likely to result from resuming the attack in Flanders by striking at Ypres and Bailleul, but chances of victory were minimal. 'On that front the enemy was now so strong in numbers that it was impossible,' commented Ludendorff. 'Before we could attack here again, the enemy must be weakened and our communications improved.'[24] Ludendorff therefore planned the first assaults to be launched further south against the Chemin des Dames in the Château-Thierry region, aimed at drawing off enemy strength from the north.

Drawbacks were fully appreciated by Ludendorff: the May offensive against the Chemin des Dames would amount to a preliminary step, with the main assault therefore delayed until at least June. Such a programme would have better suited armies which were growing in strength, rather than those becoming steadily weaker – troops lost in the first phase would be extremely difficult to replace for the second. 'We dare not risk failure, which would have taken the form of great losses, by undue haste. I could not act according to my wishes and hopes, but simply deal with the facts as they actually were.'[25] A memorandum issued by Supreme Command in May declared the task to consist of 'shaking the hostile edifice by closely connected partial blows in such a way that sooner or later the whole structure would collapse'.[26]

Publicly, Ludendorff still insisted a decisive victory could be gained. But the wording of this May memorandum failed to specify whether the intended enemy collapse would be military or political, and the plan for 'closely connected partial blows' seemed to indicate a war of attrition rather than seeking a decisive victory in battle. Yet such a drawn-out strategy would have been impossible, given the existing military and political state of Germany. Ludendorff was caught in a dilemma from which there seemed to be no escape except through complete defeat.

In mid-May Ludendorff held a revealing conversation with Colonel von Haeften, the GHQ representative at the Foreign Office who was then attempting to reconcile the views of Ludendorff and Kühlmann. According to Haeften's report, Ludendorff admitted that 'there is no chance of deciding the war in the field unless the combatant forces are reinforced by some 200,000 men of the right quality'. Haeften commented: 'Ludendorff's remarks clearly showed me the necessity of bringing the war to a rapid conclusion. Military force no longer sufficed to decide the issue, and it was necessary to have recourse to political and diplomatic means.'[27]

Ludendorff's tragedy approached its peak. For almost a month he had been exhausting himself to prepare for an offensive the success of which he doubted. At the most, all he could do was obtain military leverage for use by diplomats and politicians – in whom he had no trust. Now, at 1 am on 27 May, the German batteries again began to fire.

CHAPTER EIGHTEEN

The Threatened Fatherland

OVER 1,150 GUNS TOOK PART IN THE OPENING BOMBARDMENT ON 27 May 1918, ranging as far as 12 miles behind the enemy line. At dawn infantry in the German 1st and 7th Armies moved forward in Operation 'Blücher': a total of 17 divisions in the first assault against four French divisions and three exhausted British that had been transferred from the Amiens front which made up the French 6th Army. The Chemin des Dames was stormed within a few hours, and German troops streamed across the Aisne to reach the Vesle by evening – an advance of over 12 miles. The attackers continued to thrust forward next day, and the next: by evening on 29 May the leading units were beyond Soissons and twenty-four hours later had reached the Ourcq.

This dramatic advance caught the German GHQ by surprise. 'I had thought we should only succeed in reaching the neighbourhood of Soissons and Fismes,' wrote Ludendorff. 'By the second and third days these objectives had been left far behind.'[1] The Allies still held Reims to the south, but Paris lay less than sixty miles away. By the beginning of June the German centre had pushed up to Château-Thierry. Then, as before, Allied resistance became stronger and more troops were rushed to the threatened area – including two US divisions – and on 5 June the offensive came to a halt.

The very success of their thrust brought dangers to the attackers. The Germans occupied a salient nearly forty miles deep, in which communications were insufficient – railways were ruined by the fighting – and the flanks were extremely vulnerable to counter-attack, especially from the south. Ludendorff ordered a further offensive in this section of the Western Front, aimed at strengthening the position in the salient; but this could only be at the expense of the scheduled thrust in Flanders for which 'Blücher' had been a preliminary.

On 9 June Hutier's 18th Army attacked north of the new salient, striking at the French 3rd Army between Noyon and Montdidier. This time the enemy were well prepared, with French forces organised in depth. Hutier's infantrymen managed to advance nine miles and they captured the heights of Compiègne, but heavy Franco-American counter-attacks on 10 June prevented further moves forward. Secondary assaults south-west of Soissons also failed to make progress, while at Château-Thierry German troops suffered heavily from the 2nd US Division.

By mid-June the Western Front was again relatively quiet. Once more the Germans had obtained dramatic successes yet lacked strength to go further, and Ludendorff's plans for Flanders had had to be put aside. 'Again and again our thoughts returned to the idea of an offensive in Flanders ... But an offensive at this point still presented too difficult a problem. We had to postpone it.'[2] Instead an attack would be mounted on Reims, to strengthen the southern salient.

German resources were so deficient that the Reims operation would not be possible until July, and the delay could be disastrous. Ludendorff's optimism sounded increasingly hollow. 'There were hopes that if the offensive at Reims succeeded, there would be a very decisive weakening of the enemy in Flanders.' Yet he added: 'I gave serious thought to the question whether, in view of the spirit of the Army and the condition of our reserves, it would not be advisable to adopt the defensive.' The dilemma grasped Ludendorff in an even tighter grip. 'I finally decided against this policy, because quite apart from the bad influence it would have on our Allies, I was afraid that the Army would find defensive battles an even greater strain than an offensive, as such a policy would make it easy for the enemy to concentrate.'[3]

On 1 June, even while the latest assault had seemed to be going well, Crown Prince Rupprecht sent a letter to Hertling providing evidence of Ludendorff's fears. 'General Ludendorff shares my view that in all probability a crushing defeat of the enemy is out of the question; he is now resting his hopes upon the succour of a *deus ex machina* in the shape of an internal collapse in the Western Powers.' Rupprecht did not agree with these hopes of some kind of miraculous intervention and stressed to Hertling the necessity of taking steps to obtain peace.[4]

Ludendorff's problems multiplied daily. Spanish influenza swept through the German forces in June, with the epidemic especially severe since the men were already weakened through dietary deficiencies. By July the official field strength of each battalion was reduced still further; men reaching the front were even younger – early in 1918 the first recruits of the 1899 class were sent to divisions, now, in mid-June, the 1900 class were being called up. Manpower brought from the Eastern Front often led to detrimental results. 'The men arriving from the East,' wrote General von Kuhl in an official report after the war, 'were in many cases infected by Bolshevism.' Other newcomers had previously worked in armaments factories earning high wages, 'some of whom were inflamed with anti-militaristic ideas and exercised a fresh disintegrating influence on the Army'. Others were physically weak. 'Thrown into strange society, unknown to their superiors and comrades, they brought no accession of strength to the troops but merely increased the numbers of the unreliable.'[5] Signs of revolt among the troops were becoming increasingly common; desertion was presenting a serious difficulty, leading Ludendorff to publish a harsh order on 23 June: all deserters would henceforth be executed and their property seized.

On 24 June the Foreign Secretary rose in the Reichstag to make a speech on peace talks. Kühlmann declared: 'Without some exchange of views, considering the tremendous extent of this war of coalitions and the number of Powers ... involved in it, an absolute end can hardly be expected from military decisions alone.'[6] This public declaration was violently opposed by Ludendorff: the Foreign Secretary's words amounted to an admission of defeat. And even if Kühlmann's statements were justified, they were extremely unwise. Count Kuno von Westrap, the Conservative spokesman, immediately criticised the speech as a threat to Germany's morale at home and at the front.

Hindenburg and Ludendorff demanded Kühlmann's dismissal. The Kaiser hesitated for another two weeks, during which the Supreme Command refused to have any further dealings with the Foreign Secretary. 'His name will always be associated with the entry of the Bolsheviks into Berlin,' declared Ludendorff.[7] Chancellor Hertling was obliged to make a pathetic apology for the Foreign Secretary at a conference at Spa on 1 July: 'Von Kühlmann's speech was not delivered in happy circumstances. He was tired, and had not had time to prepare himself ... He had not even time for breakfast, which accounted for his weak delivery.'[8] Finally, on 8 July Kühlmann was replaced by Admiral Paul von Hintze, and the annexationists claimed a major victory.

The Spa Conference, which lasted from 1 to 3 July, was significant for other reasons. The Kaiser, Hertling, Hindenburg and Ludendorff found themselves in agreement over the policy to be pursued. The object of the war would be 'to exert full pressure against England'; meanwhile, Germany was ready 'to hear England if approached, with the proviso that all steps taken must be of dignity due to the German effort'.

The conference also took a firm stand on the question of war aims, with Hindenburg and Ludendorff finally clarifying their position on the crucial Belgian issue. According to the military leaders, Belgium must be brought into the closest possible relationship with Germany by measures such as customs union, community of railways and other transport systems; Flanders and Wallonia should be separated into two individual states. German occupation must continue for an extended period over the country as a whole, troops must remain in the Flanders coastal region and at Liège longer than those positioned elsewhere, and any evacuation must depend on the extent to which

Belgium bound herself to Germany. Hindenburg and Ludendorff had their way at Spa, where the conference declared: 'Belgium must remain under German influence, so that she cannot again fall under Anglo-French domination, and thus offer our enemies bases for their armies . . . There must be no Belgian army. Germany must secure for herself a long period of occupation with gradual withdrawal . . .'[9]

Ludendorff's attitude was consistent: as far as possible Germany must protect herself from a future two-front threat. This motive lay behind his demands, whether concerning territory in the East or West; contrary to claims made later by his critics, his ambitions were far different from those of Hitler in the Second World War: he believed that territory must be obtained, perhaps only temporarily, not for reasons of simple expansion and conquest, but for reasons of military security. With Belgium, Ludendorff also remembered the stiff fight put up by the defenders during the German advance in 1914 which had threatened to delay the vital thrust into France. But Ludendorff, thinking as a soldier, paid insufficient regard to the diplomatic consequences of his demands, and in fact the Spa statements were completely irreconcilable – a willingness to negotiate with Britain, yet with Germany insisting on a policy towards Belgium which would be utterly unacceptable to Britain. Any peace attempts started on such a basis would inevitably fail.

But a military solution seemed increasingly impossible. 'Talks with General Ludendorff,' noted Colonel Mertz von Quirnheim, on the GHQ staff, in his diary on 2 July. '[He] describes how there is sometimes a low ebb in the higher echelon of the command. Therefore the whole burden falls on himself. I advised him against continuing the offensive. He was straining the bow too much. But he felt he must risk it.'[10]

Military preparations entered the final stage. The plans entailed a two-pronged attack to isolate Reims: the 7th Army, under Boehn, would cross the Marne between Château-Thierry and Reims aiming for Fère-Champenoise; the 1st and 3rd Armies, under Bruno von Mudra and von Einem, would attack east of Reims with Châlons-sur-Marne the principal objective. Many of the units had previously fought in the advance over the Chemin des Dames. 'This was a heavy demand on the troops,' wrote Ludendorff, 'but the position required it.'[11]

The offensive opened on 15 July. It would be Ludendorff's last. He seemed full of confidence as the troops went forward; Colonel Mertz wrote later:

The General threw himself with all his characteristic energy on to the enemy at the Marne, and with fullest trust in the successful outcome. This energy was the more astonishing since he had had to overcome considerable doubts expressed to him by experienced colleagues. He had also to overcome some hesitations in his own mind ... It was critical for General Ludendorff that the war should be ended in 1918. No risk and no sacrifice were too great.[12]

'Who does not dare does not win,' wrote Crown Prince Wilhelm. 'We had to dare again and again since we were in the most critical situation. Until now the soldier's luck had always been with General Ludendorff – the luck of the expert ... Why should it turn its back on him now?'[13]

Leading divisions of the 7th Army west of Reims battered through French defences during the first day, and by nightfall six German divisions were across the Marne, establishing a bridgehead four miles deep. East of Reims the situation was far different: attacking troops in the German 1st and 3rd Armies were repulsed by strongly positioned French units supported by artillery beyond the accurate range of German guns. The attack in this sector failed to make ground and soon halted.

Ludendorff immediately contacted Klewitz, Chief of Staff of the 3rd Army, and declared: 'Why is the attack not continuing? It must be pushed through.' Klewitz answered quietly that the French had moved back their artillery, and German guns were insufficient to establish a strong enough rolling barrage for the advancing infantry. Ludendorff's tone immediately became less hostile. 'I agree of course with the cessation of the attack. I am the last one to order senseless bloody sacrifice. The army has done everything that was humanly possible.'[14]

The sacrifice would be too much. Yet by agreeing to the halt of the attack east of Reims, Ludendorff acknowledged that the successful advance by the 7th Army west of Reims would be largely nullified: such an advance could not continue unsupported. Ludendorff's conversation with Klewitz on the night of the 15th amounted to a recognition that the offensive as a whole had already failed. During the night he also telephoned General von Kuhl, Rupprecht's Chief of Staff on the Flanders front. Kuhl recorded that Ludendorff was 'very sad about the very small result' at Reims; Kuhl's account continued: 'I advised Ludendorff all the same to continue the attack today [16 July] with the 1st and 3rd Armies. But he thought that we would risk heavy losses.' Rupprecht's Chief of Staff criticised this decision. 'We cannot expect anything great at all – nothing great will ever be achieved without losses.'

'Fairly depressed mood,' reported Mertz in his diary on the 16th. 'Difficult question – what should happen from now on?'[15] In fact, with the abandonment of the attack east of Reims, the troops across the Marne to the west had to be withdrawn as soon as possible. Yet further complications existed: the withdrawal could not take place immediately, as the few bridges over the Marne were under incessant enemy artillery fire and were constantly being bombed or machine-gunned by enemy aircraft. 'We had to make arrangements for crossing before the retreat could even begin,' commented Ludendorff. On the 17th the withdrawal was fixed for the night of 20–21 July.

Yet Ludendorff had still to abandon his final hopes for an attack in Flanders. He drove north to Prince Rupprecht's HQ on the 17th, and urgent discussions on the possible offensive took place throughout most of the night. These were continuing next morning when news reached Ludendorff that the Allies had begun to strike back. French troops of General Charles Mangin's 10th Army had stabbed into the Marne salient south-west of Soissons; ominously, the assault was spearheaded by the US 1st and 2nd Divisions. By noon the offensive had gained four miles.

Ludendorff immediately telephoned orders for valuable reserves to be used to stem this breach in the German lines; talks with Rupprecht were ended – 'naturally in a state of the greatest nervous tension' wrote Ludendorff – and he rushed back to GHQ by train. He reached Avesnes at 2 pm on the 18th, to be met at the station by the extremely anxious Hindenburg. They hurried back to the Operations Room to hear that the French offensive seemed to be gathering frightening momentum. For the moment Ludendorff could do nothing; his reserves were being committed. 'All counter-measures that could be adopted were already under way. At that moment GHQ was unable to give any further help ... We could only await further developments.'[16]

This wait became almost unbearable. All Ludendorff's inclinations were to hit back. Yet insufficient troops were available. And Ludendorff's frustration led to startling behaviour on 19 July – a critical day which marked the General's decline in spirit and would lead critics to say he suffered from a mental breakdown during the final weeks of war.

During the morning General von Lossberg, Chief of Staff of the 4th Army, arrived at GHQ to deliver a report. Ludendorff appeared to be 'in a really agitated and nervous state'. Lossberg wrote:

To my regret, he made some very unjustified remonstrances against the Chief of the Operations Section and others of his colleagues who, he implied, had 'failed' in their assessment of the fighting forces. This scene was a really painful one. The Chief of the Operations Section, Wetzell, said nothing, like a good soldier, but obviously he found these rebukes hard to take. Tears came to his eyes from his inner emotion, which he otherwise fought down bravely.

Thirty minutes later Lossberg was called in again by Ludendorff and told that the enemy attacks had continued. 'Heavy cracks seemed to have been made ... Ludendorff seemed very depressed.' This depression deepened when Lossberg submitted his proposals: he recommended a withdrawal of all troops at the Marne salient and westwards, back to the Siegfried Line; German forces should move on to the defensive despite all the implications which this might entail. Ludendorff was silent when Lossberg finished speaking, then said: 'I find your proposals feasible. But I can't carry them through because of political considerations.' Lossberg asked what these could be, and Ludendorff answered: 'Considerations regarding the impressions on the enemy and on our army and on our Fatherland.' Lossberg declared that a commander could only be misled if he believed political factors should outweigh military reality; again Ludendorff fell silent, then suddenly said that if Lossberg was correct 'I shall ask the Field-Marshal for my dismissal.' He insisted on going to see Hindenburg but returned to say that his request to leave GHQ had been refused.[17]

Other staff officers doubted if Ludendorff did in fact make the attempt to resign. But all agreed that the General was in acute distress at this period; Mertz wrote later that Ludendorff 'suffered to the verge of emotional collapse' as a result of the French offensive, 'and at times lost control of himself'.[18] His mental turmoil undoubtedly lay behind his reaction to a proposal put forward by Hindenburg on the 19th. The Field-Marshal believed the opposite to Lossberg – rather than withdrawal, German forces must be thrown forward in the Marne area.

During dinner, with officers sitting tensely around the table and with Ludendorff barely speaking, Hindenburg suddenly turned to Mertz and declared: 'I think that the simplest and best solution would be to lead all the troops, including those from Flanders, across the heights north-west of Soissons south against the enemy's left flank.' Ludendorff interrupted: 'Such a thing would be completely unfeasible and therefore impossible. I thought I'd already made that perfectly clear.' The officers sat astonished by this outburst; Hindenburg said nothing, simply rising from the table and leaving the dining hall. Ludendorff stormed out in another direction.

But Hindenburg refused to drop his idea. During the evening conference he leant over the table and almost casually repeated the proposal, sweeping his left hand over the map in front of him. 'Nonsense,' snapped Ludendorff. Hindenburg stared at the General then muttered: 'I must speak with you.' Both men left the room and entered Ludendorff's office. The Field-Marshal later informed Mertz that he had told the First Quartermaster to remember his position, but according to Wetzell, Chief of Operations, 'the temporary discord did not tarnish the official or personal relationship', and he believed Ludendorff's behaviour stemmed from the fact that Hindenburg never usually bothered with such military matters.[19]

Allied troops continued to push forward south of Soissons. Oldershausen wrote in his diary on 20 July: 'During mealtime, conversation with His Excellency Ludendorff about difficult battles. Ludendorff inwardly very excited. Hardly eats anything.'[20] That night troops were brought back over the Marne from the bridgehead created by the 15 July advance around Reims: many of these units immediately joined the reserves now arriving to block the Allied attack near Soissons, and for the moment the defence held. Fighting died down slightly on 21 and 22 July.

Ludendorff knew this relative lull would be short, and the situation in the whole salient remained critical as far down as Reims. Communications to this salient were inadequate; Reims still held out and threatened German links to the rear; further Allied successes south of Soissons could be disastrous. During 22 July Ludendorff sent out staff officers to examine the various local positions, and these reports were presented during the evening. They confirmed Ludendorff's fears: he therefore sought and obtained Hindenburg's approval for a partial withdrawal 30 miles back from the Marne to the Vesle, with the first stage to take place on the night of 26–27 July. This would bring all forces back behind Soissons. But it also meant that Hutier's 18th Army, further north around Noyon, would be dangerously exposed and must therefore receive further reinforcements, and these could only come from Rupprecht's army group. Ludendorff had to abandon any final hope of an offensive in Flanders.[21]

Orders were issued immediately. And with the fateful decision taken, Ludendorff appeared to be calmer. 'His Excellency Ludendorff seems far quieter,' observed Oldershausen in his diary of 23 July. Then, as the dangerous time of manoeuvring back to the Vesle approached, Ludendorff's nerves again began to suffer. Colonel Mertz watched his behaviour with an agonised fascination, in common with the other officers at GHQ.

'Serious question about the nervousness of His Excellency,' noted Mertz on 24 July. 'His Excellency is working himself into the ground – he bothers too much about details. This situation is really serious.' Next day Mertz commented that Count Schwerin, Chief of Staff of the German Balkan Army, had passed through Avesnes and had also noticed Ludendorff's deterioration. 'Schwerin is highly worried by the appearance and nervousness of His Excellency. He really gives the impression of having lost all confidence. The army commanders suffer tremendously because of this.'[22]

Disengagement and withdrawal from the Marne salient began during the night of the 26th – 'according to plan and in perfect order,' noted Ludendorff with relief. Once again his tension eased slightly. 'Ludendorff's mood seems to have become better in all respects,' wrote Mertz on the 29th. 'Reason for this the comparative quietness at the front. The breakdown of his nerves has not been altogether glorious ... The Field-Marshal seemingly and unfortunately did not give any help.'

By 2 August the line had been straightened and the immediate military danger was removed. Yet Ludendorff and Hindenburg both knew that other dangers had intensified, of a political nature. The Field-Marshal wrote later: 'We could have no illusions about the far-reaching effects of this battle and our retreat. From the purely military point of view it was of the greatest and most fateful importance that we had lost the initiative to the enemy ... The effect of our failure on the country and our Allies was even greater.'[23]

Ludendorff feared that the setback on the military front could lead to domestic upheaval, and in turn bring further military catastrophe. On 23 July Mertz had written in his diary: 'His Excellency seems to feel that it is absolutely necessary for something to be done to revive his prestige. But what?' Nicolai, head of the GHQ Intelligence Section, revealed in a private letter on 28 July that Ludendorff constantly pestered him for reports on the political situation inside Germany.[24]

The General struggled to find a new strategy, acceptable to both the military and home fronts; his conclusions emerged in a directive issued from Avesnes on 2 August. The policy would be to adopt strategic defence combined with tactical offence in selected areas. 'The situation demands that on the one hand we prepare ourselves for defence, but on the other hand that we go over to the attack as soon as possible ... With these attacks ... it is less important that we should gain territory than we should inflict defeat on enemy forces and secure more favourable positions.'[25]

Even now Ludendorff refused to relinquish all hopes of gaining sufficient military success to bring about peace terms which he considered acceptable; even now his energy could be transmitted to others. Major Alfred Niemann visited GHQ on 3 August and had talks with Ludendorff. He noted signs of serious mental and physical strain, and the General's limbs seemed stiff as if the muscles were tensed. But 'into the excited red face came the expression of unbending resolution. The darkened eyes lit up ... Suddenly, for a moment, I was completely wrapped up in the infectious forces of the will for victory transmitted by this Promethean figure ... I left highly elated, full of hope – which was then again eroded by critical doubts.'[26]

Next day, 4 August, Ludendorff issued a further directive which also revealed his resurgence of spirit: 'I have a feeling that there is much concern felt by many people over enemy attacks. This is not justified, if our troops are vigilant and perform their duty ... As I have already explained, we should be pleased if the enemy *does* attack, since he will expend his strength all the quicker by doing so.'[27]

Ludendorff became increasingly enthusiastic over his new strategy: sudden, small-scale jabs from positions of defensive strength, designed to exploit enemy weaknesses and gradually sap Allied strength. This, he believed, would underline the fact that the German armies were far from beaten. His war aims remained consistent, even with the depleted resources at Germany's disposal; his optimism seemed as strong as ever. Yet these war aims were becoming almost grotesque, out of all proportion to the means of attaining them: by now Ludendorff lacked justification for his ambitions, so that his situation presented a sharp contrast to that which Hitler would apparently enjoy in 1940 – or to that of Churchill and Stalin in 1945 when they divided Europe into their respective 'spheres of influence'. By comparison, Ludendorff's objectives were relatively restricted, yet in August 1918 they were nevertheless ridiculous. Rather than toning down his demands, Ludendorff continued to insist that unless they were met Germany faced annihilation: it must be all or nothing.

Not surprisingly, subordinates at GHQ failed to understand Ludendorff's latest military policy of a series of smaller-scale assaults. 'Excellency Ludendorff still seems completely baffled,' wrote Mertz on 4 August. 'Only wants to know of smaller undertakings.'[28]

Ludendorff was sustained by his obstinacy. 'Five times I have had to lead troops back during this World War,' commented Ludendorff to Chancellor Hertling on 6 August. 'But in the end I beat the enemy. Why shouldn't this happen a sixth time?'

'Woe to us if the Allies realise our deterioration,' wrote the doubting Mertz next day, 7 August. 'We have lost the war if we cannot pull ourselves together.'[29]

But it was too late. At 4.20 am on 8 August 1918 the sky six miles to either side of Amiens suddenly flared as if lit by sheet lightning as 3,432 British and French guns opened fire. So began, in Ludendorff's later words, 'the Black Day of the German Army'.

CHAPTER NINETEEN

Defeat and Dismissal

TWENTY-SEVEN BRITISH AND FRENCH INFANTRY DIVISIONS SWEPT FORward against twenty German divisions on a ten-mile front north and south of the Somme. Over 600 tanks rolled into the enemy lines and almost immediately the defences collapsed. Within two hours troops in General Sir Henry Rawlinson's British 4th Army had taken 16,000 prisoners and 200 guns; by noon the tanks and armoured cars were nine miles to the rear of the German lines.

Final disintegration had begun. The remaining weeks of war would simply stamp the seal of Allied supremacy on to a fate which had already been decided. Amiens emphasised that Ludendorff's tools with which to fight were totally insufficient, and that the spirit of the battered German army had ebbed to a disastrous degree. Soon after the opening of the offensive Ludendorff sent Mertz forward to examine troop conditions and the subsequent report caused him intense misery.

> I was told of deeds of glorious valour but also of behaviour which, I openly confess, I should not have thought possible in the German Army; whole bodies of our men had surrendered to single troopers, or isolated squadrons. Retiring troops, meeting a fresh division going bravely into action, had shouted out things like 'Blackleg' and 'You're prolonging the war'.[1]

Ludendorff could do nothing and no shred of initiative remained. From this point of view the details of battles won, fearful casualties inflicted, ground taken, all become irrelevant. Ludendorff wrote: 'Leadership now assumed . . . the character of an irresponsible game of chance, a thing I have always considered fatal. The fate of the German people was for me too high a stake. The war must be ended.'[2]

Kaiser Wilhelm received a full briefing on 10 August at a gloomy GHQ meeting. The Allied advance had continued and other armies were moving into the attack; German troops had been pressed back on to lines stretching from Chaulnes to Roye. 'We must be clear,' declared Ludendorff at the Avesnes meeting, 'that we have received a heavy defeat. It is especially worrying that the offensive spirit of some of the divisions is not as should be.' Niemann, Wilhelm's liaison officer at GHQ, recorded: 'Outwardly the Kaiser remained calm, but if you examined his face closely you could see the tautness of the expression, the deep furrows caused by mental suffering, and the over-bright eyes which revealed the tremendous inward emotion straining for release.'

Wilhelm's comments were sparse and stark. 'I see we must balance the books. We are at the limit of our powers. The war must be brought to an end ... I shall expect you gentlemen in Spa within the next few days.'[3]

Only one strategic aim was left to Ludendorff: to salvage as much as possible for the inevitable peace talks – the stronger the army at the moment of these discussions, the stronger would be Germany's bargaining position. 'If in the long run one couldn't avoid the scales tipping in their favour, the eventual victory should be made as dear as possible to them ... I was fully conscious of the fact that with that I demanded of my own army a tremendously difficult task. It had to fight to gain time for the start of peace negotiations.'[4]

Others at the GHQ failed to understand Ludendorff's thinking. Lossberg again saw the General on 10 August and urged a general withdrawal to the Siegfried Line. 'General Ludendorff maintained his decision to continue the defensive battle in the front lines.'[5] He continued to pester the forward commanders, urging greater efforts. 'One can't reason with Ludendorff,' wrote Kuhl, Rupprecht's Chief of Staff, on 10 August. 'He meddles in any conversation and declares that one has to stay firm ... He is extremely excitable and will not listen to any argument.' Ludendorff telephoned Kuhl later in the evening and declared: 'We must not be overrun, we must win time.'[6]

It seemed as if Ludendorff's energy remained as feverish as ever. But now this incredible inner power burnt with the brightness of a guttering candle. Intense discussions took place at Spa on 13 and 14 August as the military and political leaders attempted to view the future. Just before talks began on the 13th Ludendorff had a few private words with Hintze, the new Foreign Minister; he said that in July he had been sure of being able to shatter the Allied will to fight and to force the enemy to the peace table. All this was finished. Now all that could be hoped for was 'to paralyse the enemy's desire to fight and thus slowly to make him seek peace'.

Present at the meeting on the 13th were Hindenburg, Ludendorff, Hertling and Hintze. 'We spoke clearly and decisively to each other,' wrote Ludendorff, 'agreeing that we were not in a position to win the war militarily, but that we hoped to be able to hold in France ... We spoke without nervousness.' This agreement apparently eased Ludendorff's mind. Oldershausen found the General 'in a very good mood' on the evening of the 13th. On the same day General Max von Boehn,

commander of the 7th Army, wrote in a letter: 'I admire this man –
he achieves the almost superhuman. We cannot do without him.'[7]

Encouragement also came from the Kaiser, who presided over a
second conference at Spa next morning, 14 August, and continued to
express confidence in Ludendorff's ability to wage a successful defence.
At the same time this meeting agreed that the Germans, not the Allies,
should be the first to seek peace. Hintze was the first to propose such
a step. He repeated Ludendorff's statements of the previous day, that
the army would attempt to stand fast but 'it was no longer possible to
force the enemy to sue for peace by an offensive'. Germany must therefore take the initiative, said the Admiral, and Ludendorff wrote later:
'He was manifestly moved. Tears stood in his eyes. The Emperor was
very calm. He agreed with the Secretary of State, von Hintze.' The
conference closed with the agreement that 'diplomatic negotiations
must be opened at the right moment'. Ludendorff's account added:
'Deeply moved, I shook hands with Secretary of State von Hintze.'[8]

All hopes were ruined; Ludendorff's 'superhuman' energy had
achieved nothing. Inevitably, his spirits deteriorated. During this brief
lull in the fighting, while the Allies summoned further strength for the
second stage of the Amiens offensive, Ludendorff often sneaked away
to visit the grave of his stepson Erich, now at Avesnes awaiting the
move for reinterment in Berlin. According to Dr Münter, Hindenburg's personal physician: 'There were reports of occasional crying
episodes.'[9]

Staff officers found Ludendorff calmer than in previous days, as if
he were resigned to the tragedy now surrounding him; he spoke clearly
and slowly, almost unemotionally. Major Schubert, German Military
Attaché in Moscow then visiting Avesnes, described a meeting with
the General on the 19th. 'His directions to me were clear and decisive.
His interest in my political report was very great. But how much
General Ludendorff was overburdened... Physically he did not look
like a resilient, healthy man, instead his face was obviously unhealthy
and he lacked the ability to shed the burden of his worries, even for a
moment. I emphasise explicity that ... the clarity, assurance and calm
of this great personality repeatedly imprinted themselves on my
memory.'[10]

Next day, 20 August, the Allies attacked again. Within hours it
became apparent that a further German withdrawal had become imperative. This time the main thrust came further north, in the Arras
sector; German forces pulled back three miles to their main defensive
positions, but the British C-in-C, Haig, had kept back part of his
strength to counter such a move, and on 23 August he ordered a
general advance along a 30-mile front.

Ludendorff no longer involved himself to his previous extent in
detailed military affairs, preferring to leave decisions to his subordinates: Kuhl wrote in his diary on 23 August: 'Ludendorff has now

become much more approachable. He very often asks for my point of view.' Political affairs had become more important. The Intelligence Chief, Nicolai, wrote on 24 August:

> I begin to feel that Ludendorff fears me as I come to him on the one hand with reports of the undiminished determination for destruction by the enemy Powers, and on the other hand with a warning of the imminent revolution by the Fatherland against the war. When I went to him at 11.30 pm to report again, I found him walking up and down in his rooms more sombre than I ever saw him before. Startled, he turns to me and asks: 'Is it so urgent?' I recognise for the first time that he seems to be at the end of his strength.[11]

On 25 August the British offensive threatened to sever German communications south of Cambrai. Precipitate German withdrawal could have disastrous political and diplomatic effects – yet so too could defeat in the field. These considerations forced Ludendorff to involve himself in the battle again. 'A great crisis!' noted Kuhl on the 25th. 'Hence Ludendorff's great excitement. He speaks five or six times to me during the day . . . But his prestige has sadly deteriorated.' The army groups under Prince Rupprecht and von Boehn began to fall back to lines east of Bapaume. 'Ludendorff was very ungracious last night,' declared Kuhl on the 26th. 'The Commanding-Generals had withdrawn too far. They should be more forward in order to lead better . . . It went on until 2 am . . . This morning, great crisis, a very excited morning. Ludendorff terribly excited. Everybody else is to blame.'[12]

Meanwhile Chancellor Hertling had been attempting to draw up a memorandum on possible peace terms, in which Germany declared she would surrender Belgium 'unconditionally and without any claims'; Ludendorff hesitated to agree and insisted on several qualifying clauses reserving the Flemish question for future discussions.[13] But any remaining hopes for satisfactory agreement over Belgium depended increasingly on German forces stemming the Allied advance. Foch remarked on 28 August: 'The man could escape even now if he would make up his mind to leave behind his baggage.'[14] Instead Ludendorff cursed his uncomprehending subordinates for lack of apparent determination.

'Ludendorff phoned me and raged,' complained Kuhl on the 28th. 'I should see to it that the command was improved, and so on. He was terribly excited. One has to put up with him, but . . . everywhere there has to be a scapegoat.' He added: 'It's no pleasure to work under him any more.' And on 30 August: 'We have to pull back on a large scale, bit by bit. If we try to exert ourselves at the Front, we gamble with our last and then we shall collapse completely. Then there will be no holding them any more. This is the behaviour of a gambler. I fear that ambition leads Ludendorff to do this . . .'[15]

Austria decided she must desert her ally and sue for peace independ-
ently. This news reached Berlin on 30 August, via Prince Hohenlohe,
the Austrian Ambassador, and caused fresh consternation. On 2
September defensive positions in the 17th Army sector around the
Arras-Cambrai road were penetrated; Canadian troops broke through
near Quéant. A tense meeting at Avesnes during the afternoon resulted in the decision to withdraw to the Hindenburg Line: German
forces immediately began to disengage and fall back to these final
positions. At last Kuhl seemed to sense the General's difficulties, writing on 3 September: 'It is hard for Ludendorff. I hope we consider
the consequences in relation to politics.' Also on 3 September Ludendorff issued a decree to all troops: defence lines must be held to the
last.[16]

Another lull fell over the fighting while the Allies regrouped and
while German forces struggled into their last defensive lines. Ludendorff's health slumped further, causing concern to GHQ staff. On 3
September Ludendorff received a mysterious visit from a friend named
Dr. Hochheimer, who had left GHQ only a few weeks before and now
returned unexpectedly. Hochheimer revealed his mission in a letter to
his wife: recently he had been asked to come back for 'a strictly dis-
creet conversation' with Colonel Max Bauer, a long-serving member
of Ludendorff's staff. Bauer had informed Hochheimer that 'after all
these difficult years of work and tension, under tremendous responsibilities and especially under the effects of the last eight weeks, Ludendorff is mentally deeply depressed and needs relief and recuperation.
He does not listen to those surrounding him. Even Hindenburg has
no further influence on him.'

Hochheimer was therefore asked to return to Avesnes under some
pretext and use his friendship with Ludendorff and try to assess his
mental and physical health. 'The attempt was risky considering
Ludendorff's quick temper and his suspicion . . But it had to be done
to avoid damage to the Cause and to the People.' Hindenburg had
given full agreement.

Hochheimer had therefore arrived on the 3rd; Ludendorff was surprised by the doctor's sudden return. 'What is it that is so pressing?'
he asked. Hochheimer summoned his courage and abandoned all pretence; he wrote afterwards: 'I talked earnestly, urgently and warmly,
and said that I had noticed with great sadness that for years he had
given no consideration to one matter – his own spirit. Always only
work, worry, straining his body and mind. No recreation, no joy, rushing his food, not breathing, laughing, not seeing anything of nature
and art, not hearing the rustle of the forest, nor the splashing of the
brook . . .'

Ludendorff listened in silence to this emotional declaration, then
sat still for a moment while the doctor anxiously awaited the reaction.

Suddenly Ludendorff spoke: 'You're right in everything. I've felt it for a long time. But what shall I do?'

Hochheimer rushed to give his enthusiastic answer. He wanted to take Ludendorff away from Avesnes, with its cramped rooms and feverish atmosphere, back to the more pleasant surroundings of Spa. There he would insist on Ludendorff adopting a completely different routine, and he would be obliged to rest his mind and body – 'to learn to speak with a different voice, now a taut, high voice of command, to rest his eyes, now completely glazed through continuous scrutiny of maps, to look out on to the mountains, to enjoy wind and clouds, to read.'

The General agreed. He began breathing exercises almost immediately, and on 8 September he obeyed his doctor's instructions and travelled to Spa. Treatment would last four weeks. During this time Hochheimer kept a detailed record of Ludendorff's progress, and his entries form a fascinating and even moving insight into the private Ludendorff. They also provide valuable evidence on the state of the General's mind at this time. So, while his world crumbled and the Fatherland tottered on the edge of destruction, and exhausted, emaciated troops sought strength to face the last offensive, Ludendorff sought sanctuary at his Spa villa surrounded by parkland, with the garden brimming with roses, and with the view of forests and mountains beyond.

Already, on 8 September, Hochheimer could notice an improvement. 'The man has really become quite different, fresher, freer, happier. The rigidity went ... He became relaxed and personal, asking me about my background and family.'

On 11 September he recorded:

My patient improves from day to day. Today, after deep breathing, he literally went to sleep under my hands ... I open to him the doors of worlds he has never seen ... If I tell him about our children he looks at me like a child to whom one talks about India. I avoid everything official or military. I am only interested in Ludendorff as a man. I want nothing of that side of him – the great Commander.

And on 14 September:

The man Ludendorff must first be re-born, must perhaps be created completely ... Who wakens the soul? He spoke warmly of an orderly who had given him a pound of honey as a present ... He sleeps from 12 to 5, sometimes less! Then the thoughts shuffle into order again – strategic, tactical, political, economic ... The man is utterly lonely; he has become married to his work.

Next day, 15 September, Austria published her peace note, with serious effects on German public opinion: agitation increased for Germany's own end to the war. Yet Ludendorff's improvement con-

M

tinued. Hochheimer had a long conversation with Colonel Welhelm Heye, who had succeeded Wetzell as Chief of Operations in the first week of September, and Heye also noticed the change in Ludendorff. Previously he had admired his chief as an officer and commander; now, according to Hochheimer's account, 'he can feel the inner, suppressed hidden warmth'. Hochheimer continued: 'Hindenburg will drive to the front tomorrow to visit the troops: he is fresh and firm, an old oak. Ludendorff I would compare with a strong, weathered fir tree, straight as a candle.'

Kuhl wrote in his diary on 20 September: 'Ludendorff is much quieter and friendlier on the telephone.' On the same day Hochheimer noted: 'Last night, for the first time for ages, Ludendorff slept for six hours, slept deeply right through. He gave me a delicious big pear which H. had sent him, and would not accept my refusal. "I obey you in everything. Now you have to follow me for once ..." '[17]

Meanwhile peace moves stumbled forward, with Hintze trying to induce the Netherlands to act as mediator; the Foreign Office also considered offering this role to President Wilson.[18] At GHQ, Heye believed Ludendorff should give more positive support to these peace efforts by providing politicians with more detailed information on the serious military situation. Ludendorff gave an evasive reply: 'Hintze is quite well informed. He does everything in order to reach peace.' Heye believed the General wished to stay uninvolved; the Chief of Operations and other staff officers decided to take the initiative by inviting Hintze to visit Spa.

At 5.25 am on Thursday, 26 September, the US commander General John Joseph Pershing launched the attack to begin the final Allied offensive. The US 1st Army, co-ordinating with an assault by the French 4th, smashed forward from the Verdun area towards the vital communications centre at Mézières; twenty-four hours later the British 1st, 3rd and 4th Armies and the French 1st were thrown against the Hindenburg Line in the Cambrai-St Quentin region further south; on 28 September British-Belgian forces in Flanders swept over the Ypres ridge.

'Everything is coming on L on all sides,' wrote Dr Hochheimer on the 28th. On the same day Hintze arrived at GHQ following the urgent summons from Ludendorff's subordinates. The visit would have immense results. Heye and other officers, including General von Bortenwerfter, Head of the Political Section, explained the disastrous military situation and stressed that matters could only become worse. The flow of reports from the various sections of the front revealed with frightening clarity that German forces might not be able to survive long enough for peace negotiations: total defeat was probable before these talks even began. After lunch on the 28th Heye reported to Ludendorff on the discussions with Hintze during the morning, and explained that both the officers and the Foreign Secretary believed time had almost run out. Ludendorff reacted calmly, according to Heye.[19]

Military news continued to be acutely depressing during the afternoon. Then, in the early evening, Ludendorff received information that Bulgaria was about to seek an armistice with the Allies: another gap would be torn in Germany's defences.

At 6 pm Ludendorff left his room and searched out Hindenburg. 'I could see in his face what had brought him to me,' wrote Hindenburg. Ludendorff declared that Germany must seek an immediate armistice. Fighting must be ended, before it became too late; total defeat must be averted. He declared: 'Our one task is to act definitely and firmly, and without delay.' Hindenburg, tears in his eyes, agreed without hesitation. 'As had so often happened since 22 August 1914,' he wrote, 'our thoughts were at one before they found expression in words.' The Field-Marshal said he had intended to raise this same question of the armistice later in the evening.[20]

Remaining weeks of war witnessed growing upheaval in Germany and increasing collapse of the political, economic and social structures upon which Ludendorff had so much depended. All stability had disintegrated into recriminations and intrigues, the tangle of a defeated nation trying to find excuses, scapegoats and some shreds of hope for the survival of the Fatherland. Political cohesion, always frail, finally disappeared. Hertling resigned as Chancellor at the beginning of October, to be succeeded by Prince Max von Baden on the 3rd. Next day the Prince asked President Wilson for an armistice, preliminary to a peace conference, and the succession of Notes between Germany and America began. Last-minute efforts were made to introduce a parliamentary government in Germany acceptable to the Allies, and Ludendorff supported this move: to him it seemed only just that the socialists, who had done so much to undermine his position through their lack of support, should now be called into government and should thus be smeared with blame for the imminent disaster. These political machinations led to further constitutional upheaval: Kaiser Wilhelm became increasingly eclipsed, the Chancellor was made responsible to the Reichstag, and authority over the armed forces was transferred to Ministers.

Ludendorff's *de facto* dictatorship therefore ended. But in reality his power had already disappeared and had started to do so immediately his armies could no longer offer hope of victory. His authority had depended upon his military successes, even though this authority extended far beyond the purely military field into the economic and industrial spheres. With the latter, failure had been apparent for many months. Co-operation with the unions had proved non-existent, and Ludendorff had been unable to control the workers either through persuasion or coercion. No amount of legislation or use of power could overcome the chronic shortage of men and materials which were the result of a prolonged war; Hitler was to learn a similar lesson, one which vindicated Ludendorff's original policy of a war of annihilation rather than Falkenhayn's belief in a war of attrition. As it was, by 1918 industrial output in Germany was 57 per cent of the 1913 level despite all Ludendorff's efforts, and industrial unrest had risen to even higher levels than in 1917. Colonel Bauer declared: 'We will win the war when the home front stops attacking us from behind'; Ludendorff agreed, and the ground was being well prepared for the 'stab in the back' legend.

Militarily, the situation deteriorated in whirlwind fashion. By mid-October the US-French forces had cleared the Argonne Forest, and successive German defensive positions were falling; further north the Anglo-French assaults gnawed steadily into the Hindenburg Line; German reserves were flung from one point to another.

Yet Ludendorff remained relatively calm. 'He is firm and clear,' noted Hochheimer on 3 October. Forty-eight hours later the doctor recorded the end of his treatment. 'During the last four weeks he has executed my medical plan very conscientiously and has made a tremendous recovery because of it, in spite of the fact that the world breaks into rubble around him. He is relaxed, loosened, redeemed, breathes and sleeps again. Today I took my leave of him, sat by his bed and spoke to him about the hidden recesses in his soul, of his desperate loneliness.' Hochheimer added: 'He is reserved and mistrustful, full of bad experiences with people, but with it physically so fresh and healthy again and probably looking forward to as long a life as any.'

The doctor always strongly denied that Ludendorff suffered a nervous breakdown; he said the General was 'unbroken'. Similar statements were made by senior staff officers at GHQ, including Mertz and Oldershausen, who joined together in 1919 to issue a declaration. 'None of us has made any observation which could even in the slightest sense point to a nervous breakdown, nor a diminishing of clear judgment and purposeful, strong leadership.'[21] By then, Ludendorff's enemies were using the nervous breakdown charge as one of their weapons against him, and this, like certain other criticisms, became accepted as historical truth. British detractors of Ludendorff eagerly used this accusation against their arch-enemy in the post-war years, blending wartime propaganda with their continuing hostility to brand him as 'crazy'. But no real evidence exists to support allegations that Ludendorff became a raving, incoherent, uncontrollable wreck at the end of the war; instead he was a desperately tired and disillusioned man whose over-active mind continued to push him forward.

Now, during October, Ludendorff's policy had two aims. First, if at all possible, the army must be preserved until peace talks took place; this could be secured by an armistice. Secondly, if an attempt were made to impose humiliating or crushing terms, then a last and suicidal fight must be waged. Staff officers were summoned by Ludendorff for a meeting at 10 pm, 30 September; he told them: 'We have no reserves to transfer to the West ... I should be no better than a gambler if, in view of the gravity of the situation, I did not insist upon ending the war by asking for an immediate armistice. This has been done. I have come to this conclusion in complete agreement with the General Field-Marshal.'[22]

'We felt like men who had to bury something dearly beloved,' said Ludendorff later. He therefore sought peace, but one which would retain some honour for the army and dignity for the Fatherland. German forces were undefeated in the field despite recent retreats; they still occupied more French territory than they had before Ludendorff's 1918 offensives.

Then, during October, it became increasingly apparent to Ludendorff that honour and dignity were going to be denied. On 8 October President Wilson replied to the German communication of the 4th: the US leader asked whether Germany was prepared to evacuate occupied territory, whether the German Government spoke for the whole nation, and whether his 'Fourteen Points' for peace – as announced to Congress in January 1918 – were acceptable. A non-committal reply was sent to Wilson on the 12th, resulting in the President's second Note received on the 14th. Three days later Ludendorff was summoned to attend a Berlin Cabinet Council, called to discuss this latest communication. Wilson demanded the complete cessation of submarine warfare together with extensive constitutional reforms leading to a German democracy. Wilhelm reacted strongly: 'The hypocritical Wilson has at last thrown off the mask. The object of this is to bring down my House, to set the Monarchy aside.'[23]

Ludendorff gave his views. The first aim of his policy might now have to be abandoned in favour of the second: a fight to the finish in order to avoid complete humiliation. He told the Cabinet Council: 'We are honestly trying to reach an agreement. But surely it is no crime to give up the attempt if the enemy demands the impossible. If it comes to extremes – if we are asked to surrender at discretion – it will become our duty to continue hostilities. The German nation will lend its last forces to the army.'[24]

Wilson's Third Note, received on 23 October, confirmed Ludendorff's fears, and his reaction brought his final fall. The US President declared: 'The nations of the world do not and cannot trust the word of those who have hitherto been the masters of German policy ... If the Government of the United States must deal with the military masters and the monarchical autocrats of Germany now ... it must demand not peace negotiations but surrender.'

At 10 o'clock on the night of the 24th a proclamation was issued to the army from GHQ, signed by Hindenburg. 'Wilson's answer is a demand for unconditional surrender. It is thus unacceptable to us soldiers. It proves that our enemy's desire for our destruction, which let loose the war in 1914, still exists undiminished . . . Wilson's answer can thus be nothing for us soldiers but a challenge to continue our resistance with all our strength.'[25] A last-minute change of heart failed to prevent the publication of this proclamation, and an inevitable storm of protest swept the Reichstag at noon next day, 25 October.

Unaware of this bitter criticism against the GHQ, Ludendorff and Hindenburg were seeing the Kaiser at the time of the Reichstag debate. Ludendorff repeated his belief to Wilhelm that Wilson's latest Note must be rejected and the troops must continue the struggle. 'If there is a popular rising, the war can be maintained for some months. A fortress that surrenders without having defended itself to the last is dishonoured.' Ludendorff wrote afterwards: 'His Majesty came to no decision, but he showed full confidence in me.'[26]

During the early evening Ludendorff heard of the Reichstag hostility, confirmed by stiff discussions with ministers after seeing the Kaiser. The Government had finally deserted the army; Ludendorff informed his colleagues, General von Winterfeld and Colonel von Haeften: 'There is no hope. Germany is lost.'[27]

At 8 am next morning, 26 October, Ludendorff sat in an office at the General Staff HQ in Berlin and wrote out his resignation. Hindenburg entered about an hour later, to find Ludendorff still sitting behind the desk. The Field-Marshal saw the resignation note and persuaded the General to remain at his post; the two were still talking when a summons arrived from Kaiser Wilhelm, calling them to the Bellevue Palace immediately.

The interview only took a few moments. 'Politics demanded a victim,' wrote Hindenburg. 'The victim was forthcoming.' Moreover, the departure of the most belligerent German might allow the Kaiser to stay. He received the Field-Marshal and the General with cold formality – Ludendorff noted that he 'seemed wholly changed in comparison with the previous day'. Wilhelm addressed his remarks to the General, condemning the army proclamation of the 24th. Ludendorff appreciated the situation, and according to his account: 'I said respectfully to His Majesty that I had gained the painful impression that I no longer enjoyed his confidence, and that I accordingly begged most humbly to be relieved of my office. His Majesty accepted my resignation.' Ludendorff clicked his heels, saluted, and left the room. Hindenburg remained: the Field-Marshal offered his own resignation but this was refused – the Chancellor had requested that Hindenburg should be retained as a unifying symbol for the German people.[28]

Ludendorff drove to his wife's flat in the Pension Tscheuchner in the Kürfurstenstrasse. 'I stood at the window when Ludendorff's car returned soon after 11 am,' wrote Margarethe. 'I was surprised that he had come back so soon from this important interview, and felt a strange sense of depression. Pale as death he came into the room and

sat heavily in a chair. "The Kaiser has sacked me. I've been dismissed."
For a long time he sat motionless, staring in front of him.'[29]

Two hours later Ludendorff telephoned a member of his staff, Wilhelm Breucker, who immediately rushed to see the General at the flat. He found him sitting in the chair, turning the pages of a detective novel. Ludendorff described the morning's events; he realised he had been used as a scapegoat, and believed that Wilhelm would also be sacrificed. 'You watch,' he told Breucker. 'In a fortnight we'll have no Kaiser.'

Ludendorff also revealed to Breucker and Margarethe his sudden hostility to Hindenburg. 'He felt,' wrote Margarethe, 'that he had been deserted by Field-Marshal von Hindenburg whose joys and sorrows he had shared for all those years, and who, while remaining in the Kaiser's service, had allowed him to resign alone.'[30]

Meanwhile Hindenburg returned alone to headquarters. 'I entered what had been our common office. I felt as if I had returned to my desolate quarters from the graveside of a particularly dear friend.'[31]

CHAPTER TWENTY

Exile

CINEMA AUDIENCES IN BERLIN CLAPPED WITH APPROVAL WHEN NEWS OF Ludendorff's dismissal flashed on the screens during the night of 27 October. Many months ago Ludendorff had arrived at Friedrichstrasse station in the capital, returning from the Russian front, and crowds awaited him, cheering and pushing to see the hero, jamming the streets so that his car could scarcely crawl. Margarethe laughed with delight and asked Ludendorff if he were pleased by the magnificent reception. 'Believe me,' he replied quietly, 'the people's favour is as changeable as that of their ruler. You'll see they'll stone me before I've done.'[1]

Now, in a Berlin turned dreary by the shadow of defeat, fears indeed arose for Ludendorff's safety. Daily the situation became more uncertain as German forces retreated on the Western Front, and as political disruption grew more intense in the German capital. General Wilhelm Groener, long since a rival of Ludendorff, succeeded him as First Quartermaster-General – Ludendorff had suggested Kuhl – but nothing could be done to block the multiple Allied advance. At first the Kaiser believed that with Ludendorff's dismissal the way lay open for an honourable peace. 'The operation is over,' he declared. 'I have separated the Siamese twins,' and he had confidence in being able to work with Socialists to form a suitably 'democratic' Government. His hopes were deflated almost immediately, with left-wing politicians adopting the slogan: 'If the Kaiser goes, we shall get a decent peace.' On the night of 29 October Wilhelm slipped from Berlin and hurried to Spa 'to be with the troops'.[2]

On 30 October sailors refused to obey an order to put to sea. Subsequent courts-martial led to further revolt; by 4 November the mutinous sailors had taken over Kiel, and disturbances broke out elsewhere: on 7 November a Workers' Republic was proclaimed in Munich, and on the same day Prince Max von Baden was told by Socialist Ministers that unless the Kaiser abdicated within twenty-four hours they would quit the Government. Wilhelm, after a fanciful idea of leading the army to restore order, stood down on 9 November and escaped to permanent exile in Holland.[3]

Ludendorff had been living in the Kürfurstenstrasse rooms rented by his wife. Since 28 September he had barely ventured outdoors and instead sat at a small writing-table. Outside, the streets either teemed with people or fell ominously quiet, the lull before the storm of rebellion. By early morning, 9 November, the revolution had begun, with workers streaming from their factories and marching towards the centre. News reached the capital that a separate 'social and democratic' Bavarian republic had been proclaimed in Munich the previous day by the left-wing Jewish journalist Kurt Eisner. Unrest in Berlin seethed more strongly during the morning. At 11.30 Prince Max von Baden attempted to appease the populace by declaring that the Kaiser had abdicated – in fact before Wilhelm had gone – then, only a few minutes later, Socialist politicians arrived at the Chancellery and demanded that Prince Max should hand over to the Socialist Deputy Friedrich Ebert. The Prince obliged, and the former harness-maker became Germany's leading politician.

But others also sought power. At 4 pm a republic was proclaimed from the balcony of the Royal Palace by Karl Liebknecht in the name of a new political group, the Spartacists. This organisation, named after the slave who led the rebellion against the Romans, belonged to the extreme left, if not to the Communist cause itself. Liebknecht shared the leadership with the domineering Rosa Luxemburg, small in physical stature but awesome in political skill.

Two hours before Liebknecht's appearance on the Royal balcony, the prominent Socialist politician Philipp Scheidemann had also proclaimed a republic in an attempt to forestall the more extreme groups. Scheidemann, standing on a terrace at the Reichstag building, shouted to the crowd below: 'The German people have triumphed! What was old and rotten has collapsed! Militarism is finished! The Hohenzollerns have abdicated – Long live the German Republic!'

The scramble for power intensified during the 9th and Scheidemann and his colleagues appeared to obtain the advantage. Supported by the Berlin Soldiers' and Workers' Council, a temporary government was formed consisting of Ebert, Scheidemann, a third Socialist and three representatives of the considerably more radical Independent Socialist Party – who would soon resign. During the evening of the 9th General Groener telephoned Ebert to pledge army support for the suppression of Communist uprising. Shooting nevertheless broke out.

Among the crowds now milling in the Berlin streets were Communist sailors and soldiers who began to chant Ludendorff's name. Friends warned him to escape from this hostile mob, but at first he refused to go. Margarethe wrote: 'I never joined in this advice, as that sort of solution seemed to me unworthy of him.' Then Ludendorff found the decision forced upon him: the landlady of the Kürfurstenstrasse rooms asked him to leave 'so that he wouldn't involve other guests'.[4]

So Ludendorff, who recently had commanded millions of men, was now obliged to bow to an order from his wife's landlady. He left the building after dark, wearing a false beard and blue spectacles and taking only a few belongings with him. First he went to Potsdam, where his brother – a professor at the nearby observatory – found him a room in a colleague's house. Wilhelm Breucker, recently a subordinate on the staff and rapidly becoming a confidant and trusted friend, visited Ludendorff on 10 November and persuaded him to go back to Berlin, offering accommodation in his own home. Ludendorff agreed immediately.

The deposed military dictator returned to the capital on the 11th. At 5 am on this autumn day a German peace delegation led by the Centre Party politician Matthias Erzberger agreed to Allied terms for an armistice. The scene would remain etched on Ludendorff's mind – and also on Adolf Hitler's. Erzberger signed the document in the railway carriage at Rethondes in the forest of Compiègne, then handed over a declaration which stated: 'A nation of seventy millions suffers, but does not die.' Marshal Foch replied: '*Très bien.*' He then stalked away ignoring Erzberger's outstretched hand. At 11 am the fighting stopped.

But not in Berlin. News of the armistice terms created renewed disturbances. The Germans were to hand over huge stocks of war material and the bulk of the fleet; withdrawals must take place from all occupied territory in the West and from Alsace Lorraine; Allied forces were to march into German territory on the left bank of the Rhine; the treaties of Brest-Litovsk and Bucharest were scrapped. And official peace terms had still to be discussed. All Ludendorff's worst fears were confirmed.

> The proud German army, after victoriously resisting an enemy superior in numbers for four years, performing unprecedented feats, and keeping our foes from our frontiers, disappeared in a moment ... The authorities at home, who had not fought against the enemy, could not hurry fast enough to pardon deserters and other military criminals, including among these men of their own number ...[5]

A young corporal was convalescing in a Pasewalk hospital after being temporarily blinded by British gas south of Ypres in October. He heard news of the armistice which the politicians had signed. 'Everything went black before my eyes,' wrote Adolf Hitler later, 'as I staggered back to my ward and buried my aching head between the blankets and pillow ... During these nights my hatred increased, hatred for the originators of this dastardly crime.'[6]

Almost immediately it became clear that with the renewed factional fighting in Berlin the chances of Ludendorff's survival would be slender. Anxious neighbours warned Breucker that he would carry the blame if the General fell into Spartacist hands; Breucker tried to find Ludendorff a hiding place with friends in the country, and at first those asked seemed willing, but then refused.

One evening Captain Fischer, just appointed to the German Legation in Copenhagen, suggested that Ludendorff should go with him to Denmark and then to Finland. Ludendorff agreed, but insisted that first the Government must give consent to his departure. Next morning Breucker went to see the War Minister, General Schëuch. 'I emphasised that the General was willing to return at any time, and would wait to be called to answer for himself in front of the Supreme Court.' Schëuch spoke to Ebert and within twenty-four hours Ludendorff was given necessary documents, including a Finnish passport. He objected to the fact that he was asked to use a false name, and only agreed after Schëuch told Breucker that this was essential to get past hostile workers and the so-called Soldiers' Council groups at the border. The name Ernst Lindström was adopted.

In the afternoon of 16 November Ludendorff was driven to Stettiner station in a car provided by the Finnish Ambassador. Outside the station were crowds of sailors and soldiers, most of them in tattered uniforms, and many were clearly Spartacists, shouting and screaming as they harangued the rest. Fischer and Breucker pleaded with Ludendorff to don his disguise, and eventually he agreed. He walked through the soldiers unrecognised, holding himself erect despite the bustling and shoving, and he took his seat with Fischer in a cold, draughty second-class compartment in which half the window panes were missing.[7]

Ludendorff left behind a letter for Margarethe.

My Dear Wife. My heart was torn at leaving you and having to leave you alone ... My own wife, we shall see each other again and I will be different to you. I love you and there seems to be no end to my misery. Do leave the place where you are now as knowing you're there makes me so anxious ... To me it all seems like a bad dream. I don't know if I was right to go away. Things cannot go on like this for ever. I say 'for ever', though the whole thing has only just begun ... I love you. Your Own Husband.[8]

He crossed the border safely but was recognised during the sea crossing to Denmark; news of his presence spread in Copenhagen, and for the next few days Ludendorff felt unable to escape from the stares and the murmuring as he walked through the streets. His misery was increased by the hate campaign now being waged against him in Germany, especially in the newspapers. Margarethe suffered deep unhappiness and even danger. 'The manageress of the Pension where I was staying did all she could do to protect me against those baser elements, who desired to secure me as a hostage and thereby to compel the General to return.' People living in the same building demanded her eviction, and Margarethe was finally given ten minutes in which to leave. Friends turned against her until a brave couple offered her space for herself and the faithful servant, Rudolph. 'I owe them my heartfelt thanks since not many would have the courage to offer shelter to the wife of the best hated man in all Germany.'[9]

Breucker tried to enlist Hindenburg's support in defending Ludendorff. 'I begged him to declare openly that "as Chief of the General Staff I carry full responsibility for everything that has happened. Whoever strikes a blow against Ludendorff, attacks me." ' The Field-Marshal answered on 23 November. 'I stand by General Ludendorff, my old comrade in arms and counsellor . . . You may be sure of that.' But Hindenburg continued.

> I do not think the time is right for a successful refutation of the attacks and smears against General Ludendorff . . . Today, events rush pell-mell – everything that happens is almost forgotten next day – and therefore I think that words from me in defence of General Ludendorff at the present moment would pass unnoticed. They might even increase the agitation.

A few days later Breucker was surprised by a telegram from Heye summoning him to the GHQ, now at Wilhelmshöhe. There, Breucker learnt that Ludendorff's former subordinates had managed to change the Field-Marshal's mind. After some discussion it was decided that Hindenburg would express his thanks to Ludendorff in reply to a pre-arranged telegram from the *Oberbürgermeister* of Berlin; only Ludendorff's successor, Groener, voiced objections. The plan failed, because the *Oberbürgermeister* eventually refused to co-operate.[10]

Ludendorff could stand the Copenhagen atmosphere no longer, and his letters to Margarethe became increasingly self-pitying.

> My room is small, and outside in the narrow street there is a tramway so that there won't be much sleep or work for me . . . I am at war with myself and the whole world. Dearest, it isn't easy to pull myself together again . . . My nerves are too much on edge and sometimes my speech gets out of control . . . Now I'm afraid I shall make you sad but you must know how things look to me. I never counted on being thanked but this ingratitude on the part of my country hurts me deeply . . . No human fate has been as hard as mine.[11]

In early December Ludendorff moved on, not to Finland as originally intended, but to Sweden. First he stayed in a house in Malmö, then at the Hessleholmsgaard estate at Hessleholm, two hours from Malmö, owned by a well-known Swedish horseman named Ohlsen. Back in Berlin the faithful Breucker continued his efforts on Ludendorff's behalf. One day in December he was invited to the Hotel Adlon by the financier and industrialist Hugo Stinnes for a discussion on the General's future. Stinnes had an excellent offer to make. He believed Ludendorff to be one of the most able leaders in Germany, but that he lacked 'a knowledge of the world and of foreigners'. Stinnes feared that if the General returned to Germany he would merely become embroiled in the squabbles to clear his name; it would be far better if he undertook a three-year world tour, financed by Stinnes, during which he would report to Stinnes on his observations. By the time of his return, possibly five years hence, the situation in Germany might have clarified, 'and with his contacts abroad he could take over political leadership'.

Ludendorff's subsequent career might have been vastly different if this generous offer had been accepted. Instead Ludendorff told Breucker that 'he wanted to stay an independent man – he might have become dependent upon men whom he might later have to fight'.[12] Another reason lay behind the refusal. Previously Ludendorff had sought desperately for something to occupy his mind. 'Oh for work!' he complained to Margarethe. 'This idleness and lack of independence is horrible.'[13] Now, in early December, his energy was directed into a new channel and his activity again became frenzied.

As soon as Ludendorff reached Hessleholmsgaard he began to write his memoirs and to pester Breucker for information – books, articles, documents, reminiscences. 'I am in need of much material,' he wrote on the 18th. 'My memory is not so sure, and I would dearly like to present the period correctly.' And a few days later: 'I write my memoirs with only my head to help me, and I have no possibility of time-checks. I have a good memory, but individual dates become confused.'[14]

In Berlin, confusion remained appalling. Ebert and his Social Democrats struggled to prevent the complete disintegration of governmental machinery, but though backed by the pact with Groener acting for the army, they suffered from an absence of popular support. Throughout Germany there were incidents of violence and brutality by army units against the revolutionaries, which further inflamed civilian feeling, against the military. By early December Ebert and his colleagues were unable to stop much of the administrative authority in Berlin from passing to the Executive Council of the Workers' and Soldiers' Councils – a coalition not only of radical left-wing soldiers and labourers but of Independent Socialists. This Council had already taken upon itself to enact vigorous social reforms on a local level, including the establishment of an eight-hour day, the right to organise unions, and increased benefits.

To Ludendorff and Hindenburg – and to Hitler who passed through the capital in November – these Workers' and Soldiers' Councils were tools of the Bolsheviks, with another Red revolution the final goal. Clashes between the army and the workers took place at the end of the first week in December, after which Hindenburg presented a list of political demands to Ebert including the calling of a national assembly to cancel the power of the councils. Ebert, who had witnessed the violent popular feeling against the army in Berlin, preferred to move more cautiously; riots continued.

On 18 December the Congress of Workers' and Soldiers' Councils passed a resolution calling for the creation of a people's army. The conference, which has been called – perhaps prematurely – the first Bolshevik Congress of Germany, also demanded Hindenburg's dismissal. The latter fought back. 'You may tell the Chancellor,' he told Groener, 'that I decline to recognise the ruling of Congress.'[15]

The German Communist Party had still officially to be created, and would not be so until early January. But already the more extreme members of the Workers' and Soldiers' Councils were bringing pressure on more moderate members and were moving towards Spartacist groups who shared their Communist opinions. Gradually the Spartacists began to take over the capital, with the approval of many Berliners; they controlled public utilities, transportation and the majority of factories. Anarchy seemed daily more likely.

On the international level preparations were being made for the opening of the Peace Conference in January. Already it had become abundantly clear that terms laid down by the Allied Entente would be extremely harsh; in Britain, the cry for revenge grew steadily more shrill – 'Hang the Kaiser! Make Germany pay!' Ludendorff wrote to Breucker during December: 'The Entente violates Germany. As in ancient times beaten people have vanished into history, so now our German Fatherland will be eradicated from the list of states.'

Ludendorff's heavy involvement with his war memoirs, during which he explored the reasons for failure, led him to develop a theme in his writing which emerged as a weapon to be wielded in his own defence. His letters to Breucker expanded this theme, almost as if he wanted to test the phrasing on his friend.

'The Entente rejected everything. It wanted to bow Germany down under a force of occupation, and wanted to destroy it . . . It carried a sharp sword and the German people came with clamours for peace, while the army battled on bravely and in the homeland many hands began to be busy.' He declared that the Fatherland 'let itself be swayed and put to sleep with the thought that it could bring about peace of reconciliation and of justice'. And he added: 'The war had to be fought to its bitter end. The German people had given much, but they had not given their last.'

This letter to Breucker ended with a seemingly fanatical outburst:

The end of the Nibelungen must not and will not come! Germany will be united, and will remember the achievements of the forefathers!
    Holy is religion, family and possessions . . .
    Germany, keep your army powerful and tightly in your hand and look to the horizon again.
    And your recovery will come.[16]

Such sentences can easily give the impression that Ludendorff's mind had slipped. Yet, as at other times, his apparent ravings were infrequent compared with other infinitely sane remarks and statements. Thus he switched character completely in his next letter to Breucker on 21 December:

> I sit here and write and will soon have finished the draft. Do speak to Stilke and ask him what he would give me, and also with Scherl or any other publisher. Maps are the difficulty. I don't know where I can get them from and how I can make them ... If I were in Berlin I would have finished much sooner. It is almost one o'clock in the morning ... I don't know what I'd do without you.[17]

Disturbances in Berlin continued unabated, especially clashes between the right-wing *Freikorps* groups and the Spartacists; Ebert struggled vainly to keep control, but a full-scale confrontation between the army and the Bolsheviks seemed imminent. The situation became increasingly dangerous for Margarethe, and just before Christmas she made her bid to escape from the capital to join her husband. The journey was both difficult and hazardous. Accompanied by Captain Fischer she fought for a seat on the train leaving Stettin station early on 22 December, and the description of her experience underlined the chaotic conditions throughout Germany.

> The carriages were packed with soldiers and crammed with knapsacks, trunks and suitcases. Dust and dirt reigned everywhere. The soldiers bore visible traces of their long marches and railway journeys. Perspiring and unwashed, in many cases caked with mud as they had left the trenches ... they were the last rearguard from the front.

No seats were available and Margarethe and her escort squeezed their cases into the corridor, where the Captain sat with Margarethe perched on his knees. 'It was certainly neither pleasant nor comfortable.' The stench made her giddy, and she strengthened herself with a bottle of eau-de-Cologne. Nearby squatted a huge soldier – 'a giant, heavy and brutal, with coarse features' – and Margarethe had to sit silent while he cursed the Kaiser and her husband. The journey continued throughout the day and night, with no privacy, no heat, and all the while fears of discovery; at the border Margarethe had to endure being stripped to her chemise and searched 'all down my body to the very soles of my feet'.[18]

On the day after Margarethe's departure from Berlin the Revolutionary Peoples' Marine Division rioted in the streets and broke into the Chancellery. Ebert appealed to the army for help, but before this arrived the mutinous sailors retired from the building to the Spartacist HQ in the Imperial Palace stables. On Christmas Eve regular troops from the Potsdam garrison were repulsed as they tried to seize back the stables.[19]

Also on Christmas Eve, 1918, Ludendorff's wife at last tasted freedom. She drove from Hessleholm station to the estate, pulled in a sleigh drawn by two magnificent white horses. Berlin seemed far behind. 'Great bright stars sparkled in the sky among the torn wisps of cloud ... We went at a tearing speed through a tall dense pinewood. The snow lay glittering in the branches.' And there, on the steps to the house, stood Ludendorff.

> The moment I saw Ludendorff again I realised how very great his mental agony had been. In the present state of his feelings he must have found solitude in a strange land particularly hard to bear. Hidebound, as he always was, by his temperament, he was unable to give any outward sign of his pleasure at my arrival, although I knew he must have missed me terribly.[20]

Ludendorff broke away from his writing for a few hours over Christmas to walk with his wife in the snow-covered park and to join in festivities with his host. Both he and Margarethe became depressed by the Christmas celebration; they escaped to their room and Ludendorff sat silent at his writing-table. 'We were both of us deeply immersed in our thoughts,' remembered Margarethe.

'My work will be finished within a fortnight,' wrote Ludendorff to Breucker on Boxing Day. Almost immediately the newspapers reported further disturbing events in Berlin. Two days after Christmas Ebert appointed the ex-butcher Gustav Noske as Minister of National Defence. Noske declared: 'Someone must be the bloodhound', and it became clear that firm action was intended against the Communists. 'Your leftish bourgeoisie play a dangerous game,' wrote Ludendorff to Breucker on 3 January 1919. 'They undermined authority during the war, and now they play into the hands of the Bolsheviks.'[21]

Noske moved against the Spartacists on 10 January, using soldiers of the Guards Cavalry Division, some veteran *Jäger* battalions and *Freikorps* elements: soon these troops would be known as 'Noske's Butchers'. Hindenburg claimed no responsibility since they accepted orders direct from Noske. Commander of the units was General Freiherr Walther von Lüttwitz, and with him operated Ludendorff's former close colleague, Hoffmann. Within a week the Spartacists had been apparently crushed; the Bolshevik leaders Rosa Luxemburg and Karl Liebknecht were captured and then murdered by officers of the Guards Cavalry Division.[22]

With fighting temporarily finished in Berlin, the opportunity existed for elections to be held in relative calm: these were scheduled for 19 January. And with the establishment of better order Ludendorff became increasingly anxious to return home. Breucker tried to persuade him to stay away longer, but Ludendorff retorted: 'Of course I am coming back. I have never thought it differently. I believe that my work will be finished soon ... You say that I should return after the elections. That would be too late ... I must look after M. – she can't join in the fight and she would only hinder me.'[23]

But Ludendorff's exile continued. The elections on the 19th produced 11,500,000 votes out of 30 million for the two middle-class parties, the Centre and the Democratic Parties, while the left-wing Social Democrats obtained 13,800,000 votes. From this rough balance would emerge the Weimar Constitution in five months' time.[24] Meanwhile Ludendorff was obliged to move from the pleasant Hessleholms-gaard estate: Swedish Social Democrats demanded his expulsion, and for a few days he considered travelling on to Finland where the offer of sanctuary remained open. Then this plan had to be changed. 'My wife is ill,' wrote Ludendorff to Breucker. 'At the moment she just can't travel.' They therefore remained in Sweden but changed house to a spacious building in Stockholm which had been offered by a war-time acquaintance.

Ludendorff directed all his energy to completing his book. He worked at an awesome pace, writing from early morning deep into the night, with his preoccupation continuing even during meals. 'His lips moved constantly,' remembered Margarethe, 'as he ceaselessly murmured words and sentences to himself.'[25] Letters to Breucker revealed his progress. 'The book has taken on a different shape,' he wrote in mid-January. 'It cannot avoid polemics ... It is all about saving the honour of the Fatherland, the army, my own honour and my name.' A few days later he complained: 'It is all so difficult to put together in one's head.' On 25 January he believed the finished manuscript would be 400 pages of text, 450 with maps; by 10 February this estimate had grown to 750 pages. The tone had also changed; he wrote on 31 January: 'The whole thing is not a polemic. It has become a historical work.'[26]

Interspaced with references to his work in the letters were hopes for an early return to Germany. Margarethe left in January, enduring another unpleasant journey back to Berlin where she entered a Franciscan hospital for treatment. And in the second week of February Ludendorff prepared for his own return. 'I am now busy with corrections,' he told Breucker on 14 February. 'Perhaps I've put too much personal material into it. That can easily be taken out. Other passages are to be toned down.'[27]

Ludendorff completed his *Meine Kriegserinnerungen* in the third week of February. The book totalled over 270,000 words, written in less than three months. The accomplishment was remarkable, yet typical of his energy. Equally astonishing was Ludendorff's memory: he had to write with only basic help from documents, but the detailed coverage of the war years gives no hint of the restrictions imposed upon him; inaccuracies are far fewer than might have been expected. His accounts of the campaigns are clear and concise, revealing an alert and vigorous mind.

N

Inevitably, Ludendorff sought to justify his own actions. Numerous excuses are presented for mistakes, but the book is far less egotistical than might have been expected considering the circumstances in which it was written. There exists minimal evidence of Ludendorff's personal ambition; instead the constant and sincere theme is his desire to serve the Fatherland, and his fear for its future, combined with his condemnation of the lack of support from politicians.

In a closing passage the author stated:

> In the four years of war our people did mighty deeds which bore eloquent testimony to that inherent strength which today is being wasted by the Revolution. A people of such achievements has the right to live. May it now have the strength to throw off the fetters it has laid upon itself; may it now find men to lead it who are as ready to accept responsibility as the commanders in the field, men of strong purpose and firm will, capable of breathing fresh vigour into our feeble national life...[28]

In late February Ludendorff set out for Berlin. Also during these weeks Adolf Hitler left the prisoner-of-war camp at Traunstein where he had been serving as a guard, and he travelled to Munich to begin his struggle to obtain and pervert the leadership role which Ludendorff had described.

CHAPTER TWENTY-ONE

The Kapp 'Putsch'

LUDENDORFF RETURNED TO BERLIN WITHOUT MISHAP AND FOUND ROOMS in the Hotel Adlon, where Margarethe soon joined him. For the moment he stayed quiet, calling himself Karl Neumann; the hotel proprietor, Herr Adlon, provided him with a suite enjoying a private entrance from the Wilhelmstrasse. Staying in the same building were members of the Allied Disarmament Commission, and Margarethe wrote: 'Officers of all nations swarmed round us. The khaki uniforms of the English and Americans mingled with the paper-bag blue of the French.'[1]

A few weeks later Ludendorff moved again, accepting the loan of a flat in the Victoriastrasse. The rooms were magnificently furnished, with original French Impressionist paintings on the walls – Cézanne, Manet, Van Gogh, Degas – and the windows provided a view of the Tiergarten and the beautiful houses in this elegant quarter of Berlin. Ludendorff had probably never known such comfort before, yet he barely noticed the luxury around him.

It was inevitable that Ludendorff would be drawn into politics, and that he would react in extreme fashion. His name still carried weight among large sections of the population. The Victoriastrasse flat witnessed an increasing number of visitors. 'The number of his clientèle increased from day to day,' wrote Margarethe, 'and finally it was like the consulting room of a fashionable physician.'[2]

Strangers mixed with Ludendorff's former colleagues, civilians with soldiers. Visitors included von Lüttwitz, who had played the leading role in the January battles against the Spartacists, Ludendorff's former subordinate Colonel Max Bauer, and Dr Wolfgang Kapp, founder of the Fatherland Party during the war and now a retired civil servant. Margarethe described this extreme right-wing politician as 'a man with an insinuating personality, highly gifted as an orator'. Heinz, Ludendorff's remaining stepson, also attended meetings when at home: recently he had volunteered for the police division of the Cavalry Guards – the same regiment that had put down the first Spartacist rising – and Margarethe dreaded his sudden absences. 'I had lost two of my boys at the front, was I now to lose the last of them – in street fighting in a civil war of German against German?' In March violence surged again with the second Spartacist Rising, once more suppressed by Noske with great severity: for this operation the re-organised military forces of the Weimar State, the Reichswehr, were used for the first time.

Ludendorff sought a suitable role. 'I asked myself the question: "How best can the German people be helped . . . ?" I was more and more concerned about the German. What can one give him instead of empty promises? In what way can the Germans as a whole become willing to defend themselves again and be united again?'[3]

On 7 May the terms of the Versailles Treaty were published in Berlin, laid down by the Allies without negotiation with Germany. Details came as a staggering blow, and to Ludendorff they amounted to the final act of betrayal, the result of the 'execrable armistice' signed by the politicians, and a vindication of the theme in his memoirs. The army, which even in defeat Ludendorff had wanted to lead home with honour, would be slashed to 100,000 men, to be used only for law and order and frontier duties; the magnificent General Staff would fall from 34,000 men to 4,000; arms were severely restricted, Germany's frontiers redrawn, her overseas territories lost, the Rhineland demili-tarised . . .

'The terrible destiny of Versailles lies in making us so defenceless against the violence of our enemies,' declared Ludendorff. 'It makes one shudder to think about it.'[4] Weimar politicians cried out their protests. The terms were 'unrealisable and unbearable' insisted Ebert, the Provisional President; Philipp Scheidemann, the Chancellor, de-clared: 'May the hand wither that signs this treaty!'[5] For over a month the issue received passionate debate, with the Allies becoming increas-ingly impatient for Germany's signature of acceptance. Refusal to sign would mean an Allied attack, and in June Ebert therefore asked Hindenburg for his assessment of the army's ability to resist. The Field-Marshal sent his reply from his GHQ, now at Kolberg, on the 17th: 'We can scarcely count upon being able to withstand a serious offensive.' But then Hindenburg added: 'The success of the operation as a whole is therefore very doubtful, yet as a soldier I cannot help feeling that it were better to perish honourably than accept a disgrace-ful peace.'[6]

Such a sentiment coincided with Ludendorff's own feelings, and for a moment it sounded almost as if he still stood behind the Field-Marshal's shoulder. But arguments continued in the Weimar Govern-ment, with the Cabinet increasingly divided: Erzberger argued strongly for signing; Ebert hesitated; Scheidemann resigned on 20 June. Already, on 16 June, the Allies had presented an ultimatum: either the treaty must be accepted by midnight 24 June or the armistice agreement would be terminated. During the afternoon of the 24th Ebert again telephoned Kolberg: if GHQ believed in the smallest possibility of successful resistance, he said, then he would throw all his influence against signature.

Hindenburg passed the decision to Groener: 'You know as well as I do that armed resistance is impossible.' Then he stood to leave the room. 'There's no need for me to stay. You can give the answer to the President as well as I can.' Hindenburg was doing no more than his constant practice with Ludendorff: handing over the choice of decision and its execution, and staying safely in the background himself. But Groener was no Ludendorff – and because of this, further war was avoided. Groener, already described by Ludendorff as 'that scoundrel', picked up the telephone and told Ebert that 'if fighting were resumed, the prospects of a successful issue were hopeless ... in the end even the army would approve the acceptance of the conditions'.[7] At 11.40 pm the Allies were informed that the terms would be accepted. Four days later, 28 June, the Treaty of Peace was signed in the Hall of Mirrors in the Palace of Versailles.

Ludendorff had found his cause and his crusade, and as always he would carry his convictions to the limit. 'The greatest blunder of the revolutionaries was to leave us all alive,' he told his wife. 'If I once get back to power, there'll be no quarter. I should hang up Ebert, Scheidemann and the comrades with a clear conscience and watch them dangle.'[8]

During spring 1919 Ludendorff held a conversation with General Sir Neil Malcolm, Head of the British Military Mission in Berlin. Ludendorff complained bitterly about the lack of support which he had been given during the war, and the undermining of the army's will by subversive elements. Germany would never have been defeated, he insisted, if the politicians had not been corrupt. Sir Neil asked: 'You mean that you were stabbed in the back?' Ludendorff answered: 'That's it exactly. We were stabbed in the back – stabbed in the back.'[9]

Meetings at the Victoriastrasse became more frequent and more crowded, with the visitors spilling from the living rooms into the bedrooms. Ludendorff dominated proceedings. Then, in autumn 1919, he turned aside to deal with another kind of intrigue: during September Hindenburg published his war memoirs, in which he seemed to imply that Ludendorff was tempted to disengage on 26 August 1914 during Tannenberg, and that Hindenburg rescued the battle by standing firm: 'We overcame the inward crisis, adhered to our original intention, and turned in full strength to effect its realisation.'[10] Newspapers, especially in Switzerland, took up this aspect and even reported that Ludendorff had considered a retreat at this time, with Hindenburg replying: 'We will attack.'

Ludendorff was furious, accusing Hindenburg of a 'tremendous lie' and adding: 'I have no words for this enormous act.' He demanded that the truth should be told, and Hindenburg obliged with a declaration denying any such inference. This document was then sent to the President of the State Archives, General von Haeften, for safe-keeping. A recent German historian has claimed that the offending section of Hindenburg's book was not written by the Field-Marshal, but by General von Mertz – who succeeded Haeften as President of the State Archives, after which the document denying the 'wavering' implication mysteriously disappeared.[11]

By winter 1919–20 Ludendorff's political views had hardened. He turned to writing again, spending a number of weeks preparing a book on the documents of the High Command, published later in 1920, and also helping to compose far more controversial pamphlets. Everywhere he believed he could see evidence of German demoralisation and weakness caused by the Weimar politicians. 'We look into nothingness. Self-deception, empty words, the practice of trusting to others or to phantoms, lip courage, meaning vain promises for the future and weakness in the present; all these will never help us ... Something else is needed.'[12]

Direct action seemed to be the only answer. During those dark winter evenings the Victoriastrasse sessions turned to an examination of seizure of power, with the discussions pushed forward by the *Freikorps* officer Captain Waldemar Pabst. Margarethe commented: 'One could not help feeling that he was a marvellous man, and that if a man was needed he would be the one "to deliver the goods".'[13] This dominating figure formed the *Nationale Vereinigung,* Alliance of National Union, with offices in the Schellingstrasse; Bauer worked closely with him, and the Berlin garrison commander Lüttwitz hovered nearby.

Ludendorff became increasingly preoccupied with the intrigues during the early weeks of 1920, and a breach began to appear between himself and the faithful Margarethe. A year before, he had told Breucker that she would 'only hinder' him in the fight, and this attitude grew more apparent. 'Ludendorff had not once, but often, told me not to meddle in his political affairs, in order not to hamper his freedom of movement. It would destroy his peace of mind if he felt that I bore an accomplice's share of the responsibility.' Margarethe might have accepted this reasoning, except for another aspect which now appeared. 'Women instead of men sought long and earnest conferences with Ludendorff. I was hurt by his giving other women his confidence and initiating them into his affairs, whilst I was excluded. I spoke about this to Ludendorff but he gave me a soothing reply ...'[14]

In early March the Allied Control Commission pressed Defence Minister Noske into ordering the disbandment of Lieutenant-Commander Hermann Ehrhardt's *Freikorps* Brigade. These men, praised by Ludendorff and his companions for their vigorous fighting against Bolsheviks in Munich, Brunswick and Dresden, were now camped near Berlin. The moment seemed perfect for the plotters to act. General von Lüttwitz used his authority as Potsdam commander to order

Ehrhardt to march his men into Berlin during the evening of Saturday, 12 March: the hated politicians, headed by Ebert, would be arrested, martial law would be declared, and a new government formed under the only feasible politician to attend the Victoriastrasse meetings, Dr Wolfgang Kapp.

Noske received news of the approaching brigade during the Saturday afternoon. He summoned an urgent meeting of Reichswehr officers to demand counter-action. 'Reichswehr does not shoot at Reichswehr,' declared General Hans von Seeckt, now the Chief of Staff. Nor would the police pledge support for the Republic.

Ebert fled from the capital, but before so he employed another weapon: if the troops or police refused to help, then the trade unionists might oblige. He therefore handed Privy Councillor Arnold Brecht a proclamation to be given to the press, calling for a general strike.[15]

Soon after 6 pm the 5,000 *Freikorps* troops entered the city. They sang as they marched, and on their helmets could be seen Ehrhardt's special insignia – the swastika. 'Our house was intoxicated with hopes of victory,' recalled Margarethe. 'We were all in a mood of the greatest enthusiasm.'[16] The Brigade halted in the Tiergarten, and a few minutes later Ludendorff walked down the steps of the Victoriastrasse flat to join them – he claimed later that he had merely 'been out for a stroll' when the troops approached. Then Kapp arrived. Just before 7 pm the men began to march again, this time with Ludendorff, Lüttwitz and Kapp at their head, the latter looking incongruous amongst the soldiers in his morning coat, striped trousers, spats and top hat.

Shortly after 7 pm the column wound up the Wilhelmstrasse and halted before the Reich Chancellery. Kapp and Traugott von Jagow, a former Berlin police president, entered the building and were received by the Vice-Chancellor, Dr Eugene Schiffer and by Privy Councillor Brecht. The group stood in awkward silence; Brecht commented afterwards that everyone wondered 'whether you should shake hands in such circumstances', and then the representatives of the Republican Government left the building.

But the success of the 'coup' brought its failure. Planning at Ludendorff's flat and at Pabst's office in the Schellingstrasse had been concentrated on the mechanics of seizing power, rather than what should be done with this power after it had been obtained. Progress flagged next day, Sunday, with Kapp failing to find politicians who would serve in his Cabinet. On the Monday morning the general strike proclaimed by Ebert began to take effect, and Berlin came to a standstill; fighting broke out in the city, and during the evening reports reached Ludendorff and his colleagues that army commanders in Munich, Dresden and Munster were refusing to support the 'putsch'. Military opposition to Kapp spread on Tuesday, 14 March, with a Reichswehr battalion in Berlin turning against its officers and declaring support for Ebert and his Republic; talks between Pabst and the Vice-Chancellor, Schiffer, broke down.

Ludendorff, Bauer, Ehrhardt and Pabst met in the Chancellery during Tuesday evening. Bauer, weeping with frustration, pleaded with Ludendorff to take over the leadership, but the General was shrewd enough to realise the movement had no future. He blamed the failure on 'subversive elements' and on hesitancy displayed by the officer corps. He was especially critical of the lack of support from elsewhere in Germany, notably Bavaria. Bauer and Ehrhardt also blamed the army, especially von Lüttwitz who had refused to allow the *Freikorps* to shoot strike-pickets. The group agreed that military dictatorship should be offered to General von Seeckt, but the Reichswehr Chief of Staff refused contemptuously when approached by Bauer.

The dismal meeting at the Chancellery continued until after dawn on 15 March. During this Wednesday further depressing news arrived: street fighting in Berlin, more mutinies of Reichswehr troops in support of the Republic, angry demonstrations against Kapp.

Kapp admitted defeat during the afternoon. He issued a proclamation which handed over leadership to Lüttwitz, then fled to the Tempelhof Airport *en route* for Sweden. Seeckt began to act: in the early evening he sent his chief assistant – Ludendorff's previous subordinate Heye – and ordered the conspirators to disperse. At 6 pm Lüttwitz handed in his resignation to Vice-Chancellor Schiffer and the Ehrhardt Brigade marched out of Berlin, firing at a hostile crowd as they did so. Pabst, one of the principal plotters, had already fled.

'Our hopes and illusions were shattered,' wrote Margarethe, 'and nothing remained but a bitter after-taste of disappoinment and disgust.' Now Ludendorff also left, to seek refuge in Bavaria. 'Bauer,' he said as he boarded the train, 'we are richer for a bitter experience.' He wrote later:

> I witnessed here the complete unreliability of members of the officer corps ... and the fickleness of large sections of the public ... Impressions were deep and lasting. They were connected with the decision to track down the original subversive agitators ... They must have been the same ones who profited greatly through the collapse during the World War.

Ludendorff's train pulled out of Berlin on the evening of Wednesday, 15 March. He left behind Margarethe and ruined hopes, and he took with him increased hatred for the politicians. Failure of the Kapp 'putsch' strengthened his belief in his cause and pushed him further along the extremist path.[17]

CHAPTER TWENTY-TWO

Hitler

LUDENDORFF FIRST TOOK REFUGE IN A BAVARIAN CASTLE PERCHED above the Inn valley. 'I must be alone,' he wrote to Breucker on 27 April. 'What does it matter to the world where I am? I'm a private man, but alas my name is a burden.'[1] During this temporary hibernation the gap widened between himself and Margarethe, and their relationship would never be fully restored.

Margarethe, still in Berlin and provided with a 24-man bodyguard by Ehrhardt, found another reason for the coolness between them. Among her husband's regular visitors had been 'a distinguished looking lady in deep mourning', who now asked Margarethe to pass on letters to Ludendorff from a certain Dr Lange. The request was repeated on numerous occasions, until Margarethe discovered the truth about 'this furtive business'. She wrote: 'The correspondence had not the remotest connection with politics, but consisted ... of love-letters to Ludendorff. The lady had employed me, his lawful wife, as the postmistress for her intrigue.'[2]

The abortive Kapp 'putsch' increased hostility to Ludendorff, especially in Berlin. 'The excitement of the populace knew no bounds,' remembered Margarethe, 'and all their rage and all their hate were concentrated on Ludendorff.' Typical of the vitriolic attacks on the General was a pamphlet published anonymously during the year, with the author merely describing himself as a soldier. The document accused Ludendorff of mismanagement, incompetence and even corruption during the war. 'Ludendorff, with his sharp sword, had only floundered in the fat of the enemy – hardly touching the muscles and only irritating the nerves ... To this man, alien to the people, alien to hunger, success also remained alien.' The unknown writer claimed that under Ludendorff 'lies became a narcotic. Ludendorff believes the people shy away from truth, because he himself shies away from it.'[3]

'On the whole I spit on these men,' the General told Breucker on 10 May.[4] Nevertheless he thought it prudent to keep on the move, shifting his hideaway to Stefanskirchen, near Rosenheim, where he became the guest of Baron von Halkett. He moved on again after only a few weeks, and Margarethe joined him at Augsburg where they stayed for a fortnight in the mansion of Princess Fugger-Babenhausen. Finally, on 20 August 1920 the Ludendorffs moved to the small village of Ludwigshöhe, just outside Munich, where the General had bought a villa surrounded by high walls.

Ludendorff later insisted that private reasons led him to Munich: he wanted a place of his own rather than somewhere provided for him by others, and the Bavarian capital had been chosen since his only living sister dwelt there. But politically, no other town could have suited him better. In Bavaria as a whole existed a traditional dislike of governmental interference from Berlin, and after the war this feeling increasingly found expression in demands for greater autonomy and even separatism. The power of the central Berlin Government was inevitably weakened during the unstable post-war situation, reacting in turn on affairs in Munich, where there had been extreme turbulence since1918 with assassinations, riots and short-lived Bavarian governments. It was here that Hitler came in January 1919, joining the nine-month old German Workers' Party on 14 September; by early 1920 he was already gaining control over this minuscule political group, and on 1 April he announced the organisation's new name: the National Socialist German Workers' Party. Hitler found the Munich atmosphere extremely to his liking, and his Nazi party began to grow.

The difference between Berlin and Munich had been clearly revealed in March. Whereas the Kapp putsch had failed miserably, a simultaneous coup succeeded in Bavaria. On the night of 13–14 March the Reichswehr District Commander, General Arnold von Möhl, presented an ultimatum to the Bavarian Social Democrat Premier, Johannes Hoffmann, which led to the establishment of Gustav von Kahr's right-wing government. Möhl and Kahr declined to support Kapp, prompting bitter criticism from Ludendorff, but Munich nevertheless became the natural centre for all those opposed to the Republican Central Government. Ernst Pöhner, Munich's Police President, invited the Ehrhardt Brigade to the city, where Ehrhardt himself became Chief of the Emergency Police and would soon form his 'Organisational Council', whose aim was to remove by murder or threat any individual considered to be an enemy of the German people. When asked if he knew there were political murder gangs in Bavaria, Pöhner gave the famous reply: 'Yes, but not enough of them.'

Yet despite this atmosphere, Ludendorff's career entered a quiet period in May 1920, and it almost seemed as if he had finally retired. Gradually he became reconciled with Hindenburg, who began to spend a few weeks each summer at the Ludendorff home. Margarethe commented: 'His visits were always days of rejoicing ... It is impossible to give any idea of the pleasure his presence gave us.'[5]

For almost two years Ludendorff avoided direct involvement in politics. He shunned publicity and stayed at home, writing and thinking. Yet both were directed along highly dangerous lines: his aim was to track down 'the original subversive agitators' who had ruined the Kapp putsch – and who, he believed, were the same dissidents responsible for internal collapse in the war. Inevitably, Ludendorff received visitors, mostly students, but also including some would-be politicians and other extremists. Among the latter was Frau Mathilde Kemnitz, a widow living in the nearby hamlet of Tutzig.

Ludendorff had previously met Mathilde Kemnitz in Berlin and found himself fascinated by this intellectual, rather dumpy and over-eager woman. Her ideas were sinister and twisted, and would have been considered as outrageous in normal times. But now her influence spread over Ludendorff like an evil stain; above all she seemed to hold the secret to his search for the 'subversive agitators'.

'My acquaintance with the earliest work of Dr Mathilde Kemnitz was of decisive influence on the course of my inner struggles,' wrote Ludendorff. He also declared:

Gradually I recognised the pernicious forces which had caused the collapse of the people, and in them the real enemies of the freedom of the German race ... More and more plainly I became aware of the fungi within the structure of our society ... in the form of secret supranational forces, i.e.: the Jewish people and Rome, along with their tools, the Freemasons, the Jesuit order, occult and satanistic structures ...[6]

The answer seemed simple. These forces were those alien to the German race, spreading their secret destruction within the society. And once Ludendorff came into contact with this theory, he grasped tight; as always, belief became a fervent, overpowering conviction to which Ludendorff directed all his energy and concentration. To him, the winter months of 1920–21 were extremely profitable. 'My time was filled by the study of Judaism, Freemasonry and Catholicism, and also with writing the third of my military books, *Kriegführung und Politik* [Warfare and Politics] which appeared in the autumn of 1921.'

'A growing section of the leadership of the German people,' claimed Ludendorff in this book, 'has been ruled by a veiled supranational and pacifistic feeling and intent.' Politicians had

put themselves mainly under Jewish influences, which were completely alien to the people and were in strict contrast to the Germanic nature ... The Jewish people wanted to rule over the people who had admitted them ... to castrate us as men and people, so that others with a stronger national will can rule us.[7]

While these thoughts fermented, Ludendorff also had other visitors, far more reputable than Dr Mathilde Kemnitz but at one with Ludendorff in his hopes for a better Germany. Among them was Admiral von Tirpitz. Margarethe wrote: 'He made a rousing speech on the new revival and renaissance of Germany, and as he spoke his eyes had an enraptured look which I shall remember as long as I live. It was as though he gazed into the distant future and saw Germany's glory rise again.'[8]

Hitler was also busily seeking to resurrect Germany, in his own image. By now he was receiving valuable support from Captain Ernst Röhm, the scar-faced soldier of fortune who worked on the Army District Command staff in Munich, and who pushed ex-*Freikorps* and ex-servicemen into the Nazi movement to help swell membership. On 1 April 1920 Hitler himself left the army – until then he had retained his corporal's rank – and devoted himself full-time to political affairs.[9]

Also in April 1921, the Allies fixed the figure for reparation: Germany would have to pay 132 thousand million gold marks, or £6,600 million. The German Chancellor, now Konstantin Fehrenbach, failed to secure concessions and resigned on 4 May. Next day the Allies issued an ultimatum giving Germany seven days to accept the announced sum or face occupation of the Ruhr. Josef Wirth, of the Catholic Centre Party, formed a government on 10 May and yielded to the reparation demands twenty-four hours later.

Both the exorbitant Allied demands and the new Government's capitulation fed Ludendorff's fury.

> Judah and Rome were united in the attempt to defeat the German people completely, and to assign the Fatherland to the victorious states and world capitalism. The demands of the World War enemies became more depressive and impossible to fulfil. We could not see the end of the burden imposed upon us.[10]

And, almost simultaneous with the reparation issue, another ominous development became increasingly prominent: the mark was dropping in value, from four to the dollar at the end of 1918, to 75 by summer 1921.

On 26 August Matthias Erzberger, the politician held most responsible for persuading the Government to sign the Versailles Treaty, was shot down by two of Ehrhardt's gunmen in the Black Forest near Griesbach. The murder of Erzberger, recently Reich Minister of Finance, was regarded as unfortunate but almost inevitable by Ludendorff. He called the victim 'the representative of Rome' and believed his death formed an 'expression of German misery but also of the German will to defend itself'.[11]

The murder led to an attempt by the central Government to reassert authority in Bavaria. The Kahr Ministry was obliged to dissolve Röhm's 'Citizens' Defence Force' and other para-military bodies, and the Kahr administration itself soon gave way to a new Bavarian Government formed by the more moderate Count Hugo Lerchenfeld. The extremists nevertheless continued to gain strength, despite Hitler's temporary absence serving a prison sentence: on 5 October 1921 Röhm's 'Gymnastic and Sports' division of the Nazi party changed its name to *Sturmabteilung* – the SA or Storm Section – largely composed of Ehrhardt's ex-*Freikorps* men and the Organisation Council which had carried out Erzberger's murder.[12]

Ludendorff had already made some contact with the Nazis. Some reports say Hitler himself may have been granted a brief and inconsequential interview with the hero soon after the Kapp 'putsch'. Late the previous year, 1920, Ludendorff also met nationalists at a conference in Halle, but for the moment he kept mainly to his villa, preferring people to come to him rather than himself going out. 'I am in no mood in any way to take part in public life,' he assured Breucker on 15 October 1921.

> You believe I have influence on the rightist press and on the German nationalistic circles. No, Brencker, I've not got this influence; nor do I seek it ... I am becoming philosophical in the solitude of the country. I find joy in life working in the garden with my scissors. I don't know whether this will continue, but I believe so. Life has pushed me forward into the public, against my nature.[13]

This romantic image was of course false: Ludendorff had never displayed aversion to public life, and would have welcomed the opportunity to return. And perhaps the foundations had already been laid for the peculiar and in many ways pathetic relationship which was soon to be established between Ludendorff and the Nazis, more especially between Ludendorff and Hitler. Both had many ideas in common. In addition there is every probability that Hitler's attitude of hero-worship towards the General was to a large extent sincere, and not merely manufactured in an effort to secure Ludendorff's help. Certainly Hitler continued to court the old man long after he had any real need to do so. In these early, fumbling days, Ludendorff must have seemed to Hitler as the ideal to which he himself aspired – dogged, determined, capable of ruthlessness, a figure who commanded respect, a fighter, and above all a man who had been dictator of Germany. For his part Ludendorff had never rejected adulation. Now, in his embittered loneliness, he responded to the respect and apparent worship shown to him by the Nazis and their energetic – if unorthodox – young leader.

In November 1921 the SA started to show its strength, turning upon Communists who attempted to disrupt a party meeting in the Hofbräuhaus, Munich: the incident became known as the *Saalschlacht* – Battle of the Hall. On 13 December Ludendorff revealed his latest political thoughts in another letter to Breucker: 'I see the work of the Bolsheviks in the writings of the Jews.' But he still insisted that he had no intention of mixing in active politics. 'Ambition doesn't exist with me, and I live here content and quiet. Only young students come to see me.' On 21 December he tried to explain to Breucker his attitude to the Jews. 'I have supported the Jews in Poland and Lithuania. The first Jewish soup-kitchen in Kovno was called after me ... Personally I've done nothing to them.' He added: 'However much I feel inwardly hostile to the English, I still receive Englishmen, and likewise speak with Jews. For me this is a question of race ... I cannot hurt a single person, only the race.'[14]

Inevitably, Ludendorff was drawn further into active politics. The next approach came from the *Bund Oberland* – the Oberland Defence League – one of the patriotic organisations in Bavaria, and one of the groups which Hitler was attempting to merge into alliance with the Nazi Party. But Ludendorff's early impression of Nazi aims was unsatisfactory: 'I read the programme of the National Socialist German Workers' Party, and found much which appealed to me, but unfortunately it was a rigid polemic for which I didn't have much time.' The Nazi movement seemed too much involved with polemics and not enough action; Ludendorff believed himself to be taking a more positive approach.

> I appeared more often in public ... I became deeply absorbed with the question of race ... I looked for clarity in the characteristics and mental differences of the races, and read all I could ... At the same time I occupied myself with the hereditary health question ... The evil of alcohol and its offspring in the living society was shown to me ...[15]

With re-emergence into public life, Ludendorff experienced rising hostility both locally and nationally. Amongst his opponents was Crown Prince Rupprecht of Bavaria, one of Ludendorff's Army Group Commanders during the war – whom Ludendorff had criticised in his war memoirs – and now living in his castle near Berchtesgaden. Rupprecht was closely linked with the Bavarian *Volkspartei* which had levelled extensive criticism at Ludendorff's war management, and which opposed the more extremist political views. On 24 June both Ludendorff and Rupprecht attended a ceremony at Munich University. During dinner the Crown Prince was handed a telegram; he read the words then stared at Ludendorff with undisguised contempt. The message had brought the news that Walther Rathenau, Germany's Foreign Minister who had undertaken to fulfil the Versailles provisions, had been shot dead in the street.

'Perhaps he [Rupprecht] believed that I knew about the murder,' wrote Ludendorff later. 'If so, Crown Prince Rupprecht was deeply mistaken. I have rejected such measures as political murder, even in defence of Germany.' But Ludendorff expressed similar feelings as those towards the assassination of Erzberger. 'I did not doubt that this murder was giving expression to the desire for defence against the immense violations and grievances.' These, he continued, were rightly attributed to the Jew Walther Rathenau, the Red Prophet of world revolution. Consciously, he wanted to Bolshevise the German people, with the help of the German intelligentsia. The Germans who executed the people's judgment on Walther Rathenau have acted with the thought that they have freed the German nation from vermin . . .[16]

Ludendorff's adoption of a more public political role coincided with increasing demonstrations of strength by the Nazis; Hitler's speeches became more extreme and unrestrained after his release from prison in July. On 18 September he harangued a Munich audience with the words: 'We want to call to account the November Criminals of 1918 . . . The dishonouring of the nation must cease'; and in November Hitler declared: 'The Marxists taught, "If you won't be my brother, I'll bash your skull in." Our motto shall be, "If you won't be a German, I'll bash your skull in" . . .'[17]

The National Socialists are German [wrote Ludendorff to Breucker on 28 December], but the danger exists that they will let themselves be misused, not through a precipitate coup but through political expediency. But I haven't a firm opinion about this yet. I'm pleased to be here: if I can't do anything positive, I can prevent trouble. The danger of the Jesuits is great! . . . If only people would hear my voice! That's a long way off.[18]

'The year 1923 arrived,' commented Ludendorff later, 'the year in which Jewish and cabalistic superstition hoped too much to conquer.' He had discovered why, according to him, 1923 was so important to the Jews.

It was . . . a 'Year of Jehovah'. Like the year 1914 the total sum of the digits $(1+9+2+3)$ gives the number 15; this comprises the numbers 10 and 5, which according to the Jewish superstition are the first two consonants of the word Jahweh – Jehovah – and therefore makes the actions of the Jewish and Christian cabalists successful in such years . . . The time to shatter the Reich had come.[19]

In the summer of 1922 the dollar had been worth 400 marks, an increase of over 300 since the previous year; by the beginning of 1923 the figure had risen to over 7,000. Ludendorff wrote:

The grievances had increased; the inflation and with it the misery and distress had risen; the screws of taxation had been twisted tighter; the divisions between the people had become deeper; corruption riddled official life . . . Germany could not possibly shoulder the enormous burdens . . . Poincaré, the trusted man of the Jews and Rome, had been elected chief executioner of Germany.[20]

On 11 January the French President Raymond Poincaré ordered troops into the Ruhr, using the technical excuse of German defaults in timber deliveries. The day before, Ludendorff had been visiting his old garrison town of Wesel, which would be affected by the occupation.

> The mood was depressed. One was waiting for the enemy to march in. But it was something else besides: something difficult to define was in the air. In this Catholic town, with comrades who should have been proud that I was once in their regiment, I felt rejected, as if I had been truly responsible for the outcome of the World War ... Only very slowly was the ice melted.[21]

Other, more tangible, evidence of hostility to Ludendorff emerged a few days later. He had been invited to address farm workers at Klagenfurt in Carinthia, and he journeyed by rail via Vienna; on the way the train was stopped. 'Some rather untrustworthy men stormed through the corridors of the train ... They looked into our compartment, but turned away. I heard later that my assassination had been planned ... Obviously they didn't recognise me.'[22]

Early in February, an invitation arrived from the financier Hugo Stinnes for Ludendorff to travel to Berlin for talks with the Chancellor and Seeckt on possible active opposition to the French in the Ruhr: so far only passive resistance was taking place. 'In both these leading Germans I did not see clear determination for decisive opposition ... just as I saw no preparations for resistance in all areas should the enemy advance further. We stood in different worlds ... I returned to Munich deeply disappointed. Passive resistance continued.'[23]

'Until the present day,' shouted Hitler in a speech in Munich on 13 April, 'the half-hearted and the lukewarm have remained the curse of Germany.' Ludendorff wrote to Breucker three days later:

> I believe that France wants to smash us; therefore she has to force us into war. We have no voice in it at all. Nobody helps us ...
> 'Thus we have to prepare, prepare, prepare for war.
> Who is for this is good, who is against is the enemy.'[24]

Hitler overreached himself on 1 May, attempting to disrupt the traditionalist socialist and trade-union May Day demonstrations in Munich. Röhm was prevented by his superior, General von Lossow, from providing armed support, with Lossow having recently been appointed by Seeckt to restrain the Munich garrison, and the Nazi operation failed dismally. For the next few months Hitler disappeared from the political scene, spending most of the summer at Berchtesgaden. But at the same time the Nazis attempted to broaden support; and now came the inevitable contact with Ludendorff.

One day in May Ludendorff received a visit from Rudolph Hess, the solemn and humourless Hitler disciple. He brought a message from the Nazi leader: Hitler wished to call, at the General's convenience.

Ludendorff agreed and the meeting took place a few days later; already Hitler had been preparing the way by declaring that Ludendorff was 'Germany's greatest commander'. Discussion progressed satisfactorily, with the two men sharing so many common ideas; moreover, earlier in the year Hitler had formed an alliance with other patriotic groups in Bavaria, including Ludendorff's favourite *Bund Oberland* and another organisation which he also supported, the *Reichsflagge* – Reich Banner.[25]

Later in the month Ludendorff gave an interview to an American journalist, and for the first time pledged open support for the Nazis. 'The growing aims which I follow, and which lie outside the scope of any political party, I've so far found most clearly in the principles elaborated by the German *Kampfbund* led by Hitler.' And he wrote later:

The National Socialist German Workers' Party had a tremendous attraction for the people, who found themselves in a situation of increasing distress. The battle against Jews, Marxism and Bolshevism was made easily understandable to the larger sections of the public. Adolf Hitler stepped into the foreground more and more. A sharp contrast was felt between him and the Bavarian State.[26]

By 1 July the inflation of the mark had soared still further: 160,000 to the dollar; by 1 August the figure had risen to one million; by 1 November it would be 130,000 million. The catastrophe hit everyone, rich and poor, and an increasing number of people believed Hitler and Ludendorff to be correct when they denounced the Jew-corrupted society which had allowed this inflation to come about, and the Versailles Treaty which had started the slide four years before. Hitler still kept away from Munich except for sudden, short visits, but his lieutenants remained busy.

'Our house had become the rallying-point, one could almost have called it the political centre, of the National Socialists,' wrote Margarethe. 'It was like the continual coming and going in a pigeon loft. Not merely every day, but every hour there were conferences.' Ludendorff attempted to avoid suspicion by behaving as he had done during his first months at Ludwigshöhe. 'Ludendorff, with masterly acuteness, made a point of busying himself in the garden before the eyes of everybody. He pruned the roses, watered the flowers and sprayed the lawns, as though he were the most harmless fellow in the world.'[27]

Ludendorff still found time to write, including a pamphlet published during the summer titled *The Nationalist Movement*, which obtained larger sales than any of his previous booklets. He tried to specify aims, which he believed were in danger of becoming confused.

The nationalist movement is a youthful, lively embodiment of German feeling, German thinking, German will, which combined all forces for the concentrated aim of a free greater Germany. It is the only people's movement which understands the German people in their depth, which shakes them and keeps them awake. It acts like a mighty river taking with it also those who resist ...

'I tried,' commented Ludendorff later, 'to strengthen as far as possible the nationalist movement and its readiness to fight.'[28]

Disorder in Germany increased during the summer: inflation gripped harder, and lorries and trains were looted for food by half-starved men and women; with the worsening economic situation came further instability in Berlin political affairs; disunity grew worse throughout the Reich and the gap widened between Munich and the central Government. Hitler now emerged from his Berchtesgaden retreat, and beside him stood the erect, aggressive Ludendorff.

The second of September marked the anniversary of the German victory over the French at Sedan, 1870. Hitler seized the occasion to organise a mass demonstration at Nuremberg, with the crowd numbering 100,000 according to police estimates. Ludendorff stood shoulder to shoulder with Hitler on the rostrum while the parade marched past, and he clapped enthusiastically when the Nazi leader condemned the Berlin Government in a typically vitriolic speech.

Gustav Stresemann had become German Chancellor a few weeks before, and was known to be anxious to end the policy of passive resistance in the Ruhr – a move which would have snatched away one of the sticks used by Hitler to beat the Reich Government. Moreover, other conditions were right for Nazi action; on 25 September, twenty-four hours in fact before Stresemann called off passive resistance, Hitler summoned a meeting of his subordinates and other patriotic group leaders. Present were Hermann Göring, now commander of the SA, Röhm, Captain Heiss of the *Reichsflagge,* and Friedrich Weber of the *Bund Oberland.* Ludendorff stayed away. Hitler insisted that the alliance of patriotic groups – the *Kampfbund* – must make a positive move, and as a first step he put the SA on to a state of readiness. Next day the Bavarian Cabinet proclaimed a state of emergency, and appointed Gustav von Kahr as State Commissioner with dictatorial authority; Kahr immediately banned Nazi meetings, and in reply the enraged Hitler threatened 'bloody revolution'.

Hitler was obliged to retaliate or suffer dangerous loss of prestige. Planning went ahead during October, although with no date set for action Hitler would seize any suitable opportunity. Above all, he had to seek maximum support for any takeover of power: the Nazis and other groups in the *Kampfbund* would be insufficiently strong to undertake Hitler's ambitious schemes – which envisaged nothing less than a move on Berlin supported by the whole of Bavaria. All therefore depended on the Bavarian authorities, with their support essential.

And this especially referred to Kahr and to General Otto von Lossow, the local Reichswehr commander.

Despite Kahr's action in banning Hitler's proposed meetings, hopes still remained that he would co-operate; this right-wing politician had himself assumed power by a virtual coup at the time of the miserable Kapp putsch, and he had always acted in a way hostile to the Berlin Government. This attitude emerged strongly during October. The Nazi newspaper *Völkischer Beobachter* launched a series of attacks on Berlin politicians, to which the central Government replied with orders for the suppression of the newspaper and the arrest of Heiss and Ehrhardt. Kahr refused to comply. The Defence Ministry in Berlin therefore instructed Lossow to carry out the orders, but Lossow supported Kahr and also refused. On 20 October the General was dismissed by Berlin, but Kahr insisted that he remain at his post.

Nothing could have suited Hitler better than this clash. Now he asked Ludendorff, whose name carried far more weight than his own, to act as go-between in the effort to obtain co-operation from Kahr, Lossow and Colonel Hans von Seisser, head of the Bavarian police. Ludendorff claimed later that he had no idea of any Nazi plans for a coup, and there is no firm evidence to suggest otherwise. Hitler in fact originally intended a takeover for 4 November during the annual parade for *Totengedenktag* – the Day of Homage to the Dead. This plan was abandoned, and instead Hitler decided that action should be taken on the evening of 8 November, when Kahr was scheduled to speak at the Bürgerbräukeller in Munich. Also present would be Lossow and Seisser.

On 7 November Ludendorff began his attempt to bring together Hitler and the Bavarian authorities, using Max von Scheubner-Richter as his liaison officer. At 9.30 am on the 7th Ludendorff had an inconclusive conversation with Lossow, attended by Scheubner-Richter who suggested a meeting between Kahr and Hitler. Ludendorff spent the remainder of the day trying to arrange such talks, without success, and he made a further attempt next morning, 8 November, during conversations at the Palace of Justice. These were unfinished at lunchtime. 'I had to conclude,' said Ludendorff later, 'because I had arranged talks with Herr von Kahr at 4 pm and wanted to return home for lunch beforehand.' He gained the impression that the Bavarian authorities were themselves contemplating some kind of positive move against Berlin. 'I seemed to sense from a remark by von Seisser that political action was planned for some day in the near future.' His meeting with Kahr during the afternoon was unproductive, and no mention was made of the assembly scheduled for that evening, but Ludendorff's suspicions increased that 'Kahr also had intentions to act'.[29]

Ludendorff returned home during the late afternoon. Some of Hitler's colleagues were meant to be visiting him at 8 pm, but on his arrival at the villa he found a message saying they had another engagement.

During the early evening Margarethe saw a servant hurrying out of the house, wearing uniform. Surprised, she called out to him, and he shouted back without stopping: 'A meeting in the Bürgerbräu – detailed to guard the hall. I must catch the train . . .' Half an hour later Margarethe heard the jingle of spurs. 'My son Heinz went bounding downstairs. He also was going to the meeting. The only surprising thing was that, contrary to his habit, he was wearing uniform. I wondered at that . . .'[30]

At 8.30 pm the spacious Bürgerbräukeller on the south bank of the Isar was crammed to capacity with politicians, civil servants, officers and other leading Munich citizens. Hitler stood unnoticed near one of the pillars; Kahr stood on the platform and began to speak. Hitler waited for the audience to settle, late-comers to arrive, and for Göring to assemble his twenty-five SA men outside the doors.

CHAPTER TWENTY-THREE

Munich: The Last March

AT 8.40 PM THE DOORS TO THE BÜRGERBRÄUKELLER SMASHED OPEN
and in ran Göring with his SA troopers. Kahr stopped in mid-sentence;
people in the hall stood in consternation. A shot cracked into the
ceiling and the audience turned to see Hitler standing on a chair with
pistol in hand. 'The National Revolution has begun,' he screamed.
'This hall is occupied by 600 heavily armed men! No one may leave
the hall . . .'

Many of those present believed Hitler to be merely a ludicrous little
man dressed in a dirty trench-coat over an ill-fitting morning suit.
'The poor little waiter!' thought Admiral von Hintze. Someone else
thought he looked like a 'slightly nervous sort of provincial bride-
groom' or a local tax collector in his Sunday best. But no one dared
call his bluff, and now stormtroopers wheeled a machine gun into the
aisle, swivelling the barrel across the audience. Hitler was already pushing forward to the platform, still waving his pistol. He hustled Kahr,
Lossow and Seisser into an adjoining room. He shut the door behind
him and snapped: 'No one leaves this room alive without my permission.'[1]

The telephone shrilled in the Ludwigshöhe villa. Ludendorff didn't
recognise the excited voice at the other end of the line, and the message was brief. He wrote later: 'My presence was urgently needed in
the Bürgerbräukeller. A car would come for me immediately. When
I asked what was happening, I was told that I would be informed . . .
I waited for the car to arrive.'

Margarethe heard her husband pacing up and down in his study
rather than working at his writing-table as he usually did in the evening. 'About nine that evening,' she remembered, 'he came into my room
and said: "I have to go into the town. I shall shortly be fetched by a
car. My presence is required at a national assembly." Soon after this
a motor dashed up at a tearing speed and stopped in front of the
house.'

Driving the car was Ludendorff's stepson, Heinz. Max von

Scheubner-Richter scrambled out of the back seat and hurried into the house; Ludendorff took him into his study and heard a brief outline of events, then he climbed into the car – still wearing an old tweed shooting jacket – and the vehicle screeched into the road and away towards Munich.

Meanwhile Hitler still held Kahr, Lossow and Seisser in the Bürgerbräukeller anteroom. By now he had explained his scheme: the Munich police chief, Pöhner, would be Bavarian Prime Minister, and Kahr the Chief Administrator; a move would be made on Berlin to overthrow 'the November Criminals', after which he, Hitler, would be head of the Reich Government. Ludendorff would command the army, Seisser the policy. 'If things go wrong,' exclaimed Hitler, 'I've four shots in my pistol. Three for my collaborators if they abandon me. The last is for myself.' He pushed the muzzle of his revolver against his temple and declared: 'If I am not victorious by tomorrow afternoon, I'll be a dead man.'

'You can arrest me or shoot me,' said Kahr. 'Whether I die or not is no matter.' Lossow asked Hitler if Ludendorff had given his support and the Nazi leader answered: 'Ludendorff is holding himself ready. He'll be here in a minute.' He then left the room and ran into the hall, where Göring was keeping the crowd quiet, and he shouted: 'The Bavarian Ministry is removed!' He described the roles which leading citizens would play, including Ludendorff's as head of the Reichswehr, and he ended: 'Tomorrow will see either a National Government in Germany or us dead.' Then he scuttled into the anteroom again, only to rush out once more when someone told him Ludendorff had arrived.

> Hitler greeted me [recounted Ludendorff afterwards] and begged me to take over the office of Commander-in-Chief of a National Army which must be formed. He explained the situation briefly, repeating what Scheuber-Richter had said. To me, the question was how the Bavarian State power, embodied in the three gentlemen, considered it all ... I only thought that what had happened amounted to a precipitate implementation of aims which they themselves had put forward, and I was certain that inwardly the three men would be ready to make the decision.

Hitler awaited Ludendorff's reaction with increasing impatience: the whole effort to obtain co-operation from Kahr, Lossow and Seisser would most likely fail without the Nazis being able to use the General's name. Ludendorff now had the choice of leaving the Bürgerbräukeller or joining in the confrontation of 'the three gentlemen'. He commented later: 'I've often had to make quick decisions in difficult situations. And I did so now. I stepped into the anteroom.'

Ludendorff could see no weapons, and Kahr and his colleagues seemed unguarded. He walked over to Lossow and declared: 'The stone has started to roll. The cause must now be carried forward.' Lossow reportedly answered: 'I take Your Excellency's words as a command. I shall organise the army in fighting order as Your Excellency requires.' Ludendorff then talked to Pöhner and asked if he would accept the post of Bavarian Prime Minister which had been offered to him.

Ludendorff wrote in his account:

> He said he would have to consult His Excellency von Kahr. Excellency von Kahr mentioned to me that he had been led into the anteroom at pistol point, so to speak ... The people in the hall might think he was under pressure. At last he decided, after urgent requests by Hitler to which I joined. While I was there, no pressure was put on to the gentlemen, and they did not complain about any pressure. If I had seen anything of that sort I would have intervened ... They decided for themselves, as free men, by word of mouth and shaking hands.

The group walked back into the hall, in apparent agreement; they climbed the platform, swore loyalty and shook hands again while the audience cheered and clapped. Ludendorff addressed the crowd. 'Deeply moved by the magnificence of this moment, and profoundly surprised, I place myself at the disposal of the German National Government ...' Hitler followed: 'I am going to fulfil the vow I made to myself five years ago when I was a blind cripple in the military hospital – to know neither rest nor peace until the November Criminals have been overthrown.' The crowd burst into song prompted by the stormtroopers, and the strains of *Deutschland über Alles* lifted in triumph. Ludendorff stood straight to attention, his eyes wet.

At this moment of supposed victory, the 'coup' started to collapse. Hitler was called out to settle a clash between *Bund Oberland* stormtroopers and soldiers at the Engineers Barracks; Ludendorff also hurried off, making for the War Ministry on the Schönfeldstrasse. And Kahr, Seisser and Lossow slipped away, with the latter saying he must leave to issue necessary orders. The crowd at the Bürgerbräukeller dispersed to spread the news.[2]

Lossow drove immediately to the 19th Infantry Regiment's barracks where he met Lieutenant-General von Danner, commander of the Munich garrison. 'All that of course was a bluff, Excellency?' commented von Danner, as much a threat as a question.

Ludendorff's car went first to the police HQ, where he waited in the vehicle while Weber entered to claim possession. The General arrived at the War Ministry at about midnight; Röhm and *Reichsflagge* strongmen had already occupied the building and Ludendorff climbed the stairs to Röhm's room. So began a tense and unpleasant vigil, while at home Margarethe fretted in ignorance of the whole business: Ludendorff neglected to telephone and explain his prolonged absence. 'It was long past midnight and neither my husband, my son nor our servant had returned. I waited until half-past three and then went to bed.'[3]

Ludendorff was trying to discover what was happening outside in the shadowy, lamp-lit Munich streets. First he attempted to contact Seisser, but could gain no definite news; then he tried to organise troops to protect Kahr, since in the absence of information he believed this politician must have been seized. A succession of messengers left to seek Lossow, but none returned.

News of the Munich upheaval had reached Berlin, and reaction began in the morning, 9 November: Seeckt, head of the Reichswehr, telegraphed Lossow to warn that if the army in Bavaria failed to suppress the putsch, then he would see to it himself. Orders were issued to bring in reinforcements from garrisons outside Munich.

Still unaware of this changed situation, Ludendorff made another attempt to reach Lossow. 'We did not give up hope that General von Lossow would overcome the difficulties confronting him.' Ludendorff therefore telephoned an officer at the infantry barracks and asked him to act as messenger. This officer, Oberst Leopold, saw Lossow and then came to the War Ministry shortly before dawn, by which time Hitler had joined Ludendorff in Röhm's office. 'Oberst Leopold declared that some hours earlier, around 3 o'clock, he had received the news that General von Lossow did not consider himself bound to his word, since this had been given under pressure of pistol point.' Ludendorff immediately disagreed with this claim: 'I had seen no pistol. I said that this was untrue.' Hitler, according to Ludendorff, 'did not say much'.[4]

Later Ludendorff heard that Lossow had declared: 'I do not negotiate with such trash.' And, also at dawn on the 9th, Kahr issued a statement denouncing promises extorted in the Bürgerbräukeller; Crown Prince Rupprecht recommended crushing the putsch at all costs; Kahr and his ministers escaped to Regensburg. At last Margarethe discovered her husband's activities, when her maid rushed in with the morning newspapers and the thick black headlines declared: 'Adolf Hitler just proclaimed National Dictator ... General Ludendorff nominated Commander of the National Army.' Only a few minutes later a post-office worker arrived at the villa trying to find Ludendorff: telegraph messages had been picked up which stated: 'Oath of allegiance and participation in the Hitler revolt extorted by force of arms. Hitler and Ludendorff to be arrested ...'[5]

Soon after dawn Ludendorff and Hitler returned to the Bürgerbräukeller leaving Röhm at the War Ministry. The putsch had clearly failed, but Ludendorff refused to consider backing down. 'I had pledged loyalty with Hitler and the other gentlemen. Those three broke their word. For me this was completely out of the question. Whatever happened, I belonged to my nationalist friends.' Hitler suggested retreating to Rosenheim, but the General refused: 'The nationalist movement would then have ended in the mud of the streets, and that would have been unworthy. The only honourable thing to do was to march. We ordered the guns to be unloaded – it was to be a peaceful march.'[6]

By now regular troops had besieged Röhm and his men at the War Ministry, although both sides were reluctant to open fire. Police were moving into strategic positions, including the bridges over the Isar; troop reinforcements were rushing into the city.

At 11 am the marchers began to form up outside the Bürgerbräu-keller, as many as 3,000 men with a large percentage having rifles slung across their shoulders – Ludendorff still believed these weapons to be unloaded. Shortly after 11 am the column began to move, making for the War Ministry. In front strutted an SA officer carrying a huge swastika; close behind walked Ludendorff, Hitler, Scheubner-Richter and four other nationalist leaders in the first rank. 'I said to myself,' recalled Ludendorff, 'that the *Landespolizei* or the *Reichswehr* might possibly make criminal use of their weapons. In which case duty dictated even more strongly that I should be at the head.'

Soon the marchers approached the Ludwig Bridge over the Isar, held by a police detachment: Göring persuaded this guard to stand aside, threatening that refusal to do so would mean the death of hostages taken during the night. The column swept on to the Marienplatz where a large crowd cheered the Nazis as they approached. 'We were jubilant,' commented Ludendorff. The marchers turned from the Weinstrasse into Perustrasse and then into the Residenzstrasse; the streets were now more narrow, obliging the ranks to cram together. Ahead lay the Odeonsplatz, with the Feldherrnhalle beyond. And at the opening into the square stood a strong cordon of police.

The gap narrowed between the marchers and the opposing line, and one or two outlying groups of police stood aside, but the main ranks remained blocking the route with rifles at the ready. The National Socialist, Ulrich Graf, ran forward waving his arms: 'Don't fire! Ludendorff and Hitler are coming!' Hitler cried 'Surrender!' And then the firing broke out, with responsibility for the first shot never fully established.

'Everything happened in a flash at the Feldherrnhalle,' remembered Ludendorff. 'People appeared from the steps of the hall, and they were shooting, and firing suddenly started to the left of me at the same time. I saw people shooting with guns at their hips ... The shots came from the Feldherrnhalle.'[7] First to fall was Scheubner-Richter, with whom Hitler had been marching arm in arm, and Hitler dropped to the pavement either pulled down by his companion's body or seeking shelter in the gutter. Göring crumpled, blood covering his thigh. Weber sagged against a wall, sobbing hysterically. After sixty seconds the shooting suddenly ceased, leaving sixteen marchers and three policemen dead or wounded on the cobbles, and with men milling backwards and forwards or fleeing back down the street. The lonely, isolated figure of Ludendorff continued to move forward.

Across the space between the panicked Nazis and the police walked the General, hands in his tweed coat pockets. Beside him walked his adjutant, Major Streck. Police rifles were being reloaded and the barrels pointed at the two approaching men, while in the rear Hitler was being pushed into a yellow car safe from harm. Ludendorff reached the rows of levelled rifles; he took one hand from his pocket, reached out, and pushed the barrels aside, and walked on. Police officers ran up to him, and respectfully asked him to go with them to headquarters, but first Ludendorff sent a messenger to Röhm ordering him to surrender the War Ministry, thus avoiding further bloodshed. The putsch was over.[8]

Ludendorff remained at the police HQ during the afternoon, while the Nazis continued to seek safety: Göring was smuggled across the Austrian frontier, and Hitler would be captured at Uffing on the 11th, his left shoulder dislocated from his fall to the Munich pavement. Meanwhile news of the defeat and the deaths reached Margarethe one hour after the firing at the Feldherrnhalle. At noon Heinz came home, dishevelled and exhausted; Kurt, the servant, had been killed. The telephone rang, and Margarethe and Heinz, in different rooms, both picked up separate receivers at the same time. Margarethe therefore heard the conversation between her son and General Hildebrandt. 'Heinz, do you know that your father has also been killed?' 'Yes, Your Excellency, I've already heard it, but haven't the courage to tell Mother ...' The receiver dropped from Margarethe's hand and she slumped stunned into the chair.

An hour later Margarethe heard that the report of Ludendorff's death had been a rumour. He returned home during the evening on parole, much against his will since he thought his imprisonment would have helped the cause. 'His indignation knew no bounds,' commented his wife.[9]

Mass arrests continued over the next weeks, including that of Ludendorff's stepson Heinz – he would be detained for nearly five months. Ludendorff himself was allowed to remain free, and he began organising his defence for the trial, working even harder than he had done before the takeover attempt. 'Many people, acquaintances and strangers, came to see him,' wrote Margarethe, 'and he attached importance to every story they told or any comment they made – all parts of a mosaic, as he used to call it. Often he talked for hours, his standpoint being that much, very much, could be achieved by verbal propaganda.'[10]

The trial would be an excellent vehicle for such propaganda. Ludendorff revealed his line of defence in a letter to Breucker seven days after the Bürgerbräukeller assembly. 'All the gentlemen in the adjoining room had complete freedom ... Kahr did not see pistols but imploring hands. It must also be said that Lossow and Kahr told me and others on the 6th, 7th and 8th that they had decided to start the fight.'

He continued: 'Believe me, there have never been greater scoundrels than those three! I warn everyone of these honourable men in the service of the Jesuits – for it is a battle of the Jesuits against national Germans who want nothing to do with the power of Rome. May all Germans understand this.'[11] Ludendorff wrote again on 30 November: 'Never have there been so many lies as now ... Now one talks about a "putsch". It was a Revolution, and the Government had all the power of Bavaria in its hands.'[12]

Early in the morning of 26 February, 1924, Ludendorff dressed himself carefully in full uniform, packed his papers, and waited to be driven to Munich's Blutenburgstrasse. There, just before noon, the trial of Hitler and his colleagues began in a special courtroom arranged in the old Infantry School. Ludendorff sat erect in the dock beside Hitler, Pöhner, Röhm, Weber, Kriebel and other 'putsch' leaders, all of them accused of high treason. Also being tried were a host of lesser figures, including Heinz.

As intended, the twenty-four day proceedings were filled with Nazi propaganda: coverage was extensive in all the newspapers and the defence speeches were printed in close-packed columns. Hitler's performance was amongst the most effective in his career: he took full responsibility for the attempted coup, and like Ludendorff he blamed Lossow, Kahr and Seisser for the failure – they too, he declared, had wanted to follow the same path, and they too must therefore be considered guilty.

Ludendorff spoke on the third day, and his presence and his words may well have helped to lessen Hitler's eventual sentence. He delivered an intensely detailed address to the court which described his progress towards National Socialism over the previous five years. Then he repeated Hitler's accusations of Kahr, Lossow and Seisser.

'The gentlemen, I presumed at the time, were only being obliged to continue in the same direction which they themselves had proposed ... I did not see, nor did I find, any resistance. Yes, I did help to persuade Herr von Kahr: I thought it damaging if the national will should suffer ... I believed I was associating with German men, who gave their German word and their German handshake out of their free will. If these gentlemen had said "no", then I would have said, "Well then don't do it"...'

Ludendorff expressed no regrets. On the contrary, he declared the Munich 'Revolution' to have been a victory, pushing forward the aims of National Socialism. 'Strengthened by the blood of martyrs, it received new strength. That is the result of the 8th and 9th November which the enemies did not want. May it be able to fulfil its great task, for which it has been appointed by history and by the German people! We do not want a union of the Rhine resulting from French favours, nor a state under the influence of Marxist-Jewish or supra-international powers, but a Germany that would only belong to the Germans, in which nothing rules but German will, German honour and German strength!'[13]

Ludendorff was acquitted. Hitler received the minimum sentence of five years, and few people believed he would even have to serve for this length of time; other leaders were given equally lenient terms; Heinz, charged with being an accessory since he had driven Ludendorff's car, was sentenced to a year's suspended sentence and fined 1,000 marks – Ludendorff's chauffeur was therefore punished while he himself remained untouched.

Now, while Hitler went away to spend a relatively comfortable period in prison, which he used to write *Mein Kampf*, Ludendorff became a hero again. Flowers and presents were heaped on the doorstep of his villa, and his sixtieth birthday in April became a local festival: in the evening a massive torchlight procession wound up to his house, with Nazi officials at the head and with bands thumping military marches. During this spring of 1924 Ludendorff used his popularity to gain a seat in the Reichstag, along with senior Nazi officials such as Röhm, Gregor Strasser, Feder and Pöhner's assistant Wilhelm Frick.

But a gap had begun to appear between Ludendorff and Hitler, which widened with startling and emphatic suddenness. Hitler had opposed the attempt to gain seats in the Reichstag, probably fearing that those elected would gain prominence in his absence. Once in the Reichstag, Ludendorff believed the correct policy should be to seek alliance with other patriotic groups; Hitler disagreed, giving his view in *Mein Kampf*: 'It is quite erroneous to believe that the strength of a movement must increase if it be combined with other movements of a similar kind . . . In reality the movement thus admits outside elements which will subsequently weaken its vigour.'[14]

A number of tangible reasons exist for the breach between Ludendorff and Hitler, including disagreements over future policy, over the need to gain greater power through a merger with other movements, over Hitler's temporary willingness to enlist the support of the Catholic Church of which Ludendorff was an inveterate enemy. But a more basic and more important reason was the essential difference in character between the two men. Ludendorff always lacked thrusting personal ambition: there is no evidence that he pushed himself forward for his own sake. Instead, he believed the Fatherland came first – above the people, above himself, even above the army: in the last months of war he had been prepared to sacrifice the army, if this meant the retention of some military honour and beyond this some honour for the Fatherland.

Moreover, Ludendorff never sought to lead in person. He remained content to serve under Hindenburg, even though the Field-Marshal would thereby gain the greater public acclaim for their joint victories, and even though Ludendorff would receive the greater condemnation from the Kaiser, from the politicians, and from the other officers, for their failures. Ludendorff, for good or ill, established his principles and stuck to them; Hindenburg swung with the tide; Hitler was an opportunist and a leader or nothing.

Ludendorff, for all his faults, was not a megalomaniac; rather he was an intense and misguided patriot. Hitler was also patriotic. But he saw the Fatherland as epitomised in himself alone: Germany must serve him, since only in this way could the Fatherland become truly great again. Ludendorff viewed this self-conceit with intense revulsion and he suspected Hitler's opportunism, especially since he himself lacked this type of political dexterity. Events had pushed Ludendorff forward, and he welcomed his rise to power believing his elevation to be justified; Hitler, on the other hand, seemed to manipulate events to his own purposes. The two men shared some similar methods – the Nazi appeal to the workers matched Ludendorff's own attempts to co-operate with the trade unions during the war – but Ludendorff increasingly came to suspect Hitler's motives. The Nazi leader seemed more concerned with his own success and his own image than with the good of the Fatherland, and Ludendorff refused to believe that Hitler's own acquisition of power necessarily meant Germany's return to her rightful place amongst the nations.

These suspicions seemed confirmed in the months after Munich. To Ludendorff, the immediate step should be the gathering of the widest possible amount of support through federation; instead Hitler insisted that he and his own group should continue to lead the way. In the subsequent struggle Ludendorff began to be edged into the shadows. He was tired both physically and mentally and his last hopes were apparently fading. He rarely visited the Reichstag even in the first weeks after his election, and he failed to attend any session after 29 August 1924. His disillusionment with Hitler steadily increased as he became convinced that the Nazi leader only sought to satisfy his own ambition. 'I do not love the German nationalists,' wrote Ludendorff to Breucker on 20 December 1924, 'because their politics are not honest . . . Nothing surprises me any more.'[15]

Also on 20 December 1924 Hitler obtained his release from prison, after serving merely nine months of his five-year sentence. He immediately set about removing the ban still officially imposed on his party, and he sought the help of Dr Heinrich Held, Minister-President of Bavaria. This action increased Ludendorff's antagonism, since Held was a strong Catholic.[16] On 12 February 1925 the General resigned from the *National Sozialistische Freiheitsbewegung*, which had stood in for the Nazi party while the latter had been banned, and it seemed that he and Hitler would now go their separate ways.

But suddenly the widening gap was bridged again. Ebert died on 28 February 1925 after having held office as President since the foundation of the Weimar Republic; his successor would be elected at the end of March. One evening Hitler came to see Ludendorff, and

the two men stayed talking in the General's study until almost midnight; then Ludendorff walked into his wife's room. 'I've just had an
anxious discussion with Hitler ... We've come to the conclusion that
I should stand as the National Socialist candidate. Hitler is convinced
that the risk must be run.' Margarethe wrote: 'My daughter and I
were simply horrified. It was a terrible idea.'[17]

So it was. Ludendorff's resurgence of popularity had faded. The
Nazi party was not yet strong enough throughout the country as a
whole – and, through his association with the Nazis, Ludendorff had
lost the sympathies of other political groups and of those individuals
who remembered him as a war hero. The election was held on 29
March with seven candidates standing; of the 39,226,000 people en-
titled to vote, 68.9 per cent went to the polls, and of these only a pitiful
285,793 supported Ludendorff. He came bottom of the list of candidates, with only 1.1 per cent of the valid votes.

Head of the list came Karl Jarres, recently Minister of the Interior,
with 38.8 per cent of the poll. This failure of any one candidate to
obtain more than 50 per cent of the votes necessitated a second election, according to a law passed by the Weimar Republic on 4 May
1920. New candidates were allowed to be put forward for this second
ballot, and now Hitler abandoned Ludendorff and chose Hindenburg,
who was untainted by political connections and whose prestige remained strong. Ludendorff dropped out, his bitterness and disillusionment stronger than ever.

Hindenburg had been persuaded to stand after visits to his home
by Admiral Alfred von Tirpitz and a Bavarian People's Party Reichstag deputy, Martin Loibl. The election took place on 26 April, this
time with only three candidates, and Hindenburg won although by a
narrow margin. Hitler immediately planned to make use of the new
President. Through this chain of events Ludendorff made his final
enraged break with Hitler, the Nazis and his former partner Hindenburg, and now he would struggle alone.

CHAPTER TWENTY-FOUR

A World of His Own

LUDENDORFF'S ENERGY REMAINED AS FEVERISH AS EVER, FORCING HIM further towards fanaticism in his new isolation. It also made him abandon Margarethe after a marriage of seventeen years. During these years his wife had provided Ludendorff with an element of humanity otherwise lacking in his career: with her, he became more likeable, revealing a facet of his character which was largely hidden to his fellow-officers and hence to future historians. Only the good Dr Hochheimer had been able to discover this side of his lonely patient. Now Ludendorff threw aside Margarethe for another partner who seemed more fitting to his dismal, disillusioned final years. A divorce was obtained in the summer of 1926, and with the departure of the gentle, loyal and beautiful Margarethe he seemed to extinguish the last element of warmth in his life. Instead, on 14 September, he married Dr Mathilde von Kemnitz, whose wild ideas had already contorted his thoughts against the Jews, Catholics, Freemasons. 'Hereafter,' declared Ludendorff, '[we] fought jointly against the supranational elements and their instruments and ... mutually enriched our minds.'1

Ludendorff had always been highly susceptible to a woman's flattery, and he delighted in flirting, although it seems unlikely that he ever formally took a mistress. Wilhelm Breucker wrote: 'The woman who knew how to take him could wrap this strong man around her little finger. This weakness brought the "old sinner", as he liked to hear himself called – not without a certain pride – many an inconvenience. And it brought the fall of the ageing General.'2 The fall was apparently complete, and Ludendorff became a victim of the highly eccentric Mathilde – who, according to Hitler, had already attempted to inveigle him into marrying her.

Ludendorff took up residence in his new wife's home at Tutzing. Both cut themselves off from normal existence and created a distorted and evil world of their own. For the next decade they would write a host of pamphlets and books, later printed at their own publishing house in Munich, and with each production moving further into the realms of exaggeration and hatred. In August 1927 Ludendorff attended the dedication of the Tannenberg Memorial, but then refused to stand beside Hindenburg during the ceremony: the aged Field-Marshal left before the General spoke, and at the conclusion of proceedings Ludendorff was ignored by his former colleagues. He walked back to his car alone.[3]

Hitler continued to strut along the road to power, interspacing his progress with periods of patient waiting. His moment came in late 1932 when Chancellor von Papen resigned: his successor, Kurt von Schleicher, only lasted until 28 January 1933. Two days later, 30 January, after further last-minute manoeuvring, Hindenburg was obliged to offer the Chancellorship to Adolf Hitler. Forty-eight hours later Ludendorff telegraphed the President that he had put the Fatherland into the hands of 'one of the greatest demagogues of all time'.

Hitler proceeded to use Hindenburg until death in August 1934 brought the Field-Marshal release and the Nazi leader took the ultimate step and himself became President. Ludendorff retired still deeper into his private hell shared only by Mathilde, and the pamphlets continued – *The Secret of the Might of the Jesuits and their Aims. The Destruction of Freemasonry through Disclosure of its Secrets. Salvation from Jesus Christ* . . .

'In earlier days when he was attacked,' wrote Margarethe in her memoirs, 'he used to say: "If they were not afraid of me, they wouldn't attack me. It is a good sign." But now he had reached a point when no one troubled to attack him any more. It was the last note of the song.'[4] Margarethe's observation was not quite correct: an echo of the song remained.

On 9 April, 1935, Ludendorff celebrated his seventieth birthday, and Hitler made one last effort to win his approval. The General had invited a handful of people for tea, and these guests were sitting in the lounge when a car drove up to the door. A disturbance could be heard in the hall, then the door opened and the Führer strutted in – 'with puppet-like solemnity' according to one of those present – and holding a piece of paper in his hand.

Everyone rose to their feet; Hitler went up to Ludendorff and said: 'I offer you my congratulations, Herr General, on your day of honour.' Ludendorff inclined his head slightly in acknowledgment. 'I have decided,' continued Hitler, 'yes, I have decided, to name you General Field-Marshal on this day of honour. I congratulate you on this appointment.' He thrust out the piece of paper. One of the guests wrote afterwards: 'I watched the birthday-child closely during this performance, and saw how his face twitched from the very first words. I thought, how do I get out of this? Everything happened as I feared.'

Ludendorff slammed his fist on to the table and shouted: 'You cannot yet nominate anyone General Field-Marshal, Herr Hitler! An officer is named General Field-Marshal on the battlefield! Not at a

birthday tea-party in the midst of peace!' Hitler had become as pale
as Ludendorff was crimson. He said nothing, but jerked back his hand
with the scrap of paper, turned on his heel, and stamped out of the
house.[5]

The frenzied writing continued. Then, suddenly, Ludendorff produced two books which revealed his mind still to be intact, clear-think-
ing and sane, which belied the opposites that the pamphlets over the
last decade had tended to suggest. In 1935 appeared *Mein Militärischer
Werdegang* – My Military Development – and the following year *Der
Totale Krieg*. Of the two, *Total War* is the more impressive, being an
80,000 word summary of the lessons which Ludendorff considered he
had learnt from his military career. His prejudices against Jews, Freemasons, Jesuits and Christianity are still present, but he also debates
some important aspects of modern war which would become increasingly relevant.

Ludendorff renounced the dictum of the famous nineteenth-century
Prussian theorist, Karl von Clausewitz, that direction of war should
be subjected to political will. On the contrary, declared Ludendorff,
the military leader should have all authority over both military and
political affairs in time of total war. 'The Commander-in-Chief must
lay down his instructions for the political leaders, and the latter must
follow them and carry them out in the service of warfare.' In a foot-
note, Ludendorff added:

> I can easily imagine how politicians will be excited over such an asser-
> tion, and how opposed they will be to the very idea of making politics
> subservient to the conduct of war and its requirements ... Let the
> politicians be shocked and grow excited over my assertions, and con-
> sider my views as the opinions of a hopeless 'militarist', but their con-
> victions will not alter facts. Reality demands exactly all that I demand
> for a conduct of war, and for the preservation of the existence of a
> nation.[6]

The reasoning behind Ludendorff's argument proved logical, even
if the conclusion which he reached can be disputed. Clearly, his call
for absolute military power stemmed from his own experience; he
wrote: 'The policy pursued by the German politicians during the
World War has shown how imperative my demands are.' His own
dictatorship had not been sufficiently definite. Yet apart from this,
Ludendorff based his belief on the nature of the dramatically new form
of warfare which had now come about, and which was likely to become even more evident in the future. Total war demanded total concentration on winning the war by the nation as a whole, and therefore
it seemed obvious to him that the military chief should have over-
riding authority: only he knew how best to use the resources.

Not armies, but nations wage total war, insisted Ludendorff. Effective prosecution therefore necessitated the adaptation of the economic

P

and political system to the purposes of war. He went on to say that
the participation of large masses in war made it imperative to devote
special efforts, by means of propaganda, to the strengthening of morale
at home and to the weakening of the enemy political cohesion. Again,
he spoke from his experience. His remarks on this subject were perceptive, for example his statement that: 'A good propaganda must
anticipate the development of the real events', and his belief that
morale was best helped by frankness, even regarding a military setback, since this avoided rumour-mongering.

In other sections, Ludendorff warned that the nature of total war
meant that preparations should begin well in advance of overt hostilities. Many months might be required for war machinery to move into
action, by which time it might be too late. He compared a nation at
war to the people in a besieged fortress, where the distinction between
combatant and non-combatant loses any significance.

The Second World War would soon show Ludendorff to be correct
in the basic message contained in his *Total War*: nations were indeed
besieged; all citizens were drawn into the struggle; Britain and America
paid dearly for their lack of total war preparations. The British wartime machinery for decision-making became steadily concentrated on
one man, Churchill, acting in partnership with his virtual Chief of
Staff, Alan Brooke, although both would have been unable to function without the backing respectively of Parliament and the Chiefs of
Staff Committee. The same applied in the United States, where the
bulk of the decision-making remained restricted to Roosevelt and
General George C. Marshall.

Ludendorff therefore reverted at the end of his life to the efficiency
and clarity of mind which had distinguished him during the war.
Always, he had alternated between a kind of nervous, unrealistic excitement and intensely practical ability. The former side of him lay
behind the wild and criminal theories which took hold in the post-war
years and which earned him the reputation of a madman. Yet the
other side still existed, which both then and even now have been ignored or belittled by his many detractors. The First World War imposed unprecedented problems of command and organisation in the
military and civilian fields. In Britain, the problems brought confusion
and almost chaos until Lloyd George came to power in late 1916, and
even after that the struggle to obtain a satisfactory relationship with
the military leaders continued. In Germany, the problems became concentrated on one man, Ludendorff. He failed, and has been condemned
and ridiculed ever since, yet it is probable that no man or even group
of men could have succeeded, given the German situation when he
came to power.

Ludendorff never sought to be more than a soldier. He approached
his non-military tasks from a soldierly point of view, believing correctly
that the civil and military spheres could not be separated. Whilst this

integration of the two spheres was inevitable in a total war, one man could not hope to direct the whole. Instead, Ludendorff's failings in his non-military role have been allowed to obscure his skills at the actual fighting fronts. He has been criticised for lack of strategic ability, yet the strategic decisions taken by him on the Eastern Front were undoubtedly correct, aimed as they were at keeping the Russians off-balance by striking at a multitude of different points; above all he realised the strategic limitations in the East far more accurately than did his superiors, especially Falkenhayn, and understood in particular how the nature of the terrain allowed the enemy to retreat deep into their territory. He argued for sufficient forces to back a strategy of annihilation, but these forces were denied him.

Instead the offensive continued in the West, rather than the defensive policy that Ludendorff urged, and German resources in the East were depleted. Ludendorff's own strategy in the West after his arrival on this front has been criticised as being too rigid: critics say he failed to attempt sufficient encircling movements, and instead threw his forces forward in direct attacks contrary to his methods in the East. Yet by then Ludendorff lacked the resources to make large-scale switches in direction; transport and communication difficulties were immense; troops were exhausted and lacked the abilities of those who had gone before them. Ludendorff could only continue to thrust forward at what he believed to be the enemy's weakest point. The strategy must surely have been correct, given the depleted state of both sides in 1918. 'If my attack on Reims succeeds,' said Ludendorff in July 1918, 'we have won the war.' Marshal Foch apparently agreed. 'If the German attack at Reims succeeds,' he is reported to have said, 'we have lost the war.'

Ludendorff was therefore by no means a total failure as a strategist; his abilities compared well with other commanders and were better than most. Moreover, he displayed a high level of tactical skill and perception. His encouragement of the 'Hutier' system of flexible attack opened the way for future development of this form of smashing, stormtrooper warfare, which eventually revolutionised battle with the *Blitzkrieg* concept. Ludendorff was among the first to realise the futility of frontal tactical attacks against well-sited machine guns and barbed-wire entanglements; his method for overcoming this defensive advantage proved sound.

But his military skill was greatest at another level. Germany and even the world has seen no greater Chief of Staff than Ludendorff, if only because his problems were more daunting than those which any other senior staff officer has had to face, either before or since, and to a very large extent he surmounted the difficulties. His tasks as Chief of Staff included the planning and organisation of each campaign, involving the movement of millions of men, mountains of equipment and ammunition, the sustenance of these armies in the field, possible changes in the plan during the actual operation, organisation of the subsequent advance, retirement or consolidation. All this had to be undertaken amidst appalling confusion, without adequate knowledge of enemy dispositions or intentions, often over terrible terrain in atrocious weather – and with a time limit of only a few days. Ludendorff's success was miraculous.

Ludendorff represented the culmination of the era of the Great Prussian General Staff, a body which led the military world in its planning and administrative capabilities, and which had been developed over the last hundred years by Scharnhorst, Gneisenau, then Moltke the Elder and Schlieffen. Ludendorff was the last of the line, and in many respects his name should be placed above the others. The Elder Moltke acted brilliantly during the Franco-Prussian War, but his forces were far fewer in number and hence more easily controlled, and he had only one major enemy to defeat. Future commanders would also find their tasks easier than those facing Ludendorff: on the Allied side, Eisenhower's staff managed in highly-skilled fashion during the Second World War, but by then communications were almost instantaneous.

In fact the First World War was marked by an extreme imbalance between weight and mobility, between the advantages which could be gained from recent developments in mass production and railway systems, and the need for flexibility once the railheads had been reached. Armies benefited from nineteenth-century improvements, yet had still to obtain those of the twentieth century. They had weight – millions of men, thousands of guns – and the railways could take them and their supplies to the front. But, once there, they threatened to become monstrous inert masses whose commanders were virtually helpless, lacking more tactical transport and adequate means of communication with their troops in the field. The manner in which Ludendorff handled this basic problem entitles him to a degree of recognition which he had rarely received.

Ludendorff's failure to obtain final, decisive victory should not be allowed to diminish his achievement. It is worthwhile considering what might have happened if his power had not come too late, if he had obtained his full authority in 1914 rather than 1917 and had been able to put into practice his belief in a defensive war in the West combined with all-out offensive in the East. Perhaps the war would indeed have ended before that first Christmas, millions of lives would have been saved, and the name of Ludendorff would have stood with those of Napoleon, Wellington and Marlborough.

Instead his last years were spent in lonely, twisted, semi-obscurity. In November 1937 he began to suffer severely from a bladder complaint, and he entered the Josephinium Hospital in Munich – ironically, a Catholic institution. He died on 20 December 1937, aged seventy-two. Forty-eight hours later the funeral procession moved through Munich to the Feldherrnhalle where Ludendorff had walked scornfully through the rifles while the Nazis fled. Now Hitler walked behind the coffin, and Field-Marshal von Blomberg, the Nazi War Minister, delivered the oration, and a huge swastika lay over the casket guarded by four Nazi soldiers. Hitler declined to speak publicly but is reported to have muttered: 'Now you can go to Valhalla, great commander.' Less than two years later Ludendorff's teaching in his *Total War* was put into action, but in a manner which would have appalled him. One man did indeed direct Germany's total effort, but he was an Austrian ex-corporal rather than a proud Prussian Marshal.

Sources

NOTE: The letter L in these lists refers simply to Ludendorff's *My War Memoirs*, with other books by the General noted accordingly; the letters ML refer to Frau Margarethe Ludendorff's memoirs; all references to Hoffmann are to this General's Memoirs unless otherwise stated. Full details of these and other books are to be found in the Select Bibliography.

ONE: PLANNING FOR WAR
1. Balfour, 73
2. Tempelhoff, 186, 229
3. L, I, 27
4. L, I, 24
5. L, I, 25
6. Wheeler-Bennett, 8 note
7. Earle, 195
8. Ludendorff, *Kriegsführung*, 71
9. ML, 13–15
10. ML, 17
11. Balfour, 338
12. Stone, 39
13. Kitchen, 186
14. Conrad, I, 381–382
15. ML, 31
16. Kitchen, 186
17. L, I, 26
18. Stone, 39–40
19. ML, 39, 20
20. L, I, 27; ML, 18–19

TWO: SLIDE TO CONFLICT
1. Frentz, 10

2. L, I, 27–28
3. Breucker, 30
4. Frentz, 10
5. Breucker, 30
6. ML, 39–41
7. Breucker, 32
8. Balfour, 339
9. Breucker, 33
10. Breucker, 35
11. Balfour, 340
12. Breucker, 35
13. ML, 49; L, I, 29
14. ML, 106
15. Goodspeed, 22
16. ML, 55
17. ML, 57
18. ML, 69
19. ML, 71
20. ML, 58

THREE: INVASION
1. L, I, 30
2. Goodspeed, 31
3. L, I, 31–32

4. L, I, 32
5. Tyng, 53
6. Goodspeed, 39
7. L, I, 32 ff

26. Tschuppik, 15; Evans, 112
27. Evans, 113
28. Evans, 111
29. Stone, 50, 62–63

FOUR: TO PREVENT THE WORST
1. L, I, 37–38
2. Hogg, 37–38
3. Hogg, 40–41
4. L, I, 39
5. ML, 75
6. Hoffmann, II, 150
7. Stone, 60
8. Evans, 95
9. L, I, 41–42

FIVE: MOVES FOR BATTLE
1. Hindenburg, 80
2. Wheeler-Bennett, 3–6
3. ML, 82
4. L, I, 45–46
5. Stone, 61
6. Balfour, 368
7. L, I, 46
8. Frentz, 274
9. L, I, 47
10. L, I, 12
11. Hindenburg, 84
12. ML, 83–84
13. ML, 85–86
14. Evans, 100–101
15. L, I, 47
16. Stone, 30–35
17. Stone, 54
18. Stone, 55
19. Evans, 96–97
20. Evans, 83–84
21. Evans, 109
22. L, I, 49–50
23. L, I, 49
24. L, I, 50
25. Hoffmann, II, 36

SIX: THE TRAP SPRUNG
1. L, I, 53
2. Evans, 116
3. L, I, 50
4. Stone, 64–65; Evans, 121
5. Hoffmann, II, 282
6. L, I, 58–59
7. L, I, 52
8. L, I, 52–53; Hoffmann, II, 37
9. L, I, 55
10. Tschuppik, 17
11. Knox, 86
12. L, I, 55
13. Evans, 147–148
14. L, I, 56
15. Golovine, 262–263
16. Golovine, 327
17. Hindenburg, 99
18. L, I, 57–58

SEVEN: THE MASURIAN LAKES
1. Frentz, 135
2. Frentz, 16
3. Hoffmann, I, 42
4. Frentz, 25
5. Stone, 67–68
6. L, I, 61
7. Ironside, 222
8. Hoffmann, I, 42
9. L, I, 63
10. Stone, 68
11. L, I, 64
12. L, I, 64
13. L, I, 68
14. Hindenburg, 108
15. L, I, 71
16. L, I, 72–73

EIGHT: TO THE GATES OF
WARSAW
 1. ML, 109
 2. L, I, 70, 73
 3. Hoffmann, I, 22
 4. L, I, 72
 5. Hoffmann, I, 43
 6. Hoffmann, I, 43
 7. L, I, 82
 8. L, I, 81–82; Hindenburg, 116
 9. Hoffmann, I, 46
10. L, I, 87–88
11. L, I, 95; Goodspeed, 108
12. L, I, 96
13. ML, 110–111
14. Hindenburg, 124; L, I, 94
15. L, I, 97
16. Hoffmann, II, 81
17. Hoffmann, I, 50
18. Hoffmann, I, 50
19. L, I, 107
20. Hoffmann, I, 51

NINE: THE WINTER BATTLE
 1. Breucker, 30
 2. ML, 111
 3. Falkenhayn, 54
 4. Hindenburg, 132
 5. Falkenhayn, 56
 6. L, I, 114
 7. Kuhl, *Weltkrieg*, VII, 11–12
 8. Wheeler-Bennett, 50
 9. L, I, 116–117
10. Falkenhayn, 59
11. L, I, 119; Goodspeed, 124
12. L, I, 124
13. Hindenburg, 137
14. Hoffmann, I, 54
15. L, I, 136
16. ML, 100–101
17. Breucker, 39
18. ML, 25–26
19. L, I, 148
20. Hoffmann, I, 60
21. Falkenhayn, 63–64

22. Wheeler-Bennett, 57
23. Hoffmann, I, 62
24. Hoffmann, I, 63–64
25. Hoffmann, I, 63
26. L, I, 152
27. Hoffmann, I, 71–72
28. Wheeler-Bennett, 63–64
29. ML, 140

TEN: 'WITH HEART AND
WITH HAND'
 1. L, I, 178–179
 2. L, I, 180
 3. Hoffmann, I, 94
 4. Frentz, 146
 5. Goodspeed, 138
 6. Frentz, 150 ff
 7. Frentz, 143
 8. ML, 111–112
 9. Wheeler-Bennett, 65–66;
    L, I, 208
10. Hoffmann, I, 101
11. Hoffmann, I, 105
12. Tschuppik, 80–83
13. L, I, 212
14. Hoffmann, I, 118

ELEVEN: MOVE TO THE
WEST
 1. Stone, 253
 2. L, I, 227–228
 3. Hoffmann, I, 131
 4. Stone, 261
 5. L, I, 227
 6. Stone, 261
 7. Müller, 188
 8. Hoffmann, I, 137
 9. L, I, 234
10. Stone, 263
11. Stone, 267
12. Kitchen, 204
13. Tschuppik, 56–57
14. Hoffmann, I, 141
15. Hoffmann, I, 144

16. Tschuppik, 57
17. Kitchen, 205
18. Hindenburg, 159
19. L, I, 238

TWELVE: SUPREME
COMMAND
1. Falkenhayn, 284–285
2. Hindenburg, 164
3. L, I, 239
4. L, I, 239–240
5. Tschuppik, 59–60
6. Hoffmann, I, 146
7. L, I, 246
8. Tschuppik, 82–83
9. ML, 135
10. L, I, 274
11. Hoffmann, II, 159
12. Hoffmann, II, 159;
    Goodspeed, 155
13. L, I, 275
14. Hindenburg, 187
15. L, I, 278

THIRTEEN: PERSEVERANCE
AND POWER
1. L, I, 309
2. L, I, 312
3. Tschuppik, 83–84
4. Goodspeed, 158–159;
    Tschuppik, 74–75
5. Wilhelm, 159
6. Goodspeed, 157
7. Kitchen, 206
8. Kitchen, 208
9. L, I, 332–333
10. L, I, 332–333
11. Hoffmann, II, 161–162
12. Stone, 279
13. L, I, 24
14. Howard, 43–44
15. Balfour, 370
16. Tschuppik, 86–87; L, I, 317–
    318; Bethmann Hollweg, II,
    137

17. Tschuppik, 68
18. L, I, 312

FOURTEEN: WITHDRAWAL
1. L, I, 307
2. L, I, 307
3. L, I, 348
4. Goodspeed, 170–171
5. Lutz, 63
6. Hindenburg, 265
7. L, II, 421
8. Hoffmann, II, 173–174
9. L, II, 430–431
10. Tschuppik, 121; L, II, 451
11. Hoffmann, II, 80
12. Gatzke, 189–190
13. Tschuppik, 106
14. Tschuppik, 108; Balfour, 379
15. Tschuppik, 109–110
16. L, II, 453–454
17. Hindenburg, 310–311
18. Müller, 186

FIFTEEN: STRUGGLE FOR
SURVIVAL
1. L, II, 457
2. Westrap, II, 467; Gatzke, 195
3. Goodspeed, 178
4. Gatzke, 196
5. Tschuppik, 116–117
6. L, II, 480
7. Westman, 94
8. Westman, 95
9. L, II, 480–481
10. Hoffmann, II, 196
11. ML, 114
12. L, II, 483; ML, 114
13. Breucker, 35
14. L, II, 491
15. Gatzke, 207–208
16. L, II, 463
17. Gatzke, 227–229
18. L, II, 529
19. L, II, 589–590
20. L, II, 496

21. Westman, 132
22. L, I, 339; Tschuppik, 95
23. L, II, 413
24. Goodspeed, 187

SIXTEEN: SWITCH TO THE OFFENSIVE
1. L, II, 468
2. L, II, 537
3. Gatzke, 63
4. L, II, 590
5. Hoffmann, II, 198
6. Wheeler-Bennett, 128–129
7. Wheeler-Bennett, 130
8. Wheeler-Bennett, 131
9. Wheeler-Bennett, 131
10. Balfour, 386
11. L, II, 559–561
12. L, II, 562
13. L, II, 588
14. L, II, 592
15. Lutz, 81
16. L, II, 579
17. Essame, 34
18. Lutz, 76
19. Tschuppik, 184
20. L, II, 578; Essame, 34
21. Sulzbach, 142–143
22. Hindenburg, 342
23. L, II, 596
24. L, II, 598
25. Foerster, 132–133

SEVENTEEN: ATTACK
1. Barnett, 306
2. Barnett, 307
3. L, II, 598
4. Edmonds, 254
5. L, II, 599
6. Barnett, 316
7. Edmonds, 396–397
8. Hogg, 137
9. Barnett, 317
10. ML, 131–132; L, II, 602

11. L, II, 599–600
12. Edmonds, 532
13. Barnett, 325–326
14. Rupprecht, II, 351
15. L, II, 602
16. L, II, 600–603
17. L, II, 614
18. L, II, 602
19. Balfour, 387
20. Gatzke, 254
21. Lutz, 82–83
22. Westman, 159
23. Lutz, 63
24. L, II, 615
25. L, II, 615
26. Hindenburg, 356–357
27. Tschuppik, 212

EIGHTEEN: THE THREAT-ENED FATHERLAND
1. L, II, 629
2. L, II, 639
3. L, II, 640
4. Tschuppik, 215–216
5. Lutz, 84
6. Gatzke, 278
7. L, II, 654
8. Tschuppik, 220
9. Gatzke, 279; Tschuppik, 221–222
10. Foerster, 14
11. L, II, 663
12. Foerster, 14–15
13. Wilhelm, 334
14. Einem, 419
15. Foerster, 17
16. L, II, 670
17. Lossberg, 344 ff
18. Foerster, 25
19. Foerster, 18–20
20. Foerster, 34
21. L, II, 675
22. Foerster, 28
23. Hindenburg, 386
24. Foerster, 28, 62

25. Foerster, 37
26. Niemann, 26 ff
27. Foerster, 37
28. Foerster, 37–38
29. Foerster, 133, 38

NINETEEN: DEFEAT AND
DISMISSAL
 1. L, II, 683
 2. L, II, 684
 3. Niemann, 355
 4. Ludendorff, *Die überstatt-
    lichen Mächte*, 24
 5. Foerster, 46
 6. Foerster, 44, 45
 7. Foerster, 51
 8. L, II, 687
 9. Foerster, 73
10. Foerster, 52
11. Foerster, 62
12. Foerster, 54; L, II, 695
13. Tschuppik, 239; Gatzke, 283
14. Tschuppik, 240
15. Foerster, 54–55
16. L, II, 696; Foerster, 55
17. Foerster, 76–79
18. Tschuppik, 245
19. Foerster, 87–88
20. Hindenburg, 428–429; L, II,
    721
21. Ludendorff, *Urkunden*, 526
22. Tschuppik, 251
23. Balfour, 398
24. Tschuppik, 262
25. L, II, 761
26. Tschuppik, 266; L, II, 759
27. L, II, 762
28. L, II, 763; Hindenburg, 433;
    Max, 500
29. ML, 172
30. ML, 173
31. Balfour, 61

TWENTY: EXILE
 1. ML, 170

 2. Balfour, 400–401
 3. Balfour, 405 ff
 4. Breucker, 77; ML, 177
 5. L, II, 767
 6. Bullock, 60; Hitler, 176–178
 7. Breucker, 79
 8. ML, 179
 9. ML, 182–183
10. Breucker, 81
11. ML, 180–181
12. Breucker, 81–82
13. ML, 179
14. Breucker, 164–165
15. Wheeler-Bennett, 211–213;
    Shirer, 77
16. Breucker, 165–167
17. Breucker, 167–168
18. ML, 188 ff
19. Shirer, 77–78
20. ML, 198–199
21. Breucker, 169
22. Wheeler-Bennett, 213–214
23. Breucker, 171
24. Shirer, 79–80
25. ML, 206
26. Breucker, 174–175
27. Breucker, 177
28. L, II, 770–771

TWENTY-ONE: THE KAPP
'PUTSCH'
 1. ML, 226
 2. ML, 227
 3. Ludendorff, *Auf dem Weg*, 5–6
 4. Ludendorff, *Auf dem Weg*, 16
 5. Shirer, 81
 6. Wheeler-Bennett, 218
 7. Wheeler-Bennett, 220–221
 8. ML, 177
 9. Breucker, 68
10. Hindenburg, 95
11. Frentz, 268, 276
12. L, II, 769
13. ML, 231
14. ML, 229

15. Nelson, 104
16. ML, 232
17. Ludendorff, *Auf dem Weg*, 7–8; ML, 232; Goodspeed, 230–231; Nelson, 104–105

TWENTY-TWO: HITLER
1. Breucker, 180
2. ML, 234–235
3. Anon, *Der Feldherr*, 53–55
4. Breucker, 179
5. ML, 280–281
6. Ludendorff, *Vom Felderrn*, 13
7. Ludendorff, *Kriegführung*, 40–48
8. ML, 127
9. Bullock, 66–67
10. Ludendorff, *Auf dem Weg*, 22
11. Ludendorff, *Auf dem Weg*, 22
12. Bullock, 73
13. Breucker, 181
14. Breucker, 182, 183
15. Ludendorff, *Auf dem Weg*, 23–25
16. Ludendorff, *Auf dem Weg*, 22–23
17. Bullock, 88
18. Breucker, 185–186
19. Ludendorff, *Auf dem Weg*, 25
20. Ludendorff, *Auf dem Weg*, 25
21. Ludendorff, *Auf dem Weg*, 26–27
22. Ludendorff, *Auf dem Weg*, 30
23. Ludendorff, *Auf dem Weg*, 28
24. Breucker, 187
25. Bullock, 94
26. Ludendorff, *Auf dem Weg*, 33, 36
27. ML, 245
28. Ludendorff, *Auf dem Weg*, 38, 40

29. Ludendorff, *Auf dem Weg*, 142–143
30. ML, 247–248

TWENTY-THREE: MUNICH: THE LAST MARCH
1. Bullock, 106–107
2. Ludendorff, *Auf dem Weg*, 145 ff; Hanfstängl, 100; *Der Hitler-Prozess*; Bullock, 106–109
3. ML, 248
4. Ludendorff, *Auf dem Weg*, 149–150
5. ML, 249–250
6. Ludendorff, *Auf dem Weg*, 150
7. Ludendorff, *Auf dem Weg*, 152
8. Ludendorff, *Auf dem Weg*, 152; Bullock, 112
9. ML, 252
10. ML, 260
11. Breucker, 188–189
12. Breucker, 189
13. Ludendorff, *Auf dem Weg*, 146, 153
14. Hitler, 293
15. Breucker, 190
16. Bullock, 128
17. ML, 277

TWENTY-FOUR: A WORLD OF HIS OWN
1. Ludendorff, *Vom Feldherrn*, 13
2. Breucker, 35
3. Goodspeed, 246; ML, 284
4. ML, 274
5. Frentz, 285–286
6. Ludendorff, *The Nation at War*, 182

Select Bibliography

Anon, *Der Feldherr Ludendorff, Militarpolitisch betrachet von einem Soldaten* (Berlin 1920)

Balfour, Michael, *The Kaiser and his Times* (London 1964)

Barnett, Correlli, *The Sword Bearers: Studies in Supreme Command in the First World War* (London 1963)

Bauer, Colonel Max, *Der Grosse Krieg in Feld und Heimat* (Berlin 1921)

Bethmann Hollweg, Theobald von, *Reflections on the World War* (London 1921)

Blaxland, Gregory, *Amiens 1918* (London 1968)

Breucker, Wilhelm, *Die Tragik Ludendorffs, Eine Kritische Studie* (Stollhamm 1953)

Bruchmüller, Colonel Georg, *Die Artillerie beim Angriff im Stellungskrieg* (Berlin 1926)

Bullock, Alan, *Hitler, a Study in Tyranny* (London, Pelican edition, 1962)

Carver, Field-Marshal Sir Michael (Ed.,) *The War Lords: Military Commanders of the Twentieth Century* (London 1976)

Churchill, Winston, *The World Crisis* (London 1927)

Conrad, von Hötzendorf, *Aus Meiner Dienstzeit 1906–18* (Vienna 1921)

Craig, Gordon A., *The Politics of the Prussian Army 1640–1945* (Oxford 1964)

Der Hitler-Prozess (Munich 1924)

Earle, Edward Meade (Ed.,) *Makers of Modern Strategy* (Princeton 1943)

Edmonds, Brigadier-General Sir J. E. (Ed.,) *The Official History of the War: Military Operations in France and Belgium 1914–1918. Vol. IV 1918* (London 1922–1949)

Einem, General von, *Ein Armee Führer erlebt den Weltkrieg* (Leipzig 1938)

Essame, H., *The Battle for Europe, 1918* (London 1972)

Evans, Geoffrey, *Tannenberg 1410/1914* (London 1970)

Falkenhayn, General Erich von, *General Headquarters 1914–16 and its Critical Decisions* (London 1919)

Feldman, Gerald D., *Army, Industry and Labour in Germany 1914–18* (Princeton 1966)

Fischer, Fritz, *Germany's Aims in the First World War* (New York 1967)

Foerster, Wolfgang, *Der Feldherr Ludendorff im Unglück* (Wiesbaden 1952)

Frentz, Hans, *Der unbekannte Ludendorff, Der Feldherr in seiner Umwelt und Epoche* (Wiesbaden 1972)

Gatzke, Hans W., *Germany's Drive to the West* (Baltimore 1950)

Generalny Shtab RKKA: Sbornik dokumentov mirovoy voyni na russkom fronte (Moscow 1939)

Golovine, Lieut.-General Nicholai N., *The Russian Army in the World War* (Yale 1931)

Goodspeed, D. J., *Ludendorff* (London 1966)

Görlitz, Walter, *The German General Staff* (London 1953)

Hanfstängl, Ernst, *Hitler, the Missing Years* (London 1957)

Hindenburg, Field-Marshal Paul von, *Out of My Life* (London 1920)

Hitler, Adolf, *Mein Kampf*, trans. James Murphy (London 1939)

Hoffmann, General Max, *My War Diaries and other Papers* (London 1929)

Hoffmann, General Max, *Tannenberg, wie es wirklich war* (Berlin 1925)

Hogg, Ian, *The Guns 1914–18* (London 1973)

Howard, Michael (Ed.), *Soldiers and Governments* (London 1957)

Hubatsch, W., *Hindenburg und der Staat* (Göttingen 1966)

Ironside, Major-General Sir Edmund, *Tannenberg: The First Thirty Days in East Prussia* (London 1925)

Janssen, Karl-Heinz, *Der Kanzler under der General* (Göttingen 1967)

Kitchen, Martin, *A Military History of Germany* (London 1975)

Knox, Major-General Sir Alfred, *With the Russian Army, 1914–17* (London 1921)

Krebs, A., *Tendenzen und Geschichte der NSDAP* (Berlin 1959)

Kuhl, General H. von, *Der Weltkrieg 1914–1918* (Berlin 1930)

Kuhl, General H. von, *La Campagne de la Marne* (Paris 1927)

Lossberg, General Fritz von, *Meine Tätigkeit im Weltkriege 1914–1918* (Berlin 1939)

Ludendorff, General Erich, *My War Memoirs* (*Meine Kriegserinnerungen*) 2 vols. (London 1919)

Ludendorff, General Erich, *Kriegsführung und Politik* (Berlin 1921)

Ludendorff, General Erich, *Urkunden der Obersten Heeresleitung über ihre Tätigkeit 1916–1918* (Berlin 1922)

Ludendorff, General Erich, *Die überstaatlichen Mächte im letzten Jahre des Weltkrieges* (Leipzig 1927)

Ludendorff, General Erich, *Mein Militärischer Werdegang* (Munich 1935)

Ludendorff, General Erich, *The Nation at War (Der Totale Krieg)*; trans. A. S. Rappoport (London 1936)

Ludendorff, General Erich, *Auf dem Weg zur Feldherrnhalle* (Munich 1937)

Ludendorff, General Erich, *Vom Feldherrn zum Weltrevolutionär und Wegbereiter Deutsche Volksschöpfung: Meine Lebenserinnerungen von 1919–25* (Munich 1940)

Ludendorff, Margarethe, *My Married Life with Ludendorff* (London 1930)

Lutz, R. H., *The Causes of the German Collapse* (Stanford 1934)

Max, Prince of Baden, *Memoirs* (New York 1931–32)

Nelson, Walter Henry, *The Berliners* (London 1969)

Niemann, Alfred, *Kaiser und Revolution, Ereignisse im Grossen Hauptquartier* (Berlin 1922)

Muller, Admiral Georg von, *The Kaiser and his Court* (London 1961)

Palmer, Alan, *Bismarck* (London 1976)

Reichsarchiv: Der Weltkrieg (Berlin 1925)

Ritter, Professor Gerhard, *The Schlieffen Plan* (New York 1958)

Ropponen, K., *Die Kraft Russlands* (Helsinki 1968)

Rupprecht, Crown Prince of Bavaria, *Mein Kriegstagebuch* (Berlin 1929)

Savant, Jean, L'époée russe (Paris 1945)

Shirer, William, *The Rise and Fall of the Third Reich* (London, Pan Edition, 1964)

Stone, Norman, *The Eastern Front 1914–1917* (London 1975)

Sulzbach, Herbert, *Zwei Lebende Mauern* (Berlin 1935)

Tempelhoff, Henny von, *Mein Glück im Hause Ludendorff* (Berlin 1918)

Tschuppik, Karl, *Ludendorff: the Tragedy of a Specialist*; trans. W. H. Johnston (London 1932)

Tyng, Sewell, *The Campaign on the Marne, 1914* (London 1935)

Verzhkhovski, D., and Lyakhov, V., *Pervaya mirovaya voyna* (Moscow 1964)

Westman, Stephen, *Surgeon with the Kaiser's Army* (London 1968)

Westarp, Count Kuno von, *Konservative Politick im letzten Jahrzehnt des Kaiserreichts*, II (Berlin 1935)

Wheatley, Eliot B., *Prelude to Calamity, the Nazi Revolution 1933–35* (London 1969)

Wheeler-Bennett, J. W., *Hindenburg, the Wooden Titan* (London 1967)

Wilhelm, Crown Prince, *Memoirs* (New York 1922)

Index

Compiled by Robert Urwin